JAPANESE CANDLESTICK CHARTING TECHNIQUES

JAPANESE CANDLESTICK CHARTING TECHNIQUES

A CONTEMPORARY GUIDE TO THE ANCIENT INVESTMENT TECHNIQUES OF THE FAR EAST

SECOND EDITION

STEVE NISON

NYIF

NEW YORK INSTITUTE OF FINANCE

NEW YORK • TORONTO • SYDNEY • TOKYO • SINGAPORE

NEW YORK INSTITUTE OF FINANCE
NYIF and NEW YORK INSTITUTE OF FINANCE are trademarks of Executive
Tax Reports, Inc., used under license by Penguin Putnam Inc.

Library of Congress Cataloging-in-Publication Data

Nison, Steve.
    Japanese candlestick charting techniques : a contemporary guide to the ancient investment techniques of the Far East / Steve Nison.—2nd ed.
        p. cm.
    Includes bibliographical references and index.
    ISBN 0-7352-0181-1 (cloth)
    1. Stocks—Charts, diagrams, etc. 2. Investment analysis. I. Title.

HG4638 .N57 2001   2001026704
332.63'222'0952—dc21

Printed in the United States of America
30 29 28 27 26

PREFACE

能ある鷹は爪を隠す

A clever hawk hides it claws.

It's hard to believe that Japanese candlestick charts, the "claws" of Japanese technical analysis, were completely unknown to the Western world before I revealed them to the Western hemisphere in 1989. Candlestick charts are now so prevalent that it is hard to imagine that before the first edition of this book, no one in the West knew about these wonderful techniques and not one charting service had candlestick charts. This is amazing to me, considering that candlestick charts are now available on almost every charting service.

I am proud to say that *Japanese Candlestick Charting Techniques* quickly became the foundation of all candlestick charting work in the West. The first edition of this book is why you now have candlestick charts on the Internet and anywhere else they are available. Illustrating the universal popularity and effectiveness of candle charts, the book has been translated into six languages and has gone through thirteen printings.

The tools, techniques, and topics offered in the first edition of this book are ageless and useable in all markets and time frames. But through cogent logic (and holding my dog hostage!) the editor of this edition convinced me it was time for a new edition.

Some of the fresh aspects of this book include updated charts, more equity markets, a focus on active trading via intraday charts, new refinements and strategies, and fresh combinations of Western technical analysis with candlestick charting tools.

In a public seminar, I asked the audience to write what they hoped to get from the seminar. Someone wrote, "To make big $$$." While I can't guarantee "big $$$" I expect that the tools, strategies, and techniques in this book will go a long way to improve your trading and decrease risk exposure.

Thank you for making the first edition of this book so popular. I know you will find this one as valuable, practical, and entertaining.

I would enjoy hearing your comments, experiences, and ideas with candle charts. I welcome your e-mail at info@candlecharts.com and invite you to visit our site at www.candlecharts.com. While I can't guarantee a reply, all your e-mails and letters will be read.

ACKNOWLEDGMENTS

小さな親切は忘れず小さな過ちは忘れよ。

Do not forget little kindnesses and do not remember small faults.

I want to thank all of you who have helped ignite the flames of interest in candle charts. The overwhelmingly positive feedback keeps the lights of the candles growing ever brighter.

To my institutional and public seminar attendees, advisory clients, and online clients, I want to thank you for your continued support and kind words.

A Japanese proverb says that, "One evening's conversation with a superior man is better than ten years of study." It is my pleasure to acknowledge the superior men and women who have so generously helped me.

Many of those who deserve recognition for their help are mentioned in Chapter 1. There are others whom I would like to thank for their help in lighting my path. There were so many who contributed to this project that if I have forgotten to mention anyone I apologize for this oversight.

The underpinnings for all my research on candles are the translations provided by Richard Solberg. His acquisitions of the Japanese candle charting books, his ideas, and his work provided the scaffolding for the rest of my candle endeavors.

The Market Technicians Association (MTA) deserves special mention. It was at the MTA's library that I first discovered candle material written in English. This material, albeit scant, was extremely difficult to obtain, but the marvelously complete MTA library had it.

Yoji Inata spent many hours answering my more advanced questions. He was also kind enough to contact his peers in Japan to get more detailed answers if necessary.

The Nippon Technical Analysts Association (NTAA) deserves utmost praise for their assistance. Mr. Kojiiro Watanabe helped me to contact NTAA members who have been especially helpful. They are: Mr. Minoru Eda and Mr. Yasushi Hayashi Nori Hayashi.

There are many candle charting software programs available. For this book I used two of what I consider the best: Aspen Graphics (www.Aspenres.com) and CQG (www.cqg.com). Their products and support are top-notch.

Just as I did in the first edition, I again want to thank "idea a day" Bruce Kamich. Bruce is a friend and a fellow technician with over 25 years' experience. He continues to provide many valuable ideas and suggestions.

Mark Tunkel, a friend and a colleague for many years, has powerful insights into candle charts. His help on this book is much appreciated.

Susan Barry, the editor for the first edition of this book, had the foresight to convince her boss that candles would be popular enough to take a chance on a book. The increasing sales since its initial publication in 1991 have confirmed her thinking.

For this edition, Ellen Schneid Coleman and Sybil Grace at Prentice Hall have taken the coal of this book and made it into a diamond.

Of course, there is my family. It's hard to believe that my son was just born when I wrote the first edition. (He's now 11.) I told him that I came close to calling him Candlesticks Nison. That name would be appropriate. Evan's a very quick learner—especially when it comes to finances—and can't absorb candle charting fast enough. I think we will put our family finances in his hands.

Rebecca, four years old when the first edition was published, is a very bright young lady now. She makes me proud to be her father. If we put our finances in her hands, we would be homeless, but would have lots of clothing and make-up.

My wife Bonnie continues to be our cornerstone. Without her, everything would fall apart and there would be no way this book could have been done.

ABOUT THE
AUTHOR

先人の跡をたどる

If you wish to know the road, inquire of those who have traveled it.

Steve Nison, CMT, was the very first to reveal the startling power of candlestick charts to the Western Hemisphere. He is acknowledged as the leading authority on the subject.

His two books, *Japanese Candlestick Charting Techniques* and *Beyond Candlesticks*, are international best-sellers and are the foundation of all candlestick research and analysis.

Steve has trained professionals in almost every major investment firm in eighteen different countries on how to apply these methods. He has also taught at the Federal Reserve, The World Bank, and numerous universities. He is an instructor at the New York Institute of Finance.

Steve was among the first to receive the Chartered Market Technician (CMT) designation from the Market Technicians Association (MTA). He was previously a senior technical analyst at Merrill Lynch and senior vice president at Daiwa securities. He holds an M.B.A. in Finance and Investments.

Steve is president of Candlecharts.com, which offers institutional on-site and public seminars, educational products, and advisory services. To learn all that Candlecharts.com has to offer, see page 287 or visit their Web site at www.candlecharts.com.

CONTENTS

PART 1: THE BASICS   21

CHAPTER 1

INTRODUCTION

始めは大事
The beginning is most important.

Japanese candlestick chart analysis, so called because the lines resemble candlesticks, has been refined by generations of use in the Far East. Until the publication of *Japanese Candle Charting Techniques*, the "claws" of Japanese charting analysis—that is, candle charts—were a hidden secret from the Western world for over a century. That book revealed in detail, for the first time to the Western hemisphere, these "secrets of the Orient."

Since the term "candlesticks" is often shortened to "candles," I will use both terms interchangeably throughout this book.

I am flattered that my work has been credited with revolutionizing technical analysis and that all subsequent books, articles, etc. by other authors have used the first edition of this book as their underpinning. This is what I had hoped. The premise of that book was to lay the foundation for future candle charting material. It is thus very gratifying to have this book often called the "bible of candle charting."

Before the publication of this book in 1991 B.C. (Before Candlesticks), who ever heard of a candlestick chart? Now, who hasn't?

Online traders, day traders, institutional propriety traders, and market makers are just some of the candle charting enthusiasts. Web sites, real-time trading systems, and technical analysis software packages include candle charts. This attests to the popularity and universal appeal candles have to trading today's volatile markets. Candles are hotter than ever.

My 11-year-old son Evan (who was almost called Candlesticks Nison when he was born) saw an online charting service that had candle charts. He said, "Daddy, so if it wasn't for you, there would be no candle charts on the Web or anywhere in America. Is that right?" I said that was true. He hesitated and then said, "Cool, I want a raise in my allowance."

WHAT'S NEW IN THIS BOOK

While the format and underlying concepts are the same as the first edition (if it ain't broke don't fix it), the trading environment and players in the market have changed since that edition. Consequently, besides having all new charts, this edition has:

- more intraday markets
- more focus on active trading for swing, online, and day traders
- new tactics for getting maximum use from intraday charts
- new Western techniques in combination with candles
- a greater focus on capital preservation

WHY HAVE CANDLE CHARTING TECHNIQUES CAPTURED THE ATTENTION OF TRADERS AND INVESTORS AROUND THE WORLD?

Year after year the flames of interest grow ever brighter for these charting tools. This is because candle charts:

- *Are easy to understand:* Anyone, from the first-time chartist to the seasoned professional, can easily harness the power of candle charts. Don't let the simplicity of these tools fool you. Their power to analyze the health of the market is unmatched by any other charting methodology.

- *Provide earlier indications of market turns:* Candle charts often send out reversal signals well before those of traditional indicators on bar or point and figure charts. This should help you to enter and exit the market with better timing.

- *Furnish unique market insights:* Candle charts not only show the trend of the move, as does a bar chart, but, unlike bar charts, candle charts also show the force underpinning the move.

- *Are enjoyable to learn:* The picturesque terms such as *dark-cloud covers*, *hammers*, and *windows* make candle charts fun to use. But don't let the "picturesque" names fool you. These techniques will be potent weapons in your battle with the markets.

- *Enhance Western charting analysis:* Candle charts are so versatile, they can be fused with any Western technical tool. For our clients, we merge the insights given by the candle charts with the most potent Western technical analysis tools. If you are a seasoned technician, you will discover how joining Japanese candles with your favorite technical tools can create a powerful synergy of techniques. This merging of Eastern and Western analysis will give you a jump on those who use only traditional Western charting techniques.

- *Will increase efficiency of your analysis:* Because of the immediate visual information sent out by the candle charts, they will make your market analysis faster and more efficient.

As the Oriental proverb states, "The journey of a thousand miles begins with the first step." This chapter is that first step, albeit an important one, on the road to candle chart analysis. Yet, even after this introductory chapter, you will discover how the candles will help make your market analysis more efficient, improve entry and exit timing, and open new, effective, and unique avenues of analysis.

I made a bold forecast in the first edition of this book. I said, "In the near future, candle charts may become as standard as the bar chart. As more technical analysts become comfortable with candle charts, they will no longer use bar charts." This, indeed, is what is unfolding.

At the conclusion of my institutional and public seminars, I often ask the audience, "How many of you will now use bar charts?" Of the thousands of traders who have taken my seminars, no one has ever raised a hand. If you are new to candles, you will understand why after reading this book (or even the first few chapters).

Using candle charts instead of bar charts is a win–win situation. As we will see in the chapter on drawing candle lines, the same data is required to draw the candle charts as for the bar charts (open, high, low, and close). This is very significant. It means that any of the technical analyses used with bar charts (such as moving averages, trendlines, retracements, etc.) can be employed with candle charts. But, and this is the key point, candle charts can send signals not available with bar charts. This aspect will give you a jump on those who use only traditional Western charting techniques. By employing candle charts instead of bar charts, you have the ability to use all the same analyses as you could use with bar charts. But candle charts send out insights into the health of the market that are unavailable anywhere else.

WHO IS THIS BOOK FOR?

This book is for you if:

- Your charting service has candle charts and you want to unlock their full potential.
- You want to get a jump on the competition.
- You would like to enter and exit the market with better timing.
- You want added value techniques to complement trading tools you now use.
- You want to have fun while you learn.
- You are new to candle charts or are a seasoned pro.

SOME BACKGROUND

"Why," I have often asked myself, "has a system that has been around so long been almost completely unknown in the West?" Were the Japanese trying to keep it secret? I don't know the answer to this, but it took years of research to fit all the pieces together. I was fortunate in several ways. Perhaps my perseverance and serendipity were the unique combination needed that others did not have.

I became acquainted with a Japanese broker in 1987. One day, while I was with her in her office, she was looking at one of her Japanese stock chart books (Japanese chart books are in candle form). She exclaimed, "Look, a window." I asked what she was talking about. She told me a window was the same as a gap in Western technicals. She went on to explain that while Western technicians use the expression "filling in the gap," the Japanese would say "closing the window." She then used other expressions like "doji" and "dark-cloud cover." I was hooked. I spent the next three years exploring, researching, and analyzing anything I could about candle charts.

It was not easy. My initial education was with the help of a Japanese broker and through drawing and analyzing candle charts on my own. Then, thanks to the Market Technicians Association (MTA)[1] library in New York City, I came across a booklet published by the Nippon Technical Analysts Association called *Analysis of Stock Price in Japan*. It was a Japanese booklet that had been translated into English. Unfortunately, there were just ten pages on interpreting candle charts. Nonetheless, I finally had some English candle material.

A few months later, I borrowed a book that provided some more basic candle charting information. Once again I had found it at the MTA library. The MTA office manager, Shelley Lebeck, brought a book back from Japan entitled *The Japanese Chart of Charts* by Seiki Shimizu and translated by Greg Nicholson (published by the Tokyo Futures Trading Publishing Co.) back from Japan. It was an important find since it contained about seventy pages on candle charts and is written in English.

As I discovered, while the book yielded a harvest of information, it took some effort and time to get comfortable with its concepts. They were all so new. I also had to become comfortable with the Japanese terminology. The writing style was sometimes obscure. Part of this might have to do with the difficulty of translation. The book was originally written in Japanese about twenty-five years ago for a Japanese audience. I also found out, when I had my own material translated, that it is dreadfully difficult to translate such a specialized subject from Japanese to English.

Nonetheless, I had some written reference material. I carried the book with me for months, reading and rereading, taking copious notes, applying the candle methods to the scores of my hand-drawn candle charts (since there wasn't any candle charting software, all my charts had to be constructed by hand). I chewed and grinded away at the new ideas and terminology. I was fortunate in another way—I had the help of the author, Seiki Shimizu, to answer my many questions. Although Mr. Shimizu does not speak English, the translator of the book, Greg Nicholson, graciously acted as our intermediary via fax messages. *The Japanese Chart of Charts* provided a base for the rest of my investigation into candles.

In order to expand my nascent abilities in candle charting techniques, I sought out Japanese candle practitioners who would have the time and inclination to speak with me about the subject. I met a Japanese trader, Morihiko Goto, who had been using candle charts and who was willing to share his valuable time and insights. This was exciting enough! Then he told me that his family had been using candle charts for generations! We spent many hours discussing the history and the uses of candle charts. He was an invaluable storehouse of knowledge.

My real treasure trove of information is the Japanese candle charting literature that I had translated. For this I had the extreme good fortune to find a translator, Richard Solberg. His ability to track down all the candle charting books in Japan (to my knowledge, I have the largest collection outside Japan) and his translating skills were invaluable.

In December 1989, I authored a two-page article on candle charts. This was the first information on the subject ever written by a non-Japanese. In early 1990, as my thesis for the Chartered Market Technician exam for the MTA, I wrote a paper on candle charts. This was the first detailed article ever authored by an Occidental about Japanese candle charts. A pamphlet at Merrill Lynch (which had over 10,000 requests) soon followed.

Japanese Candlestick Charting Techniques was published in 1991, followed in 1994 by *Beyond Candlesticks* (John Wiley). As of this writing, these books have been translated into eight languages and have gone through many printings.

My work has been highlighted in financial media around the world including *The Wall Street Journal*, *The Japan Economic Journal*, *Barron's*, *Worth Magazine*, *Institutional Investor*, and scores of other publications. An appearance on FNN (the predecessor to CNBC) drew the largest audience that station ever had.

I've had the privilege of revealing my trading strategies to thousands of traders and analysts in over seventeen countries, including, of all places, Hanoi, Vietnam. I also had the honor of speaking before the World Bank and the Federal Reserve.

I founded Nison Research International in 1997 to provide institutional on-site customized seminars and analytical services.

I formed Candlecharts.Com in 2000, which offers Web-based seminars, videos, and other services. I invite you to visit our site at www.candlecharts.com.

WHAT IS IN THIS BOOK?

In the first part of the book, you'll learn how to draw and interpret scores of candle lines and formations. This will slowly and clearly lay a solid foundation for Part 2 where you will discover the value of integrating candles with Western technical techniques. My goal is not to give you market omniscience. My hope is that the ideas in this book will show how Japanese candles can "enlighten" your trading.

The best way to explain how an indicator works is through marketplace examples. The Japanese say, "One seeing is better than a hundred hearings." Therefore, there will be numerous real-world examples of each technique.

My focus will be mainly on the U.S. markets, but the tools and techniques in this book are applicable to any market and time frame. This is attested by the fact that candle charts are used on weekly (for hedgers), daily (for swing and intermediate term traders), and intraday charts (for swing and day traders). The tactics addressed in this book can be used for equities, futures, options, foreign exchange—anywhere and in any time frame in which technical analysis is applied.

I have drawn illustrations of candle patterns to assist in the educational process. These illustrations are representative examples only. The drawn exhibits should be viewed in the context that they show certain guidelines and principles. The actual patterns do not have to look exactly as they do in the exhibits in order to provide you with a valid signal. This is emphasized throughout the book in the many chart examples. You will see how variations of the patterns can still provide important clues about the state of the markets.

Thus, there is some subjectivity in deciding whether a certain candle formation meets the guidelines for that particular formation, but this subjectivity is no different from that with other charting techniques. For instance, if a stock has support at $100, is support considered broken if prices go under $100 intraday, or do prices have to close under $100? Does a 50-cent penetration of $100 substantiate broken support or is a larger penetration needed? You will have to decide these answers based on your trading temperament, your risk adversity, and your market philosophy. Likewise, through text, illustrations, and real-world examples I will provide the general principles and guidelines for recognizing the candle formations. But you should not expect the real-world examples to always match their ideal formations.

Two glossaries are at the end of the book. The first includes candle terms and the second, Western technical terms used in the book. The candle glossary includes a visual glossary of all the patterns.

SOME CAUTIONS

As with any subjective form of technical analysis, there are, at times, variable definitions that will be defined according to the users' experience and background. This is true of some candle patterns. Depending on my source of information, there were instances in which I came across different, albeit usually minor, definitions of what constitutes a certain pattern. For example, one Japanese author writes that the open has to be above the prior close in order to complete a dark-cloud cover pattern. Other written and oral sources say that, for this pattern, the open should be above the prior high.

In cases where there were different definitions, I chose the rules that increased the probability that the pattern's forecast would be correct. For example, the pattern referred to in the prior paragraph is a reversal signal that appears at tops. Thus, I chose the definition that the market should open above the prior day's high. This is because it is potentially more bearish if the market opens above the prior day's *high* and then fails, versus if the market opens above the prior day's *close* and then failed.

Much of the Japanese material I had translated is less than specific. Part of this might be the result of the Japanese penchant for being vague. The penchant may have its origins in the feudal ages when it was acceptable for a samurai to behead any commoner who did not treat him as expected. The commoner did not always know how a samurai expected him to act or to answer. By being vague, many heads were spared. However, I think the more important reason for the somewhat ambiguous explanations has to do with the fact that technical analysis is more of an art than a science.

One should not expect rigid rules. Most forms of technical analysis are guideposts. For instance, if one of the Japanese books says that a candle line has to be surpassed to forecast the next bull move, I equate "surpassed" with "on a close above." That is because, to me, a close is more important than an intraday move above resistance or below support. This is another example of subjectivity: In the Japanese literature many candle patterns are described as important at a high-price area or at a low-price area. Obviously what constitutes a "high-price" or "low-price" area is open to interpretation. One of the techniques I suggest using to gauge "low" or "high" price is an oscillator to see if the market is oversold or overbought. This is an example of why it is valuable to add classic Western technical tools (such as oscillators) to those of candle charts.

As with all charting methods, candle chart patterns are subject to the interpretation of the user. Extended experience with candle charting in your market will show you which of the patterns, and variations of these patterns, works best in your markets. In this sense, subjectivity may not be a liability. This may give you an advantage over those who have not devoted the time and energy in tracking your markets as closely as you have.

As discussed in Chapter 3, drawing the individual candle chart lines requires a close. Therefore, you may have to wait for the close to get a valid trading signal. This may mean a market on close order may be needed or you may have to try and anticipate what the close will be and place an order a few minutes prior to the close. You may also prefer to wait for the next day's opening before placing an order.

This aspect of waiting for a close is not unique to candle charts. There are many technical systems (especially those based on moving averages of closing prices) that require a closing price for a signal. This is why there is often a surge in activity during the final few minutes of a trading session as computerized trading signals, based on closing prices, kick into play. Some technicians consider only a close above resistance a valid buy signal so they have to wait until the close for confirmation.

Candle charts provide many useful trading signals. They do not, however, provide price targets. This is why it is so important to use Western technical techniques on candle charts. This will be a focus of Part 2.

With the hundreds of charts throughout this book, do not be surprised if you see patterns that I have missed within charts. There will also be examples of patterns that, at times, did not work. No technical tool, including candles, is infallible.

Candles are not designed to be a complete system; they are just one weapon, albeit a powerful one, to use in your trading battles.

Before I delve into the topic of candle charts, I will briefly discuss the importance of technical analysis as a separate discipline. For those of you who are new to this topic, the following section is meant to emphasize why technical analysis is so important. It is not an in-depth discussion. If you are already familiar with the benefits of technical analysis, you can skip this section. Do not worry if you do not read the following section; it will not interfere with later candle chart analysis information.

THE IMPORTANCE OF TECHNICAL ANALYSIS

The importance of technical analysis is multifaceted. First, while fundamental analysis may provide a gauge of the supply/demand situations (i.e., price/earnings ratios, economic statistics) and so forth, there is no psychological component involved in such analysis. Yet the markets are influenced at times, to a major extent, by emotionalism. As John Maynard Keynes stated, "There is nothing so disastrous as a rational investment policy in an irrational world."[2] Technical analysis provides the only mechanism to measure the "irrational" (emotional) component present in all markets.

Here is an entertaining story about how strongly psychology can affect a market. It is from the book *The New Gatsbys*.[3] It takes place at the Chicago Board of Trade.

> Soybeans were sharply higher. There was a drought in the Illinois Soybean Belt. And unless it ended soon, there would be a severe shortage of beans. . . . Suddenly a few drops of water slid down a window. "Look," someone shouted, "rain!" More than 500 pairs of eyes [the traders—editor's note] shifted to the big windows. . . . Then came a steady trickle, which turned into a steady downpour. It was raining in downtown Chicago.
>
> Sell. Buy. Buy. Sell. The shouts cascaded from the traders' lips with a roar that matched the thunder outside. And the price of soybeans began to slowly move down. Then the price of soybeans broke like some tropic fever.
>
> It was pouring in Chicago all right, but no one grows soybeans in Chicago. In the heart of the Soybean Belt, some 300 miles south of Chicago the sky was blue, sunny and very dry. But even if it wasn't raining on the soybean fields it was in the *heads of the traders, and that is all that counts* [emphasis added]. To the market nothing matters unless the market reacts to it. *The game is played with the mind and the emotions.*" [Emphasis added.]

In order to drive home the point about the importance of mass psychology, think about what happens when you exchange a piece of paper called "money" for some item like food or clothing. Why is that paper, with no intrinsic value, exchanged for something tangible? It is because of a shared psychology. Everyone believes it will be accepted, so it is. Once this shared psychology evaporates, when people stop believing in money, it becomes worthless.

Second, technicals are also an important component of disciplined trading. Discipline helps mitigate the nemesis of all traders, namely, emotion. As soon as you have money in the market, emotionalism is in the driver's seat and rationale and objectivity are merely passengers. If you doubt this, try paper trading. Then try trading with your own funds. You will soon discover how deeply the counterproductive aspects of tension, anticipation, and anxiety alter the way you trade and view the markets—usually in proportion to the funds committed. Technicals can put objectivity back into the driver's seat. They provide a mechanism to set entry and exit points, to set risk/reward ratios, or stop out levels. By using them, you foster a risk and money management approach to trading.

As touched upon in the previous discussion, the technicals contribute to market objectivity. It is human nature to see the market as we want to see it, not as it really is. How often does the following occur? A trader buys. Immediately the market falls. Does he take a loss? Usually no.

Although there is no room for hope in the market, the trader will glean all the fundamentally bullish news he can in order to buoy his hope that the market will turn in his direction (as one of our advisory clients put it, "You root for your position.") Meanwhile prices continue to descend. Perhaps the market is trying to tell him something. The markets communicate with us. We can monitor these messages by using the technicals. This trader is closing his eyes and ears to the messages being sent by the market.

If this trader stepped back and objectively viewed the price activity, he might get a better feel of the market. What if a supposedly bullish story is released and prices do not move up or even fall? That type of price action is sending out volumes of information about the psychology of the market and how one should trade in it.

I believe it was the famous trader Jesse Livermore who expressed the idea that one can see the whole better when one sees it from a distance. Technicals make us step back and get a different and, perhaps, better perspective on the market.

Third, following the technicals is important even if you do not fully believe in their use. This is because, at times, the chart actions are the major reason for a market move. Since they are a market-moving factor, they should be watched.

Fourth, random walk proffers that the market price for one day has no bearing on the price the following day. But this academic view leaves out an important component—people. People remember prices from one day to the next and act accordingly. To wit, people's reactions indeed affect price, but price also affects people's reactions. Thus, price, itself, is an important component in market analysis. Those who disparage technical analysis forget this last point.

Fifth, the price action is the most direct and easily accessible method of seeing overall supply/demand relationships. There may be fundamental news not known to the general public, but you can expect it is already in the price. Those who have advance knowledge of some market-moving event will most likely buy or sell until current prices reflect their information.

Notes

1. For anyone seriously interested in technical analysis, I strongly recommend joining the MTA. Their web site is www.mta.org.
2. Smith, Adam. *The Money Game* (New York: Random House, 1986, p. 154).
3. Tamarkin, Bob. *The New Gatsbys* (Chicago: Bob Tamarkin, 1985, pp. 122–123).

CHAPTER 2

A HISTORICAL BACKGROUND

古きを訪ねて新しきを知る

Through inquiring of the old we learn the new.

This chapter provides the framework through which Japanese technical analysis evolved. For those who are in a rush to get to the "meat" of the book (that is, the techniques and uses of candlesticks), you can skip this chapter, or return to it after you have completed the rest of the book. It is an intriguing history.

Among the first and the most famous people in Japan to use past prices to predict future price movements was the legendary Munehisa Homma.[1] He amassed a huge fortune trading in the rice market during the 1700s. Before I discuss Homma, however, I want to provide an overview of the economic background in which Homma was able to flourish. The time span of this overview is from the late 1500s to the mid-1700s. During this era Japan went from sixty provinces to a unified country where commerce blossomed.

From 1500 to 1600, Japan was a country incessantly at war as each of the daimyo (literally "big name" meaning "a feudal lord") sought to wrestle control of neighboring territories. This 100-year span between 1500 and 1600 is referred to as "Sengoku Jidai" or, literally, "Age of Country at War." It was a time of disorder. By the early 1600s, three extraordinary generals—Nobunaga Oda, Hideyoshi Toyotomi, and Ieyasu Tokugawa—had unified Japan over a 40-year period. Their prowess and achievements are celebrated in Japanese history and folklore. There is a Japanese saying: "Nobunaga piled the rice, Hideyoshi kneaded the dough, and Tokugawa ate the cake." In other words, all three generals contributed to Japan's unification but Tokugawa, the last of these great generals, became the Shogun whose family ruled Japan from 1615 to 1867. This era is referred to as the Tokugawa Shogunate.

The military conditions that suffused Japan for centuries became an integral part of candlestick terminology. If you think about it, trading requires many of the same skills needed to win a battle. Such skills include strategy, psychology, competition, strategic withdrawals, and, yes, even luck. So it is not surprising that throughout this book you will come across candlestick terms that are based on battlefield analogies. There are "night and morning attacks," the "advancing three soldiers pattern," "counterattack lines," the "gravestone," and so on.

The relative stability engendered by the centralized Japanese feudal system led by Tokugawa offered new opportunities. The agrarian economy grew, but more important, there was expansion and ease in domestic trade. By the seventeenth century, a national market had evolved to replace the system of local and isolated markets. This concept of a centralized marketplace was to lead indirectly to the development of technical analysis in Japan.

Hideyoshi Toyotomi regarded Osaka as Japan's capital and encouraged its growth as a commercial center. Osaka's easy access to the sea, at a time where land travel was slow, dangerous, and costly, made it a national depot for assembling and disbursing supplies. It evolved into Japan's greatest city of commerce and finance. Its wealth and vast storehouses of supplies provided Osaka with the appellation "the Kitchen of Japan."

Osaka contributed much to price stability by smoothing out regional differences in supply. In Osaka, life was permeated by the desire for profit (as opposed to other cities in which money making was despised). The social system at that time was composed of four classes. In descending order they were the Soldier, the Farmer, the Artisan, and the Merchant. It took until the 1700s for merchants to break down the social barrier. Even today the traditional greeting in Osaka is "Mokarimakka" which means, "Are you making a profit?"

In Osaka, Yodoya Keian became a war merchant for Hideyoshi (one of the three great military unifiers). Yodoya had extraordinary abilities in transporting, distributing, and setting the price of rice. Yodoya's front yard became so important that the first rice exchange developed there. He became very wealthy—as it turned out, too wealthy. The Bakufu (the military government led by the Shogun) confiscated his entire fortune in 1705 on the charge that he was living in luxury not befitting his social rank. The Bakufu was apprehensive about the increasing amount of power acquired by certain merchants. Certain officials and merchants tried to corner the rice market in 1642. The punishment was severe: Their children were executed, the merchants were exiled, and their wealth was confiscated.

The rice market that originally developed in Yodoya's yard was institutionalized when the Dojima Rice Exchange was set up in the late 1600s in Osaka. The merchants at the Exchange graded the rice and bargained to set its price. Up until 1710, the Exchange dealt in actual rice. After 1710, the Rice Exchange began to issue and accept rice warehouse receipts. These warehouse receipts were called rice coupons. These rice receipts became the first futures contracts ever traded.

Rice brokerage became the foundation of Osaka's prosperity. There were more than 1,300 rice dealers. Since there was no currency standard (the prior attempts at hard currency failed due to the debasing of the coins), rice became the de facto medium of exchange. A daimyo needing money would send his surplus rice to Osaka where it would be placed in a warehouse in his name. He would be given a coupon as a receipt for this rice. He could sell this rice coupon whenever he pleased. Given the financial problems of many daimyos, they would also often sell rice coupons against their next rice tax delivery (taxes to the daimyo were paid in rice—usually 40 to 60 percent of the rice farmer's crop). Sometimes the rice crop of several years hence was mortgaged. These rice coupons were actively traded. The rice coupons sold against future rice deliveries became the world's first futures contracts. The Dojima Rice Exchange, where these coupons traded, became the world's first futures exchange. Rice coupons were also called "empty rice" coupons (that is, rice that was not in physical possession). To give you an idea of the popularity of rice futures trading, consider this: In 1749, there were a total of 110,000 bales (rice used to trade in bales) of empty-rice coupons traded in Osaka. Yet, throughout all of Japan there were only 30,000 bales of rice.[2]

Into this background steps Homma, called "god of the markets." Munehisa Homma was born in 1724 into a wealthy family. The Homma family was considered so wealthy that there was a saying at that time, "I will never become a Homma, but I would settle to be a local lord." When Homma was given control of his family business in 1750, he began trading at his local rice exchange in the port city of Sakata. Sakata was a collections and distribution area for rice. Since Homma came from Sakata, you will frequently come across the expression "Sakata's Rules" in Japanese candlestick literature. These refer to Homma.

When Munehisa Homma's father died, Munehisa was placed in charge of managing the family's assets. This was in spite of the fact that he was the youngest son. (It was usually the eldest son who inherited the power during that era.) This was probably because of Munehisa's market savvy. With this money, Homma went to Japan's largest rice exchange, the Dojima Rice Exchange in Osaka, and began trading rice futures.

Homma's family had a huge rice farming estate. Their power meant that information about the rice market was usually available to them. In addition, Homma kept records of yearly weather conditions. In order to learn about the psychology of investors, Homma analyzed rice prices going back to the time when the rice exchange was in Yodoya's yard. Homma also set up his own communications system. At prearranged times he placed men on rooftops to send signals by flags. These men stretched the distance from Osaka to Sakata. After dominating the Osaka markets, Homma went to trade in the regional exchange at Edo (now called Tokyo). He used his insights to amass a huge fortune. It was said he had 100 consecutive winning trades.

His prestige was such that there was the following folk song from Edo: "When it is sunny in Sakata (Homma's town), it is cloudy in Dojima (this Dojima Rice Exchange in Osaka) and rainy at Kuramae (the Kuramae exchange in Edo)." In other words, when there is a good rice crop in Sakata, rice prices fall on the Dojima Rice Exchange and collapse in Edo. This song reflects Homma's sway over the rice market. In later years Homma became a financial consultant to the government and was given the honored title of samurai. He died in 1803. Homma's books about the markets (*Sakata Senho* and *Soba Sani No Den*) were said to have been written in the 1700s. His trading principles, as applied to the rice markets, evolved into the candlestick methodology currently used in Japan.

Notes

1. His first name is sometimes translated as Sokyu and his last name is sometimes translated as Honma. This gives you an idea of the difficulty of translating Japanese into English. The same Japanese symbols for Homma's first name, depending on the translator, can be Sokyu or Munehisa. His last name, again depending on the translator, can be either Homma or Honma. I chose the English translation of Homma's name as used by the Nippon Technical Analysts Association.
2. Hirschmeier, Johannes, and Tsunehiko, Yui. *The Development of Japanese Business 1600–1973* (Cambridge, MA: Harvard University Press, 1975, p. 31).

PART 1
THE BASICS

千里の道も一歩から

Even a thousand-mile journey begins with the first step.

CHAPTER 3

CONSTRUCTING THE CANDLESTICK LINES

櫓櫂がなくて舟で渡れぬ

Without oars you cannot cross in a boat.

Candle charts use the same open, high, low, and close data as the traditional Western bar chart. With this in mind, a bar chart is shown in Exhibit 3.1. Exhibit 3.2 is a candle chart of the same price information as the bar chart.

Prices seem to jump off the page on the candle chart. It presents a stereoscopic view of the market as it pushes the flat, two-dimensional bar chart into almost a three-dimensional aspect. Candle charts are visually stimulating. Exhibit 3.3 shows how the same data looks on a bar chart and then a candle chart.

EXHIBIT 3.1. Lucent—Daily (Bar Chart)

EXHIBIT 3.2. Lucent—Daily (Candle Chart)

Chapter 3 • Constructing the Candlestick Lines

Time Period	Open	High	Low	Close
1	20	30	15	25
2	25	25	10	15
3	30	35	15	20
4	45	50	35	40
5	25	40	25	35

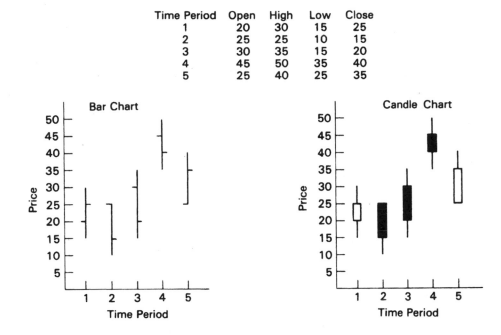

EXHIBIT 3.3. Bar Chart and Candle Chart

DRAWING THE CANDLE LINES

The rectangular sections of the candle lines in Exhibits 3.4 to 3.6 are called the *real body*. The real body represents the range between the session's open and close. When the real body is black (i.e., filled), it means the close of the session was lower than the open. If the real body is white (i.e., empty), it shows the close was higher than the open.

The thin lines above and below the real body are the *shadows* (these names are almost lyrical—the real body and the shadows of these real bodies.) These shadows represent the session's price extremes. The shadow above the real body is called the *upper shadow* and the shadow below the real body is the *lower shadow*. Accordingly, the peak of the upper shadow is the high of the session and the bottom of the lower shadow is the low of the session.

If a candle line has no upper shadow, it is said to have a *shaven head*. A candle line with no lower shadow has a *shaven bottom*.

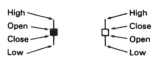

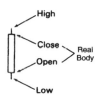

EXHIBIT 3.4. White Candle Line

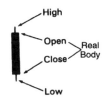

EXHIBIT 3.5. Black Candle Line

EXHIBIT 3.6. Spinning Tops

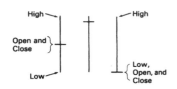

EXHIBIT 3.7. Examples of Doji

We see why these are named candle or candlestick charts; the individual lines often look like candles with their wicks. As mentioned in the Introduction, we will use the terms candles and candlesticks interchangeably throughout the rest of the book.

The Japanese say the real body is "the essence of the price movement." This reflects a central concept about the power of the real bodies: By looking at the height and color of the real body, we get an immediate visual clue whether it's the bulls or bears who are in control.

As such, candle charts will make market analysis faster and more efficient. Using the long white candle in Exhibit 3.4 as an example, who is in charge? The bulls or bears? Obviously, it's the bulls since on that session the market opened near its low and closed near its high. Likewise, a long black candle (Exhibit 3.5) is a visual representation that, at least for that session, the bears were in control since the market opened near its high and closed near the session lows.

Candle lines can be drawn using any time frame—from intraday to daily to weekly charts. For example, a white candle, as shown in Exhibit 3.4, if based on a daily chart, would mean that the bottom of the real body is the first trade of the day (remember, a white real body signifies the open is at the bottom of the real body) and the top of the real body is the day's close. The intraday peak and trough are the tip of the upper shadow and the bottom of the lower shadow, respectively.

Similarly, a five-minute black candle line tells us that the open of that five-minute period is at the top of the black real body and the close is at its bottom. The high and low of that five-minute session will define the upper and lower shadows.

A practical application of the real body is using its size as a barometer of the market's momentum.

While a long white and black candle shows the action is one-sided, we get a clue that the prior momentum may be losing force as the real body becomes smaller. The Japanese term for a small real body (black or white) is a *spinning top*. Exhibit 3.6 shows examples of spinning tops. The lines illustrated in Exhibit 3.6 have upper and lower shadows, but the sizes of the shadows are not important. It is the small size of the real body that makes these spinning tops.

Spinning tops are components of candle formations including morning and evening stars, harami, hammers, and others that will be discussed at length in the appropriate sections.

Notice something about the real bodies in Exhibit 3.7? There aren't any! These lines are named *doji* (the plural of doji is also doji) and they represent a session when the open and close are the same (or very close to one another). Doji have implications as a reversal signal. We will look at this aspect later in this chapter and in greater detail in Chapter 8.

In Exhibit 3.8, during the week of April 1 a descent began near 315 via a series of black candles. As the decline ensued the real bodies increased in length, reflecting increasing bearish momentum. The emergence of the spinning top on April 7 changed the technical picture from one in which the bears had complete control to a market where the bears were losing domination. Since the small real body was only one session's activity, it should be viewed as a tentative clue. Nonetheless, it was the first sign of a potential reversal. This represents a major advantage of candle charts: They will often let you spot potential market turns as quickly as one session.

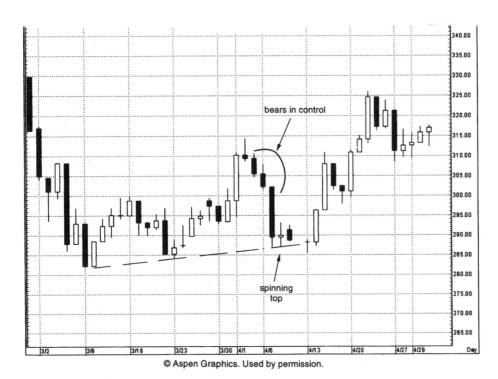

© Aspen Graphics. Used by permission.

EXHIBIT 3.8. Semi-Conductor Index—Daily (Spinning Top)

While the April 7 spinning top was a candle signal, it also helped confirm a traditional western technical analysis tool—specifically, a rising support line constructed by connecting the March 10 and March 23 lows. Thus, we have two signals, the support line and spinning top, reinforcing support near 285. This concept of combining Eastern and Western techniques will be the focus of Part 2.

Another example of a spinning top hinting of a turn is the point where the decline from 315 began—the April 2 spinning top (remember, the color of the small real body is not important) that followed a tall white candle (at which time the bulls were in control).

One of the fascinating aspects of the candles is that they can send out warning signals not evident on bar charts. For example, look at the prior chart in Exhibit 3.2 and the rally the week of January 18. Notice the two candles lines as the stock approached the $60 level. If this was a bar chart, this stock would look healthy since it was making higher highs, higher lows, and even higher closes. However, the candle lines give us a different perspective. To wit, those small real bodies are hinting that the bulls do not have full control. Also, note that the high during the week of January 18 was also near a resistance area. As such, the small real bodies, via the candles, were confirming that resistance area.[1]

As we've seen, the Japanese place great emphasis on the relationship between the open and close because they are the two most emotionally charged points of the trading day. The Japanese have a proverb: "The first hour of the morning is the rudder of the day." Likewise, the opening is the rudder for the trading session. It furnishes the first clue about that day's direction. It is a time when all the news and rumors from overnight are filtered and then joined into one point in time.

The more anxious the trader, the earlier he or she wants to trade. Therefore, on the open, shorts may be scrambling for cover, potential longs may want to emphatically buy, hedgers may need to take a new or get out of an old position, and so forth.

After the flurry of activity on the open, potential buyers and sellers now have a benchmark. There are frequent analogies to trading the market and fighting a battle. In this sense, the open provides an early view of the battlefield and a provisional indication of friendly and opposing troops.

The other pivotal price point is the close. We can thus expect heavy emotional involvement into how the market closes. The close is also a critical price point for many technicians. They may wait for a close to confirm a breakout from a significant chart point. Margin calls in the futures markets are also based on the close. Many computer trading systems (for example, moving average systems) are calculated from closes.

Typical of the military analogies used by candle chart analysis is the way the Japanese refer to unusually big orders on the open or close. If a large buy or sell order is pushed into the market at or near the close, with the intention of affecting the close, the Japanese call this action a "night attack." If this is done on the open, it is called, not surprisingly, a "morning attack."

CANDLE TERMINOLOGY AND MARKET EMOTION

Technical analysis is the only way to measure the emotional component of the market. We know that many times an ounce of emotion can be worth a pound of facts. How else to explain a sudden shift in the market without a change in the fundamentals?

A fascinating attribute to candle charts is that the names of the candle patterns are a colorful mechanism describing the emotional health of the market at the time these patterns are formed. After hearing the expression "dark-cloud cover," would you think the market is in an emotionally healthy state? Of course not! As we will see later, this is a bearish pattern and the name clearly conveys the unhealthy state of the market.

There are many patterns and ideas in this book, and the descriptive names employed by the Japanese not only make candle charting fun, but easier to remember if the patterns are bullish or bearish. For example, in Chapter 5 you will learn about the "evening star" and the "morning star." Without knowing what these patterns look like or what they imply for the market, just by hearing their names, which do you think is bullish and which is bearish? The evening star (the nickname for the planet Venus), which comes out before darkness sets in, sounds like the bearish signal—and so it is! The morning star, then, is bullish since the morning star (the planet Mercury) appears just before sunrise.

NOTES

1. Spinning tops are discussed in more detail in my book *Beyond Candlesticks* (New York: John Wiley and Sons, 1994).

CHAPTER 4

REVERSAL PATTERNS

一寸先は闇

Darkness lies one inch ahead.

Technicians watch for price clues alerting them to a shift in market psychology and trend. Reversal patterns are these technical clues. Western reversal indicators include double tops and bottoms, reversal days, head and shoulders, and island tops and bottoms. Yet the term "reversal pattern" is somewhat of a misnomer. Hearing that term may lead you to think of an old trend ending abruptly and then reversing to a new trend. This rarely happens. Trend changes usually occur slowly, in stages, as the underlying psychology shifts gears. A trend reversal signal implies that the prior trend is likely to change, but not necessarily reversing. Compare a trend to a car traveling forward. The car's red brake lights go on and the car stops. The brake light was the reversal indicator showing that the

EXHIBIT 4.1. Top Reversal

EXHIBIT 4.2. Top Reversal

EXHIBIT 4.3. Top Reversal

prior trend (that is, the car moving forward) was about to end. But now that the car is stationary, will the driver then decide to put the car in reverse? Will he or she remain stopped? Will he or she decide to go forward again? Without more clues we do not know.

Exhibits 4.1 through 4.3 are some examples of what can happen after a top reversal signal appears. The prior uptrend, for instance, could convert into a period of sideways price action. Then a new trend lower or higher could start (see Exhibits 4.1 and 4.2). Exhibit 4.3 illustrates how an uptrend can abruptly reverse into a downtrend.

Remember that when I say "reversal pattern," it means only that the prior trend should change but not necessarily reverse. It is prudent to think of reversal patterns as trend change patterns. Recognizing the emergence of reversal patterns can be a valuable skill. Successful trading entails having both the trend and probability on your side. The reversal indicators are the market's way of providing a road sign, such as "Caution— Trend in Process of Change." In other words, the market's psychology is in transformation. You should adjust your trading style to reflect the new market environment. There are many ways to trade in and out of positions with reversal indicators. We shall see many examples of this throughout the book.

An important principle is to initiate a new position (based on a reversal signal) only if that signal is in the direction of the major trend. Let us say, for example, that in a bull market, a top reversal pattern appears. This bearish signal would not warrant a short sale. This is because the major trend is still up. It would, however, signal a liquidation of longs. We could then look for a bullish signal on the correction to buy since the prevailing trend was higher.

I have gone into detail about the subject of reversal patterns because most of the candle indicators are reversals. Now, let us turn our attention to the first group of these candle reversal indicators, the hammer and hanging man lines.

UMBRELLA LINES

Exhibit 4.4 shows candles with long lower shadows and small real bodies (black or white) near the top of the daily range. The lines in Exhibit 4.4 are called *umbrella lines* because they look like umbrellas. Umbrella lines are candles with very long lower shadows and a small real body at the top end of the range. These umbrella lines are fascinating in that these lines can be either bullish or bearish according to the market environment.

If an umbrella line emerges during a downtrend, it is a signal that the downtrend should end. In such a scenario, this umbrella line is labeled a *hammer*, as in "the market is hammering out" a base (see Exhibit 4.5). The actual Japanese word for the hammer is *takuri*. This word means "trying to gauge the depth of the water by feeling for its bottom." This is a perfect analogy for the hammer line as the market attempts to grope for a bottom. Coincidently, the hammer line looks likes a hammer with its head and handle.

As mentioned above, the character of umbrella lines changes based on the prevailing trend before the umbrella line. We saw that an umbrella line after a decline is a bullish signal called a hammer. However, if either of the lines in Exhibit 4.4 emerges after a rally, it is a potential top reversal signal ominously called a *hanging man* (see Exhibit 4.6). The name "hanging man" is derived from the fact that it looks like a hanging man with dangling legs.

It may seem unusual that the same candle line can be both bullish and bearish. Yet, for those familiar with Western island tops and bottoms, you will recognize that the identical idea applies here. The island formation is either bullish or bearish depending on where it is in a trend. An island after a prolonged rising trend is bearish, while the same island pattern after a falling trend is bullish.

To give a sense of the challenge of unraveling candle charting techniques, one of the books I used for my research described the umbrella lines in Exhibit 4.4 by saying, "buy from below and sell from above." What did that mean? Remember that I did know about hammers and hanging man lines at the time I read this. It took some time and some research to figure out that the author meant that it's bullish after a falling market ("buy from below") and potentially bearish after a rising market ("sell from above"). The years of research required into unlocking these "secrets of the Orient" were due to the fact that most of

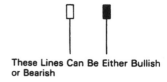

These Lines Can Be Either Bullish or Bearish

Exhibit 4.4. Umbrella Lines

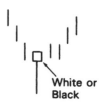

White or Black

Exhibit 4.5. Hammer

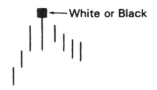

White or Black

Exhibit 4.6. Hanging Man

the candle patterns and techniques were described in similarly vague descriptions. It's a good thing I like challenges!

The hammer and hanging man can be recognized by three criteria:

1. The real body is at the upper end of the trading range. The color of the real body is not important.
2. It has a long lower shadow that should be at least twice the height of the real body.
3. It should have no, or a very short, upper shadow.

There are three aspects that differentiate the hanging man from the hammer—trend, extent of the move before the candle line, and confirmation. Specifically:

- *Trend:* A hammer must come after a decline. A hanging man must come after a rally.
- *Extent of the move before the candle line:* A hammer is valid even if it comes after a short-term decline, but a hanging man should emerge after an extended rally, preferably at an all-time high.
- *Confirmation:* As will be addressed later, a hanging man should be confirmed, while a hammer need not be.

The longer the lower shadow, the shorter the upper shadow; the smaller the real body, the more meaningful the bullish hammer or bearish hanging man. We will now focus on the hammer and then the hanging man.

Hammer

The real body of the hammer can be white or black. This is because even if the real body of the hammer is black, we can see in Exhibit 4.5 that it still closed near the session highs. We can say it is slightly more bullish if the real body of the hammer is white (because it closed at the high). The Japanese nickname for a white hammer is a "power line." In my experience, the success of the hammer is not dependent on the color of its real body.

The hammer's long lower shadow and close at, or near, the high of the session graphically relays that the market sold off sharply during the session and then bounced back to close at, or near, the session's high. This could have bullish ramifications. This aspect of closing at or near the highs is why the hammer should have no, or a minuscule, upper shadow. If there was a long upper shadow, this would mean the market closed well off its highs, which is an important criterion for the hammer.

Since the hammer is a bottom reversal signal, we need a falling trend to reverse.

In Exhibit 4.7 we see a hammer on February 24. It's classic because of its extended lower shadow and small real body at the top end of the trading range. It also followed a decline. This is a necessary condition for a hammer.

The line on February 22 would not be defined as a hammer because it didn't have the required lower shadow of two or three times the height of the real body. Such a lower shadow is necessary because it would display that the market had been pushed down sharply lower during the session, but by the end of the session, as the Japanese would say, there was a

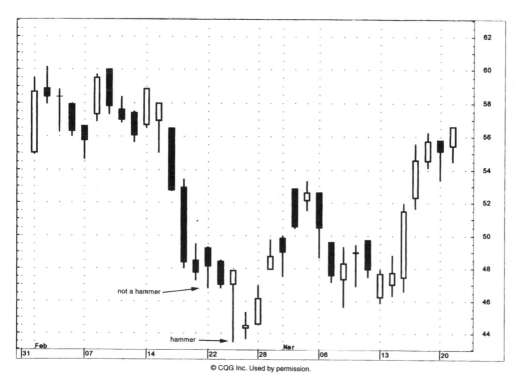

© CQG Inc. Used by permission.

Exhibit 4.7. Wal-Mart Stores—Daily (Hammer)

"kamikaze fight" as the bears lost control as adduced by the fact that the market closed at, or near, its session highs. This was visually shown with a classic hammer on the 24th. You can bet that after a day like this classic hammer, the bears are having second thoughts.

Exhibit 4.7 brings out a vital aspect of candle charting. Successful trading with candle charts requires an understanding not only of the candle patterns, but also of where the candle pattern appears and in the context of risk/reward analysis. One should always consider the risk/reward aspect before placing a trade based on a candle pattern or candle line. Let's look at the ideal hammer on the 24th keeping this aspect of risk/reward in mind.

By the time the hammer was completed (remember, we have to wait for the close), the stock closed near $48. Thus, if one bought at the completion of a hammer (around $48), the risk would be under the hammer's lows of near $43. That is around $5. We now have a $5 risk. There is nothing wrong with that if your target is much greater than $5. However, for some active traders $5 might be too large a risk.

As such, to help lower the potential risk of the trade, one could wait for a correction to within the hammer's lower shadow (of course, there will be many times when the market will not correct after the hammer). By using the hammer's lows as a potential purchase area, we have bought closer to the stop out area.

Let's imagine Trader A recognizes the hammer on February 24. He is so excited by this beautifully defined hammer that he buys at the hammer's close near $48. The next session, the market gaps down to $44.50 on the opening. Trader A is now underwater by $3.50. He may decide to exit the prior day's long position with a $4.50 loss. In such a scenario Trader A may have said the candles did not work.

Trader B recognizes the hammer's potential turning signal, but remembering the aspect of risk/reward does not buy on the hammer's close (because the risk would be too much for her). The next day, when the market opened lower, it was then near a potential support area at the lower end of the long lower shadow. Trader B recognizes the stock is now near potential support and decides to buy. After the stock rallied from this support area, Trader B would sing the praises of candles.

Of course, there will be times when a market fails to hold potential support or resistance areas as well as they did with this hammer. How you personally utilize the power of the candle charts will be an important component of how successful the candles turn out to be for you.

In the prior chart we saw how a hammer can become a potential support. In Exhibit 4.8 we show how a hammer can also be used to help confirm support. In this chart of the NAS-DAQ-100 (NDX), there is a rally that started at area A. The first sign that the ascent was slackening were the two small black real bodies (at 1 and 2) near 3723. The market retreated steeply from there. As it neared the potential support area near 3680 (support at A), a hammer formed. If the support is solid, the hammer should then become a support, as it was for the next two sessions. Of course, if the NDX had closed under the 3680 support area, our bullish outlook would have been voided. That is an important aspect of technicals—there should always

© Aspen Graphics. Used by permission.

Exhibit 4.8. NDX—Five Minutes (Hammer)

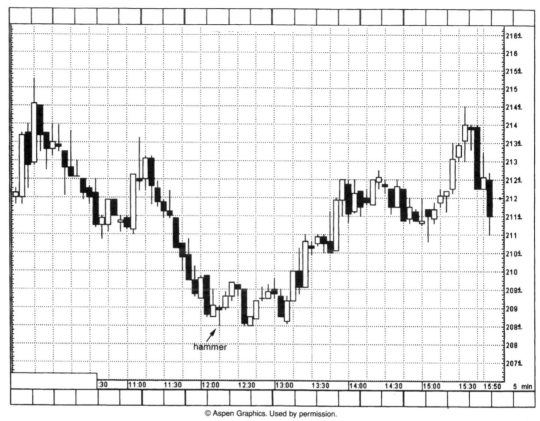

© Aspen Graphics. Used by permission.

Exhibit 4.9. IBM—Five Minutes (Hammer)

be a price that says we are wrong. In this case it would have been under 3680.

In Exhibit 4.9 we see a hammer with an extended lower shadow whose diminutive real body is at the top end of the session. We should note that a hammer can have a little upper shadow, as is the case here. This hammer became a solid floor of support.

Hanging Man

The hanging man has the same shape as the hammer; the only difference is that a hanging man comes after an advance (see Exhibit 4.6). Because a long lower shadow is viewed as a plus, and since the hanging man has such a shadow, it is especially important that one wait for bearish confirmation with the hanging man. At a minimum this would be a lower opening under the real body of the hanging man. But I usually recommend a close beneath the hanging man.

The reason for waiting for a close under the hanging man's real body is that if the market closes lower the next day, those who bought on the open or close of the hanging man day (and lots of trading occurs at these two times) are now left "hanging" with a losing position. This is why I would also like to see the hanging man at an all-time high, or at least at a high for a significant move. In this scenario the longs entering on the hanging man session are in their position at new highs, thus making them more nervous. Consequently, those longs might decide to back out of their now losing position. That could cascade into more selling pressure. Note how the second small real body in Exhibit 4.8 (line 2) was a hanging man whose bearish implications were confirmed by a lower close the next session.

Exhibit 4.10 is an excellent example of how the same line can be bearish (as in the hanging man line on January 29) or bullish (the hammer on February 22). Although both the hanging man and hammer in this example have white bodies, the color of the real body is not of consequence.

© Aspen Graphics. Used by permission.

Exhibit 4.10. Microsoft—Daily (Hanging Man and Hammer)

The first line was a hanging man because the trend preceding it was a rally. The hanging man was made at new highs for the move. The next day (February 1) the market closed lower than the hanging man's real body, leaving all those new longs—who bought on the hanging man's open or close—in pain.

The line on February 22 was a hammer because it followed a downtrend. The session before the hammer was a small real body. This was an early clue that the bears' drive was being inhibited. The hammer was more bullish proof of this.

In Exhibit 4.11, on December 13, we see an upside breakout from a short-term *box range* (the Japanese term for a lateral trading range). The rally from this breakout continued with three extended white real bodies, each of which opened near its low and closed at or near its highs. This underscored the bulls' domination. Some cautionary signals emerged after the third long white candle when a series of candles with upper shadows arose. Note also what was happening with the slope of the highs as we got these upper shadows. The slope from one high to the next was decreasing (shown by the curving line). That

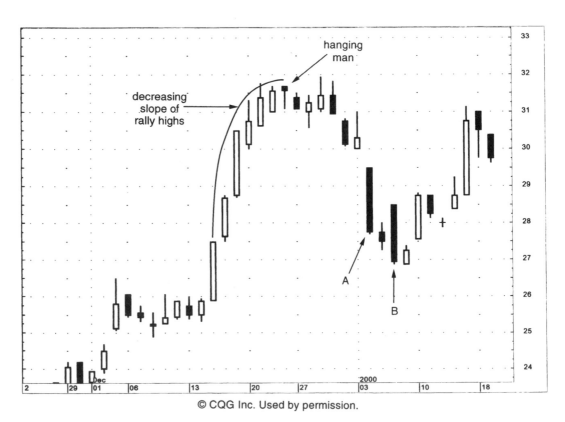

Exhibit 4.11. Unibanco Uniao de Bancos Brasileros—Daily (Hanging Man)

meant although new highs were still being made, the pace of the rally was slackening.

The real hint that the bulls were losing control of the market was with a hanging man session. Not only was this a hanging man session, but it was also the first black real body and the first spinning top of the rally. Confirmation of the hanging man came at the next session's close under the hanging man's real body. An attempt a couple days later to push the market higher stalled near $32 via a series of long upper shadows.

The descent from the hanging man at $32 lost bearish momentum near $27. We were able to tell this by what happened after long black real bodies at A and B. Specifically, on the day after each of these long black real bodies there was a small real body. We would think that after each bearish session at A and B, the market would continue lower the next session. But it didn't as shown by the spinning tops. This showed that the bears, as shown by the two long black candles at A and B, had tried to take control twice but on both occasions failed. This probably gave the bears second thoughts about selling and more encouragement for those thinking about buying.

Exhibit 4.12 highlights the importance of waiting for bearish confirmation with a hanging man. Candle lines at 1, 2, and 3 were hanging man lines (their upper shadows were small enough to keep them as hanging man lines). Each of these lines made a new high close for the move and thus kept the bullish momentum in force. To confirm the bearishness of any of these hanging lines, and to convert the trend from up to less positive, we would need a close under any of these hanging man real bodies. That did not occur. Remember, anybody who bought on the opening and closing of the hanging man session bought at the highs of the move. If the market continues higher after the hanging man session (as it did here), are these longs in pain? Of course not. They're happy because the market is higher than where they bought. As such, as shown in this example, if the market does not close under the hanging man's real body, then the bull trend remains entrenched.

© Aspen Graphics. Used by permission.

Exhibit 4.12. Gabelli Asset Management—Daily (Hanging Man and Confirmation)

Exhibit 4.13. Bullish Engulfing Pattern

Exhibit 4.14. Bearish Engulfing Pattern

THE ENGULFING PATTERN

The hammer and hanging man are individual candle lines. As previously seen, single candle lines through the color, length, and size of the real bodies and the shadows can send important signals about the market's health. Most candle signals, however, are based on combinations of individual candle lines. The engulfing pattern is the first of these multiple candle line patterns. The engulfing pattern is a major reversal signal with two opposite color real bodies composing this pattern.

Exhibit 4.13 shows a *bullish engulfing pattern*. The market is falling. Then a white bullish real body wraps around, or engulfs, the prior period's black real body (hence its name). Another nickname is a "hugging line" for obvious reasons. (Maybe on Valentine's Day I will refer to the engulfing pattern as a hugging pattern.) This shows buying pressure has overwhelmed selling pressure.

Exhibit 4.14 illustrates a *bearish engulfing pattern*. Here the market is trending higher. A white real body engulfed by a black real body is the signal for a top reversal. This shows that supply has overwhelmed demand.

There are three criteria for an engulfing pattern:

1. The market has to be in a clearly definable uptrend (for a bearish engulfing pattern) or downtrend (for a bullish engulfing pattern), even if the trend is short term.

2. Two candles comprise the engulfing pattern. The second real body must engulf the prior real body (it need not engulf the shadows).

3. The second real body of the engulfing pattern should be the opposite color of the first real body. (The exception to this rule is if the first real body of the engulfing pattern is a doji. Thus, after an extended fall, a doji engulfed by a very large white real body could be a bottom reversal. In an uptrend, a doji enveloped by a very large black real body could be a bearish reversal pattern).

The closest Western analogy to the Japanese engulfing pattern is the outside reversal session. In classic Western technicals, this occurs when, during an uptrend (or downtrend), a new high (or low) is made with prices closing under (or above) the prior day's close.

Some factors increasing the likelihood that an engulfing pattern could be an important turning signal are:

1. If the first day of the engulfing pattern has a very small real body (i.e., a spinning top) and the second day has a very long real body. The small first real body candle reflects a dissipation of the prior trend's force and the large second real body proves an increase in force behind the new move.

2. If the engulfing pattern appears after a protracted or very fast move. A fast or extended move creates an overextended market (either overbought or oversold) and makes it vulnerable to profit taking.

3. If there is heavy volume on the second real body of the engulfing pattern. Volume will be discussed in Part 2.

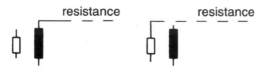
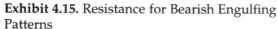

Exhibit 4.15. Resistance for Bearish Engulfing Patterns

Exhibit 4.16. Support for Bullish Engulfing Patterns

A prime use of the engulfing pattern is utilizing them as support or resistance. This is illustrated in Exhibits 4.15 and 4.16. In Exhibit 4.15 I use the high of the two candle lines that make the bearish engulfing pattern. That high becomes our resistance (based on a close). As shown in Exhibit 4.16, the same concept is used for the bullish engulfing pattern. With that I have found that the lowest low of that pattern should become support.

This technique of the bearish engulfing pattern as resistance and support is especially useful if the market has moved too far from the lows (with a bullish engulfing pattern) or highs (with a bearish engulfing pattern) to be comfortable selling or buying. For example, by the time a bullish engulfing pattern is completed (remember, we need to wait for the close of the second session before we know it's a bullish engulfing pattern), the market may be well off its lows. As such, I would feel that it has gotten away from an attractive buying area. In such a scenario, we can wait for a possible correction to our support area at the lows of the bullish engulfing pattern and then consider stepping in from the long side. The same would be true, but in reverse, for a bearish engulfing pattern.

In Exhibit 4.17 we see that the first white candle after six sessions of black descending candles emerged early on May 5. This white candle completed the bullish engulfing pattern. We then use the low of the bullish engulfing pattern (the lowest low of the two sessions that comprise the pattern) as support near $56. Lucent rallied from this bullish engulfing pattern and then stalled at a bearish engulfing pattern. Note how the high of this bearish engulfing pattern became resistance the next session. With the descent from this bearish engulfing pattern, a doji sent a tentative clue that the stock was trying to stabilize near the potential support at the bullish engulfing pattern. The stock rallied from this successful test of the bullish engulfing

Exhibit 4.17. Lucent—60 Minutes (Bullish Engulfing Pattern)

pattern's support, hesitated for a few sessions at the bearish engulfing pattern's resistance, and then continued its ascent along a rising support line.

In Chapter 1, I addressed the significance of real bodies, but shadows should be a pivotal part of your analysis. We look at an example of this aspect in Exhibit 4.18.[1] A series of long upper shadows—otherwise known as bearish shadows—arose during the weeks of November 2 and 16. These long upper shadows sent a strong visual clue that the market was rejecting the 1.1850 area. The decline that began after the second set of long upper shadows ended with a hammer (a candle with an extended lower shadow—another example of the shadow's significance). A few days after the hammer, the stock pulled back via a long black real body (that marginally broke the hammer's support). The next day a tall white candle completed a bullish engulfing pattern. The rally that began from the bullish engulfing pattern terminated at the doji at 1.1950. Note how the doji confirmed a resistance area defined by the late October's series of long upper

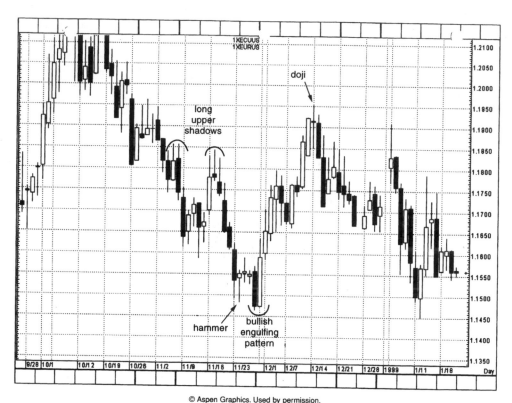

© Aspen Graphics. Used by permission.

Exhibit 4.18. Euro/Dollar—Daily (Bullish Engulfing Pattern)

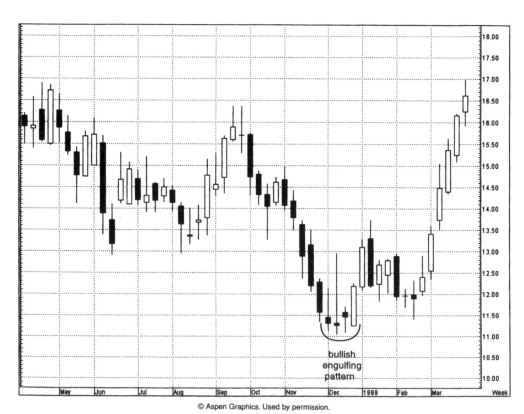

© Aspen Graphics. Used by permission.

Exhibit 4.19. Crude Oil—Weekly (Bullish Engulfing Pattern)

shadows. Remembering the concept of the bullish engulfing pattern as potential support, we look to the November 27 and 28 bullish engulfing pattern near 1.1470 as support. A successful test at this area occurred the week of January 11.

A major low in crude oil came with a classic bullish engulfing pattern as shown in Exhibit 4.19. This was a classic pattern insofar as the first real body was a small black real body (this showed the bears were losing a foothold) and the second candle was a vibrant long white real body that opened on its low and closed near its high. What was so significant about this particular bullish engulfing pattern was that the white real body engulfed not only one black real body, but three black real bodies. Keep in mind that while this clearly showed the bulls had taken full control from the bears, it does not signify the extent of the move following the bullish engulfing pattern. Candles, while unexcelled at sending out early reversal signals, do not provide price targets. This is why Western technicals are so important, as they can be used to help forecast price targets. This is an aspect we will look at in Part 2.

© CQG Inc. Used by permission.

Exhibit 4.20. Citibank—Daily (Bearish Engulfing Pattern)

In Exhibit 4.20 a rally that began at area A hesitated for a few sessions in late March near $43.50 with some long upper shadows and a doji. With a push over this five-day resistance area, as the Japanese would say, "The dirt was blown away." The rally resumed in earnest until it was short-circuited at the bearish engulfing pattern on April 13 and 14. Note the extreme size of the black real body of that pattern. This underscored how the bears had wrested control of the market from the bulls. This bearish engulfing pattern was confirmed as resistance a few weeks later with the emergence of another bearish engulfing pattern. This echoed the fact that each time the bulls were able to propel the stock toward $51.50, they couldn't hold control of the market.

Let's look at these two bearish engulfing patterns and compare them to a Western outside reversal session. In a Western outside reversal session (I'll focus on a top outside reversal session), the market makes a new high for the move and then closes the next day under the previous day's close. The first bearish engulfing pattern, if in bar chart form, would also be a traditional Western outside reversal day since the stock made a new high for the move with the top of the black candle session and then closed under the prior day's close.

Now, let's look at the second bearish engulfing pattern in late April. Note how the second candle in that bearish engulfing pattern failed to obtain a new high (its high was $51 and the prior session's high was $51.75). Consequently, if this was a traditional bar chart, it would not have been a reversal signal via an outside reversal session (since it didn't make a new high). But with a candle chart, all that is needed for the bearish engulfing pattern is for a black real body to wrap around a white real body, which is what happened in this instance. This is a good example of how the candles will provide a timing advantage on those who just use traditional bar chart analysis.

In Exhibit 4.21 a bearish engulfing pattern in early July took the force out of the preceding rally. This bearish engulfing pattern became resistance for the next week and a half. Once Cisco closed over the highs of this bearish engulfing pattern on July 15, it was a bullish breakout (even though it was a doji, the fact that it was a new high close is a positive). For those who are momentum players, the break above a bearish engulfing pattern could

Exhibit 4.21. Cisco—Daily (Bearish Engulfing Pattern)

be viewed as an indication of a new upleg and a time to consider buying. To confirm a breakout, I recommend waiting for a close over that resistance area, not just in intraday break. Another bearish engulfing pattern was completed on July 21 became resistance that was tested in late August. Notice as prices approached the bearish engulfing pattern's resistance area, a group of small real bodies reflected hesitation.

DARK-CLOUD COVER

Our next reversal pattern is the *dark-cloud cover* (see Exhibit 4.22). It is a dual-candle pattern that is a top reversal after an uptrend or, at times, at the top of a congestion band. The first day of this two-candle pattern is a strong white real body. The second day's price opens above the prior session's high (that is, above the top of the upper shadow). However, by the end of the second day's session, the market closes deeply within the prior day's white body. The greater the degree of penetration into the

Exhibit 4.22. Dark-Cloud Cover

THE IMPORTANCE OF PROTECTIVE STOPS

One of the more powerful aspects of technical analysis is that it can be used as a mechanism for a risk and money management approach to trading. Defining risk means using protective stops to help protect against unanticipated adverse price movements.

A stop should be placed at the time of the original trade, since this is when one is most objective. Stay in the position only if the market performs according to expectations. If subsequent price action either contradicts or fails to confirm these expectations, it is time to exit. If the market moves opposite to the chosen position, you may think, "Why bother with a stop? It is just a short-term move against me." Thus, you stubbornly stay with the position in the hope the market will turn in your direction. Remember two facts:

1. All long-term trends begin as short-term moves.
2. There is no room for hope in the market. The market goes its own way without regard to you or your position.

The market does not care whether you own it or not. The one thing worse than being wrong is staying wrong. Lose your opinion, *not* your money. Be proud of the ability to catch mistakes early. Getting stopped out concedes a mistake. People hate to admit mistakes since pride and prestige get involved. Good traders will not hold views too firmly. It has been said that famous private investor Warren Buffet has two rules:

1. Capital preservation.
2. Don't forget rule 1.

Stops are synonymous with rule 1. You have limited resources. These resources should be maximized, or at a minimum, preserved. If you are in a market that has moved against your position, it is time to exit and find a better opportunity. Think of a stop as a cost of doing business.

Since so much of the Japanese candle terminology is grounded on military terminology, we will look at stops in this context as well. Each trade you make is a battle—and you will have to do what even the greatest generals have to do: Make temporary, tactical retreats. A general's goal is to preserve troops and munitions. Yours is to save capital and equanimity. Sometimes you must lose a few battles to win the war. The Japanese have a saying, "A hook's well lost to catch a salmon." If you are stopped out, think of it as you would a lost hook. Maybe you will catch your prize with the next hook.

white real body, the more likely this is a top. Some Japanese technicians require more than a 50-percent penetration of the black session's close into the white real body. If the black candle does not close below the halfway point of the white candlestick, it may be best to wait for more bearish confirmation following the dark-cloud cover. In some circumstances I will also view it as a dark-cloud cover even if the open is over the prior session's close instead of the prior session's high.

The rationale behind this bearish pattern is readily explained. On the first session of the dark-cloud cover, the market is ascending with a strong white candle. This is followed by a gap higher on the next session's opening. Thus far, the bulls are in complete control. But then the whole technical picture changes as, on the second day of this pattern, the market closes not only beneath the prior close, but well within the prior day's real body, offsetting much of the gain of the first session. In such a scenario, the longs will have second thoughts about their position. Those who were waiting for selling short now have a benchmark to place a stop—at the new high of the second day of the dark-cloud cover pattern.

Some factors intensifying the importance of dark-cloud covers include:

1. The greater the penetration of the black real body's close into the prior white real body, the greater the chance for a top. (If the black real body covers the prior day's entire white body, it would be a bearish engulfing pattern rather than a dark-cloud cover.) Think of the dark-cloud cover as a partial solar eclipse blocking out part of the sun (that is, covers only part of the prior white body). The bearish engulfing pattern can be viewed as a total solar eclipse blocking out the entire sun (that is, covers the entire white body). A bearish engulfing pattern, consequently, can be a more meaningful top reversal. If a long white real body closes above the highs of the dark-cloud cover, or the bearish engulfing pattern it could presage another rally.

2. During a prolonged ascent, if there is a strong white day that opens on its low (that is, a shaven bottom) and closes on its high (that is, a shaven head) and the next day reveals a long black real body day, opening on its high and closing on its low, then a shaven head and shaven bottom black day has occurred.

3. If the second body (that is, the black body) of the dark-cloud cover opens above a major resistance level and then fails, it

would prove the bulls were unable to take control of the market.

4. If, on the opening of the second day, there is very heavy volume, then a buying blow off could have occurred. For example, heavy volume at a new opening high could mean that many new buyers have decided to jump aboard ship. Then the market sells off. It probably won't be too long before this multitude of new longs (and old longs who have ridden the uptrend) realize that the ship they jumped onto is the *Titanic*. For futures traders, very high opening interest can be another warning.

Just as a bearish engulfing pattern can be resistance, so too the highest high of the two sessions that formed the dark-cloud cover should be resistance. This is shown in Exhibit 4.22.

A dark-cloud cover in Exhibit 4.23 stopped a rally. The day after this pattern, Intel pushed up and failed near the high of this pattern near $71. The stock stalled again near $71 a week and then two weeks later. Observe how Intel poked its head above the resistance line on January 20, but the failure to close over the resistance keeps resistance intact.

Exhibit 4.23. Intel—Daily (Dark-Cloud Cover)

© Aspen Graphics. Used by permission.

Exhibit 4.24. Wolverine Tube—Daily (Dark-Cloud Cover)

In Exhibit 4.24 we see a rally that began mid August. On August 22 the stock gapped higher and formed a hanging man session, but its potential bearish implications were not confirmed the next session since the next day's close was over the hanging man's real body. The stock had a final push with a gap higher opening on August 28 at $43.25. On that opening it looked fine from the bulls' perspective. It closed down at $40.62 by the end of that session. This completed a dark-cloud cover since the black candle pulled well into the prior session's white real body.

While this was a well-defined dark-cloud cover, from a risk–reward perspective it may not have been a good place to sell. This is because the dark-cloud cover was finalized on the close of the second day of the pattern, and by then it was well off its highs. Using the concept of the dark-cloud cover as potential resistance, one could wait for a bounce to near the dark-cloud cover to sell (assuming this occurs). In early October a rally to the high of the dark-cloud cover showed signs of running out of steam with a small black real body and

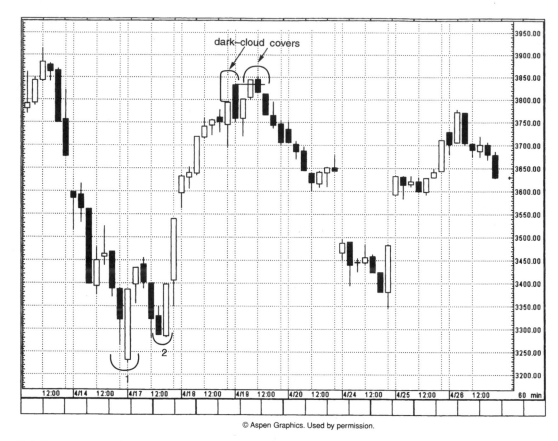

dark-cloud covers

© Aspen Graphics. Used by permission.

Exhibit 4.25. NASDAQ Composite—60 Minutes (Dark-Cloud Cover)

the same highs for four consecutive sessions at $43.25. The decline from early October ended with a hammer that confirmed a late September support area.

Dual bullish engulfing patterns at 1 and 2 in Exhibit 4.25 underscored the solidity of support in the 3275/3250 area. The rally from the second bullish engulfing pattern hesitated at the dark-cloud cover. Immediately after this pattern, a white real body marginally penetrated the dark-cloud cover's resistance (shown at the horizontal line). While not a decisive breakout, it was a close above resistance and as such a positive signal.

Exhibit 4.25 reflects the importance of adapting to changing market conditions. To wit, the breakout above resistance at the first dark-cloud cover puts the trend higher, but the next session our market view changes from positive to a more cautionary one. Why? Because the day after the breakout a black candle completed another dark-cloud cover. This second black candle reflected an inability by the bulls to hold the new highs.

support

Exhibit 4.26. Piercing Pattern

PIERCING PATTERN

As is true with most candle patterns, for each bearish pattern there is an opposite bullish pattern. So it is with the bearish dark-cloud cover. The dark-cloud cover's counterpart is the bullish *piercing pattern* (see Exhibit 4.26). The piercing pattern is composed of two candles in a falling market. The first candle is a black real body day and the second is a white real body. This white candle opens lower, ideally under the low of the prior black day. Then prices rebound to push well into the black candle's real body.

The piercing pattern is akin to the bullish engulfing pattern. In the bullish engulfing pattern, the white real body engulfs the entire previous black real body. For the piercing pattern, the white real body pierces, but does not wrap around, the prior black body. In the piercing pattern, the greater the degree of penetration into the black real body, the more likely it will become a bottom reversal. An ideal piercing pattern will have a white real body that pushes more than halfway into the prior session's black real body. The psychology behind the piercing pattern is as follows: The market is in a downtrend. The bearish black real body reinforces this view. The next session the market opens lower via a gap. The bears are watching the market with contentment. Then the market surges toward the close, managing not only to close unchanged from the prior day's close, but sharply above that close. The bears will be second-guessing their position. Those who are looking to buy would say new lows could not hold and could view it as an opportunity to buy.

The piercing pattern signal increases in importance based on the same factors 1 through 4 as with the dark-cloud cover, but in reverse. (See previous section.) With the dark-cloud cover we would like to see the black real body closing more than midway in the prior white candlestick. But there is some flexibility to this rule. There is less flexibility with the piercing pattern. The piercing pattern's white candlestick should push more than halfway into the black candlestick's real body. The reason for less latitude with the bullish piercing pattern than with the bearish dark-cloud cover pattern is the fact that the Japanese have three other patterns called the *on-neck*, the *in-neck*, and the

Exhibit 4.27. On-Neck Pattern

Exhibit 4.28. In-Neck Pattern

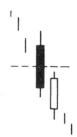

Exhibit 4.29. Thrusting Pattern

thrusting pattern (see Exhibits 4.27 to 4.29). They have the same basic formation as the piercing pattern. The difference among them is in the degree of penetration by the white candle into the black candle's real body. The on-neck pattern's white candle (usually a small one) closes near the low of the previous session. The in-neck pattern's white candle closes slightly into the prior real body (it should also be a small white candle). The thrusting pattern should be a longer white candle that is stronger than the in-neck pattern, but still does not close above the middle of the prior black real body.

It's not important to remember the individual patterns in Exhibits 4.27 to 4.29. Instead, just remember the concept that the white candle should push more than halfway into the black candle's real body to send out a more potent bottom reversal signal.

A series of long lower shadows shown in Exhibit 4.30 at areas 1 and 2 denoted potential support near $56. But on September 8 Dayton-Hudson pummeled through this support as it opened near $54. The bears had gained control—or so they thought. By the end of September 8, the bulls had successfully propelled the

© Aspen Graphics. Used by permission.

Exhibit 4.30. Dayton-Hudson—Daily (Piercing Pattern)

stock to well above the prior session's close. The candle lines of September 7 and 8 built a piercing pattern. A week after the piercing pattern, a hammer on September 16 reinforced the pattern's support near $54. More confirmation emerged the week after the hammer with a series of long lower shadows.

A rally that started from a bullish engulfing pattern in mid March in Exhibit 4.31 displayed a hint of trouble with the March 24 spinning top near $59. A close over $59 on April 3 with a long white real body put the bulls back in charge, at least until the next session. On this session (April 4) the stock formed a variation of a dark-cloud cover. It was a variation of the dark-cloud cover because with that pattern we like to see an open on the second day above the prior session's high. In this case, the open was above the prior day's close. Nonetheless, since the black candle on April 4 pulled so deeply into the white candle's real body, it increased the likelihood that this would be as effective as a more traditional dark-cloud cover.

The piercing pattern on April 17 and 18 presaged a rally. The rally from this piercing pattern continued until another dark-cloud cover on April 24 and 25. This second dark-cloud cover

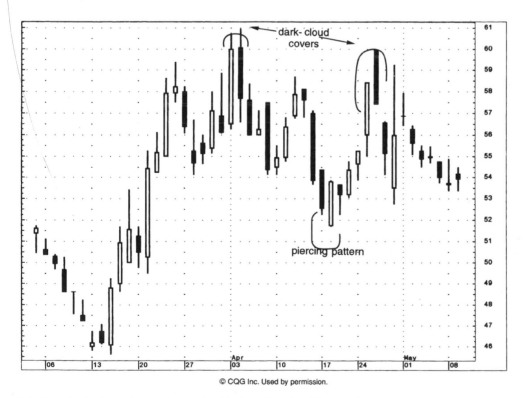

Exhibit 4.31. American General—Daily (Piercing Pattern)

could also be viewed as a variation of a classic dark-cloud cover. Why? Because the black real body did not push more than halfway into the white real body. Once again, while this wasn't a classic dark-cloud cover, there were two factors that led me to believe it was just as negative as a traditional dark-cloud cover. Specifically, (1) the black candle on April 25 opened sharply above the prior day's high and then closed under the prior day's close, and (2) this pattern was also a failure, and hence confirmation of resistance at the early April dark-cloud cover.

This chart highlights the general concept that one should view a non-ideal candle pattern by (1) how it was formed and (2) within the overall market picture. These two factors will help us gauge if the less-than-perfect pattern could have the same implications as a more classicly defined candle pattern. It is this subjectivity that makes computer recognition of candle patterns so difficult. For example, the two dark-cloud covers discussed in this exhibit did not meet the classic definition of the dark-cloud cover, but I viewed them as dark-cloud covers

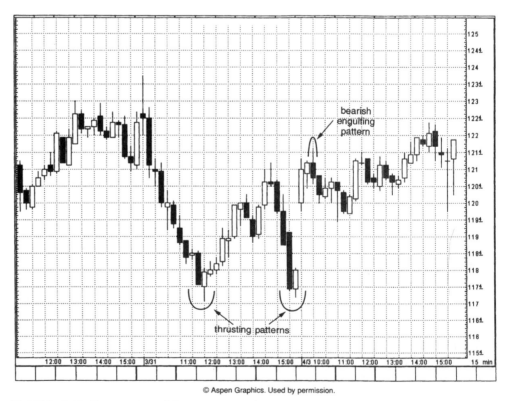

© Aspen Graphics. Used by permission.

Exhibit 4.32. International Business Machines—15 Minutes (Thrusting Patterns)

because of how and where they were formed, as discussed in the prior paragraph.

With a piercing pattern that doesn't push deeply into the prior black candle, I usually suggest waiting for confirmation with a higher close the session after the white candle. In Exhibit 4.32, late in the morning of March 31, a white candle pushed into the black candle. Since it did not close above the middle black candle, it wasn't a piercing pattern. It was a thrusting pattern. The higher close the session after this thrusting pattern helped reinforce that this could be a bottoming signal. Late in the session of March 31 another thrusting pattern was formed near $117. Normally with a thrusting pattern (as we saw earlier that day) one should wait for some bullish confirmation. But with this second thrusting pattern, because it confirmed a prior support area, one would need less bullish confirmation (i.e., less reason to wait for higher close the next session). As such, for active momentum traders, the close of the white candle of the second thrusting pattern could have been used as a buying opportunity. An exit signal was given with the bearish engulfing pattern early the next morning.

Note

1. Shadows are examined in detail in my book *Beyond Candlesticks* (New York: John Wiley, 1994).

CHAPTER 5
STARS

用人に飽きはない

One cannot be too cautious.

One group of fascinating reversal patterns is those that include *stars*. A star is a small real body (white or black) that gaps away from the large real body preceding it (see Exhibit 5.1). In other words, the star's real body can be within the prior session's upper shadow; all that is needed is that the real bodies don't overlap (there are some exceptions to this rule, which are addressed later in this section). If the star is a doji instead of a small real body, it is called a doji star (Exhibit 5.2). The star, especially the doji star, is a warning that the prior trend may be ending.

The star's small real body represents a stalemate between the bulls and bears. The bulls are obviously in charge in a briskly

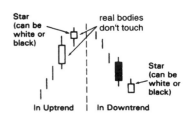

EXHIBIT 5.1. Star in an Uptrend and a Downtrend

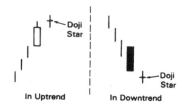

EXHIBIT 5.2. Doji Star in an Uptrend and a Downtrend

ascending market. With the emergence of a star in such an environment, it is a signal of a shift from the buyers being in control to a deadlock between the buying and selling forces. This deadlock may have occurred either because of a diminution in the buying force or an increase in the selling pressure. Either way, the star tells us the rally's prior power has slightly dissipated. This means the market is vulnerable to a setback.

The same is true, but in reverse, for a star in a downtrend (sometimes a star during a downtrend is labeled a *raindrop*). The long black candle during the downtrend visually reflects that the bears are in command. A change is seen in the advent of the star, which signals an environment in which the bulls and the bears are more in equilibrium. In other words, the downward energy has thus been cooled. This is not a favorable scenario for a continuation of the bear market.

The star is part of four reversal patterns including:

1. the morning star;

2. the evening star;

3. the doji stars; and

4. the shooting star.

THE MORNING STAR

The *morning star* (Exhibit 5.3) is a bottom reversal pattern. Its name is derived because, like the morning star (the nickname for the planet Mercury) that foretells the sunrise, it presages higher prices. There are three candle lines comprising this pattern:

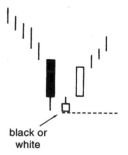

black or white

EXHIBIT 5.3. Morning Star

- *Candle 1.* An extended black real body. This pictorially proves that the bears are in command.

- *Candle 2.* A small real body that doesn't touch the prior real body (these two lines comprise a basic star pattern). The small real body means sellers are losing the capacity to drive the market lower.

- *Candle 3.* The concluding candle of the morning star is a white real body that intrudes deeply into the first session's black candle. This is the indication that the bulls have seized control.

The lowest low of the three lines that form this pattern should be support as shown by the dashed line in Exhibit 5.3.

An ideal morning star would have a gap between the second and third real bodies. From my experience, a lack of a gap does not seem to weaken the power of this formation. The decisive factor is that the second candle should be a spinning top and the third candle pushes well into the black candle.

Exhibit 5.4 is an example of this. In late July/early August we see three candle lines that make up the requisite criteria of a morning star: a long black candle, a small real body, and then a tall white candle. Of course, this pattern has to follow a decline. An aspect that kept this from an ideal morning star pattern was that the third real body wrapped around the second candle. However, from my experience, even if the second and third candles overlap, it doesn't mitigate the effectiveness of this pattern. In fact, the second and third lines of this morning star pattern created a bullish engulfing pattern.

EXHIBIT 5.4. Wheat—Weekly Continuation (Morning Star)

This chart is also a good example of how candle charts will frequently give turning signals before the more traditional signals derived from a bar chart. A bear channel that began in February remained in force until the third quarter that year. The close over the top of the bear channel was the traditional Western signal that the downtrend had been broken. By using the light of the candles (via the morning star), we had obtained an early warning beacon of a turn many sessions prior to the break over the bear channel.

A limitation with the morning star is that since this is a three-candle pattern, one has to wait until the close of the third session to complete the pattern. As is usually the case, if this third candle is a tall white one, we would get the signal well after the market already had a sharp bounce. In other words, the completion of the morning star may not present an attractive risk/reward trading opportunity. An option is waiting for a correction to the morning star's support area to start nibbling from the long side. As shown in Exhibit 5.5, there was a morning star in early February. If one bought on the completion of this pattern near $74, by the next day he or she would have had a loss. By waiting for a correction to anywhere near the low of the morning star (toward $65.50) before buying, a trader would decrease his or her risk since the stop would be under the low of the morning star. As this stock ascended, it did so along a rising support line. (Trend lines are the focus of Chapter 11.)

While the ideal morning and evening stars should have none of their three real bodies touching, there is even more flexibility to the definition of the morning star (and also the evening star) in markets where the open and close are either the same or close to one another. This would include:

1. Foreign exchange markets where there is no official open and close.

2. Many indexes such as the Semi-Conductor or Drug Indexes.

3. Intraday charts. For instance, on a 15-minute chart the open of a 15-minute session is usually not much different from the close of the prior 15-minute session.

© Aspen Graphics. Used by permission.

EXHIBIT 5.5. Merrill Lynch—Daily (Morning Star)

Let's use the intraday chart in Exhibit 5.6 to see an instance of the value of being flexible in interpreting the candle patterns. Mid-day on December 27 the index made a new low for the move and in doing so broke under the support from early that day of 3535/3530. The bears thus took control. But at 13:00 a small real body and the next session's long white candle made a morning star. Notice how all three bodies touched one another (the open of the second candle was the same as the close of the first candle and the open of the third candle was the same as the close of the second session). Because this was an intraday chart where the open/close difference is usually minor, I still viewed this as a viable morning star. This pattern took on more credibility since the third candle, which finalized this pattern, also pushed the index back above the previously broken support area near 3530. When a market makes a new low and the bears can't maintain these new lows, it is frequently a hint of a reversal.

© Aspen Graphics. Used by permission.

EXHIBIT 5.6. NASDAQ Composite Index—15 Minutes (Morning Star)

THE EVENING STAR

The *evening star* is the bearish counterpart of the morning star pattern. It is aptly named because the evening star (the nickname for the planet Venus) appears just before darkness sets in. Since the evening star is a top reversal, it should be acted upon if it arises after an uptrend. Three lines compose the evening star (see Exhibit 5.7). The first is a long white real body, the next is a star. The star is the first hint of a top. The third line corroborates a top and completes the three-line pattern of the evening star. The third line is a black real body that closes sharply into the first period's white real body. I like to compare the evening star pattern to a traffic light. The traffic light goes from green (the bullish white real body) to yellow (the star's warning signal) to red (the black real body confirming the prior trend has stopped).

In principle, an evening star should have a gap between the first and second real bodies and then another gap between the second and third real bodies. But, as detailed earlier in the section on the morning star, this second gap is rarely seen and is

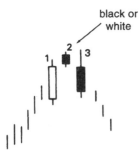

EXHIBIT 5.7. Evening Star

not necessary for the success of this pattern. The main concern should be the extent of the intrusion of the third day's black real body into the first day's white real body.

At first glance Exhibit 5.7 is like an island top reversal as used by Western technicians. Analyzing the evening star more closely shows it furnishes a reversal signal not available with an island top (see Exhibit 5.8). For an island top, the low of session 2 has to be above the highs of sessions 1 and 3. However, the ideal evening star only requires real body 2 to be above the high of real bodies 1 and 3 to be a reversal signal.

Some factors increasing the likelihood that an evening or morning star could be a reversal would include:

1. If there is no overlap among the first, second, and third real bodies.

2. If the third candle closes deeply into the first candle's real body.

3. If there is light volume on the first candle session and heavy volume on the third candle session. This would show a reduction of the force for the prior trend and an increase in the direction force of the new trend.

The highs of the evening star become resistance as displayed by the dashed line shown in Exhibit 5.7.

Let's look at Exhibit 5.9. A classic evening star was completed in early January. This evening star had the ideal prerequisite of the three real bodies not intersecting. Intersecting the star portion (that is, the second candle line of the evening star pattern) was a hanging man line whose bearish confirmation came the next day. The descent from the evening star culminated a week later near 1210 at area A. The rally from A hesitated a week later via a doji near the resistance area created by the evening star. This doji hinted the rally was exhausting itself. (Dojis are discussed in Chapter 8.)

The next time the market rallied to this resistance in the first week of February, it formed a bearish engulfing pattern at B. I mention this bearish engulfing pattern to bring out the importance of trend in helping to define a candle pattern. I have discussed how a bearish engulfing pattern is when a black real body engulfs a white real body. There was a black real body at A that

EXHIBIT 5.8. Western Island Top

wrapped around a prior white candle. Was this a bearish engulfing pattern? No, because it came after a price decline; whereas a bearish engulfing, as a top reversal, needs a rally to reverse. This is why I define B as a bearish engulfing pattern, but not A.

Another doji in late February echoed continued supply near the evening star's resistance level. The long black candle after this doji formed another evening star pattern. This evening star had a doji as a second candle line instead of a spinning top. This is a special type of evening star called an *evening doji star*, which is discussed later in this section. The second evening star is an example where the second and third candles overlapped. From my experience this works as well as the more classic pattern in which none of the real bodies touch.

A challenge with some of the candle patterns is that by the time the pattern is completed, the market may be well off its highs or lows. The evening star, because of the need to wait for its completion with a long black real body, may give a reversal signal well after the market has already turned. We look at this aspect in Exhibit 5.10.

As shown in this chart, the high of the move was near $34, with the evening star's completion on the close of the third session at $31. As such, if one sold based on the evening star at $31, the risk would be to the high of evening star toward $34. There is no problem with a $3 risk if the target is many times that risk. Only then would it be an attractive risk/reward trade.

If this $3 risk is too large, one can improve the risk/reward aspect of this trade by waiting for a bounce to near the resistance area at the top of the evening star (of course, there is no guarantee of a bounce). In this example, two sessions after the evening star we got a $2 rebound which took the stock very close to its pivotal resistance at $34. After this stock resumed its decline, it moved into the April–May period. The shrinking real bodies presaged that chances for a turnaround had increased.

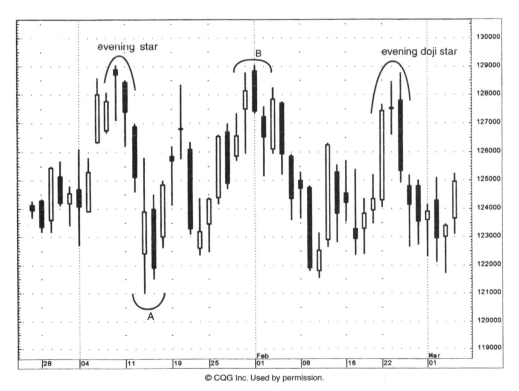

EXHIBIT 5.9. S&P Index—Daily (Evening Star)

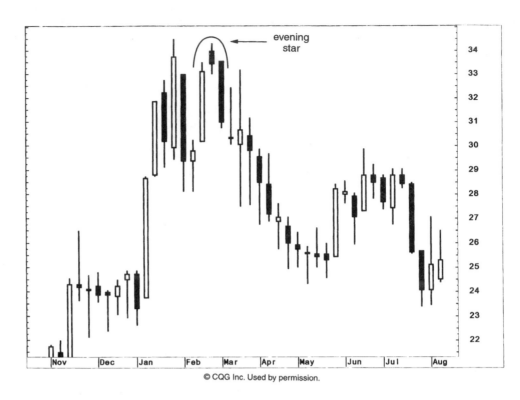

© CQG Inc. Used by permission.

EXHIBIT 5.10. Roger Communications—Weekly (Evening Star)

EXHIBIT 5.11. Evening Doji Star

EXHIBIT 5.12. Morning Doji Star

THE MORNING AND EVENING DOJI STARS

An evening star that has a doji instead of a small real body as the second candle is called an *evening doji star* (see Exhibit 5.11). The evening doji star is a distinctive form of the regular evening star. We saw an example of this pattern in Exhibit 5.9.

A morning star that has a doji as the star portion (i.e., the middle candle of the three candle lines) is a *morning doji star* (see Exhibit 5.12). This type of morning star can be a meaningful bottom.

If there is an evening doji star in which the bottom shadow of the doji session does not overlap with the shadows of the first or third candles (that is, the shadows do not touch), it is considered a top reversal signal known as an *abandoned baby top* (see Exhibit 5.13). This pattern is very rare.

The same is true, only in reverse, for a bottom. Specifically, if there is a doji that has a gap before and after it (where the shadows do not touch), it should be a bottom. This pattern is referred to as an *abandoned baby bottom* (see Exhibit 5.14). It is also extremely rare. To give an idea on the rarity of this pattern, consider that the abandoned baby is the same as a Western island top or bottom where the island session would be a doji.

Because the middle line of the morning star in Exhibit 5.15 was a doji, this is an example of a morning doji star. Here we see how the third candle line slightly overlapped the second real body (i.e., doji line). The ascent from this morning doji star ran out of force with the series of spinning tops (a.k.a. small real bodies). As is the case with the traditional morning star, the lowest low of the morning doji star (in this case near $92) should act as a base on pullbacks. That is what happened in mid October as the morning doji star held its ground as support. The doji portion of the morning star had long upper and lower shadows. This further reflects that the market is losing its prior directional bias (which in this example was down). This doji, called a *long-legged doji*, is discussed in Chapter 8.

An evening doji star is shown in Exhibit 5.16. Ideally, I would have liked to see the last black candle of this pattern close more into the white real body of the first session. However, the fact that this occurred at a "century" mark of $400 (a "century

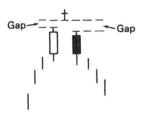

EXHIBIT 5.13.
Abandoned Baby Top

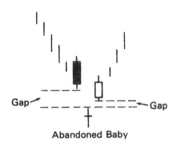

EXHIBIT 5.14.
Abandoned Baby Bottom

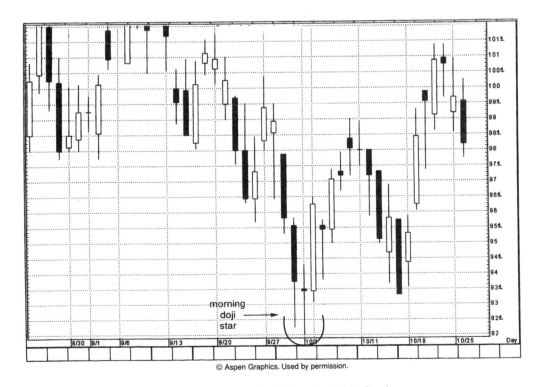

© Aspen Graphics. Used by permission.

EXHIBIT 5.15. Procter & Gamble—Daily (Morning Doji Star)

EXHIBIT 5.16. Drug Index—Daily (Evening Doji Star)

mark" is a round $100 figure that can become support or resistance) and then the failure to push over the resistance area of this pattern a few days later (via a long upper shadow candle) helped substantiate this as an evening doji star. This $400 level remained an upside barrier over the next few weeks with the long black real body on November 30 providing the "death blow" in forming a bearish engulfing pattern.

In Exhibit 5.17 an evening doji star pattern formed in late February. Because the market gapped before and then after the doji, this pattern was an abandoned baby top. Also troubling about this particular scenario was the third day's abandoned baby (gapped down). This showed the prior day's new high close above $56 could not be sustained. When a new high is made and the bulls can't maintain the new highs, it often had bearish consequences. This is discussed in Chapter 11.

The ideal abandoned baby bottom has a doji as the second real body. In Exhibit 5.18 there was a diminutive real body as the second session instead of the requisite doji needed for the ideal abandoned baby. However, the real body was so small

EXHIBIT 5.17. CVS—Daily (Abandoned Baby Top)

EXHIBIT 5.18. Soybean Oil—Daily (Abandoned Baby Bottom)

that it could be viewed as a doji and thus a variation of this pattern (this second session was also a hammer). The advance from this bottom reversal persisted until a series of longer upper shadows (at the arrows) alerted us that the bulls were not calling all the shots. This further buttressed the outlook that the market had hit a ceiling. A rebound commenced after the bullish engulfing pattern of April 6 and 7.

THE SHOOTING STAR AND THE INVERTED HAMMER

As shown in Exhibit 5.19, the *shooting star* has a small real body at the lower end of its range with a long upper shadow. We can see how this line's name is derived. It looks like a shooting star with its long tail blazing across the sky. The Japanese aptly say that the shooting star shows trouble overhead. Since it is one session, it is usually not a major reversal signal as is the bearish engulfing pattern or evening star. Nor do I view the shooting star as pivotal resistance as I do with the two previously mentioned patterns.

As with all stars, the color of the real body is not important. The shooting star pictorially tells us that the market opened near its low, then strongly rallied and finally backed off to close near the opening. In other words, that session's rally could not be sustained.

Since the shooting star is a bearish reversal signal, it must come after a rally. An ideal shooting star has a real body that gaps away from the prior real body. Nonetheless, as will be seen in several chart examples, this gap is not always necessary. A lack of a rising gap is more of a reason to be negative on the shooting star. This is because, as addressed in Chapter 7, an ascending gap, called a "rising window" in Japan, is a positive signal. As such, I am more comfortable saying the trend could be turning less bullish if the shooting star has no gap. If a shooting star–shaped candle line comes after a downturn, it could be a bullish signal. Such a line is called an inverted hammer. The inverted hammer line is discussed later in this chapter.

EXHIBIT 5.19. Shooting Star

The Shooting Star

If Exhibit 5.20 were formed as a bar chart instead of a candle chart, sessions A, B, and C would reflect a healthy environment because they each had higher highs, higher lows, and higher closes. But from a candle charting perspective, we get visual warnings with these sessions of trouble overhead. Specifically, the bearish upper shadows at A, B, and C strongly indicate a stock that is, as the Japanese say, "rising in agony." Final confirmation of a top came at session C, the shooting star. You may have noticed that a gravestone doji looks like a shooting star. The gravestone doji is a specific version of a shooting star. The shooting star has a small real body but the gravestone doji—being a doji—has no real body. The gravestone doji is thus more bearish than a shooting star.

In Exhibit 5.21, the first shooting star—in what was to be a series of shooting stars—arose on March 10 at $34.50. A few weeks later, three consecutive shooting stars appeared at this

EXHIBIT 5.20. Mail Well—Daily (Shooting Star)

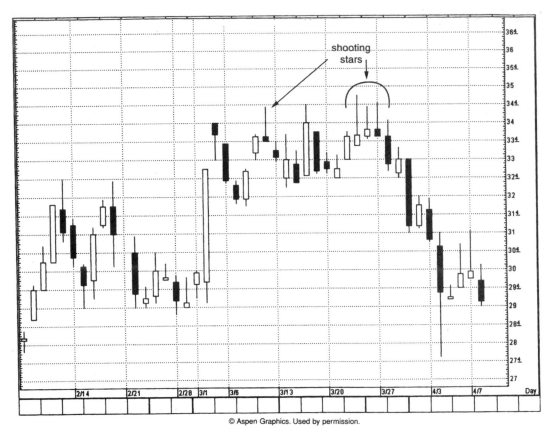

EXHIBIT 5.21. Unibanco Uniao de Bancos Brasileros—Daily (Shooting Star)

same $34.50 level. This told us that try as they might, each time the bulls had been able to push the stock up to $34.50, they couldn't sustain these intraday highs into the close. In other words, the shooting stars were visually showing us that the market was rejecting higher prices. When, as in this example, we get signal after signal at the same price level, it reinforces that resistance area. In this case the confluence of shooting stars dramatically increased the likelihood that this would be a reversal. Of course, if the bulls had enough force to close this stock over the highs of the shooting stars, then we would reassess any bearish views.

A shooting star early on August 22 in Exhibit 5.22 reinforced trouble near $304 since it was the third consecutive session that failed there. The 30-minute period following the shooting star gave more proof of a top since it produced a bearish engulfing pattern. Corning then settled into a box range defined by the support of the hammer at $294 from late on August 23 (which was successfully defended with another hammer early the next

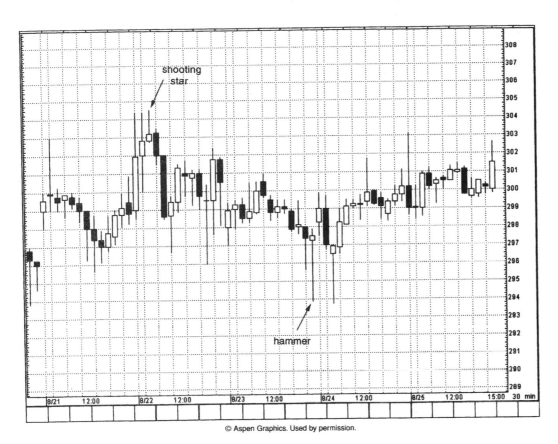

EXHIBIT 5.22. Corning—30 Minutes (Shooting Star)

day). The rally from the second hammer at $294 hit a ceiling with the shooting star's resistance near $304.

The Inverted Hammer

While not a star pattern, I want to discuss the *inverted hammer* in this section because of its resemblance to the shooting star. Exhibit 5.23 demonstrates how an inverted hammer has the same form as a shooting star with its long upper shadow and small real body at the lower end of the range. The only difference between the shooting star and inverted hammer is that the inverted hammer comes after a decline. As a result, while the shooting star is a top reversal line, the inverted hammer is a bottom reversal line. The color of the inverted hammer's real body doesn't matter. This is similar in concept to the hammer and hanging man concept (see Chapter 4) in which the same shape line is bullish or bearish depending on the preceding trend.

EXHIBIT 5.23. Inverted Hammer

Just as a hanging man needs bearish confirmation, the inverted hammer needs bullish confirmation. This confirmation could be in the form of the next day opening above the inverted hammer's real body or especially a close the next day over the inverted hammer's real body.

The reason for the required bullish verification of the inverted hammer is because its long upper shadow gives the inverted hammer a bearish hue. To wit, on the inverted hammer session the market opens on, or near, its low and then rallies. The bulls fail to sustain the rally and prices close at, or near, the lows of the session. Why should negative action like this be a potentially bullish reversal signal? The answer has to do with what happens over the next session. If the next day opens, and especially closes, over the inverted hammer's real body, it means those who shorted at the opening or closing of the inverted hammer are losing money. The longer the market holds above the inverted hammer's real body, the more likely these shorts will cover. This could spark a short covering rally that could lead to bottom pickers going long. This could feed upon itself with the result being the beginning of a rally.

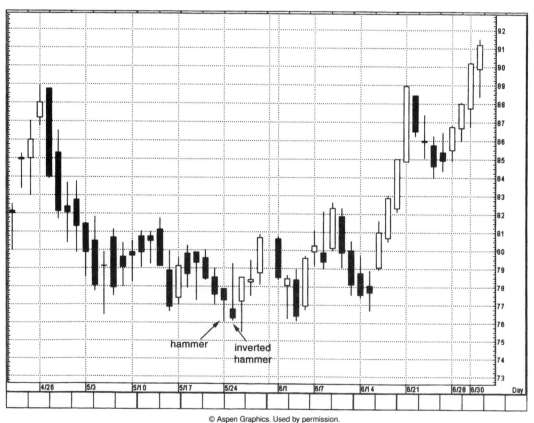

EXHIBIT 5.24. Microsoft—Daily (Inverted Hammer)

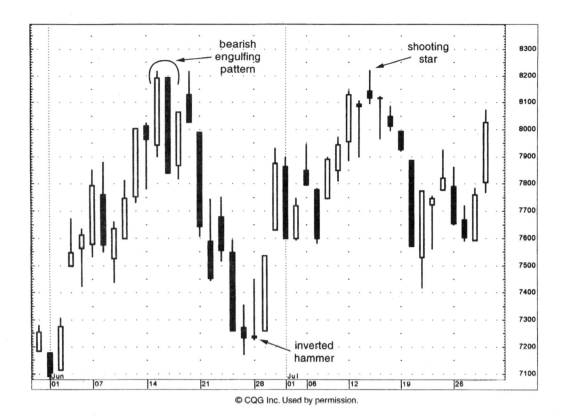

EXHIBIT 5.25. Oil Service Index—Daily (Inverted Hammer)

On May 24 in Exhibit 5.24, a hammer generated support at
$76. The next day an inverted hammer formed. This was a new
low close for the move, and as such kept the short-term trend
pointing down. However, the hammer's support was still being
maintained. The May 26 close accomplished two plusses: It
once again confirmed the hammer's support and it provided
bullish confirmation of the inverted hammer since it was a
close over that line's real body. If more bullish confirmation
was needed of the solidity of support at $76, it came on June 2
with another hammer.

A bearish engulfing pattern in mid June in Exhibit 5.25 developed into resistance a few days later. The descent from this failure at resistance near $82 culminated with an inverted hammer.
This line was confirmed by a higher opening the next day, and
especially with that session's higher close. The rally from this
inverted hammer continued into the week of July 12 when a
shooting star implied that the bearish engulfing pattern's resistance was still in force.

CHAPTER 6

MORE REVERSAL PATTERNS

臭い物に蓋

Put a lid on what smells bad.

Most of the reversal formations in Chapters 4 and 5 are comparatively strong reversal signals. They show that the bulls have taken over from the bears (as in the bullish engulfing pattern, a morning star, or a piercing pattern) or that the bears have wrested control from the bulls (as in the bearish engulfing pattern, the evening star, or the dark-cloud cover). This chapter examines more reversal indicators that are usually, but not always, less powerful reversal signals. These include the harami pattern, tweezers tops and bottoms, belt-hold lines, the upside-gap two crows, and counterattack lines. This chapter then explores more potent reversal signals that include three black crows, three mountains, three rivers, dumpling tops, frypan bottoms, and tower tops and bottoms.

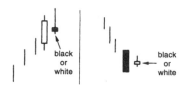

EXHIBIT 6.1. Harami

THE HARAMI PATTERN

Spinning tops (that is, small real bodies) are components in certain formations. The harami is one of these formations (the star, examined in Chapter 5, is another). The *harami pattern* (see Exhibit 6.1) is a small real body that is contained within what the Japanese call "an unusually long black or white real body." "Harami" is an old Japanese word for pregnant. The Japanese nickname for the long candle is the "mother" candle and the small candle is the "baby" or "fetus." The second candle of the harami can be white or black. If, for example, both the first and second candles of the harami are white, it would be expressed as "white–white harami."

The Japanese will say that with a harami the market is "losing its breath." The bearish harami displays a disparity about the market's health. Specifically after a bull move, the long white real body's vitality is followed by the small real body's uncertainty. Additionally, the small real body opening and closing within the prior open–close range is another indication that the bulls' upward drive has weakened. Thus, a trend reversal is possible. During a bear move, the selling force reflected by a long black real body is followed by the second day's vacillation. This could portend a trend reversal since the second day's small real body is an alert that the bears' power has diminished.

The combination of candle lines in the harami pattern, with its first tall real body followed by a small real body, is the reverse of the engulfing pattern. In the engulfing pattern, a lengthy real body engulfs the preceding small real body.

Another difference between the harami and engulfing patterns is that for the two candles of the engulfing pattern, the color of the real bodies should be opposite. This is not necessary for the harami. You should find, however, that in most instances, the real bodies in the harami are oppositely colored.

The harami formation is comparable to the Western inside day. For a Western inside day (see Exhibit 6.2), the entire range of the second session has to be within the entire range of the first session. This is not necessary for harami. For harami all that is required is that the second real body be within the first real body, even if the shadow of the second day is above or below the prior day's high and low. Notice the bearish harami

EXHIBIT 6.2. Inside Day

on the left of Exhibit 6.1. On the second session the upper shadow moved over the prior white real body. This is still a harami because the second session's real body was contained within the first real body.

Harami Cross

The regular harami has a tall real body followed by a small real body. Yet, there are no rules as to what is considered a "small" candle. This, like many other charting techniques, is subjective. As the general principle, the more diminutive the second real body, the more potent the pattern. This is usually true because the smaller the real body, the greater the ambivalence and the more likely a trend reversal. In the extremes, as the real body becomes smaller as the spread between the open and close narrows, a doji is formed. A doji preceded by a long black real body during a decline (or a tall white real body during a rally) is a distinctive type of harami referred to as a harami cross (Exhibit 6.3).

The harami cross, because it contains a doji, is viewed as a more potent reversal signal than the regular harami pattern by the Japanese. The harami cross is sometimes referred to as the *petrifying pattern*. My best guess as to why it has that nickname is that the preceding trend has been frozen or petrified in preparation for a reverse move. A harami cross occurring after a very long white candle is a pattern a long trader ignores at his or her own peril. Harami cross can also call bottoms, but they seem more effective at tops.

Exhibit 6.4 shows a brisk rally that started October 26. The third white candle of this rally on October 31 pushed the index over the October 23–24 bearish engulfing pattern's resistance (at B). However, whatever cause for optimism the bulls had on the 31st was short-lived as a harami pattern was completed with the November 1 candle. That candle's real body was so small that it could be considered a harami cross. The series of spinning tops after the harami reinforced that the trend had changed from up to neutral. The long black candle on November 8 completed a tower top (see later in this chapter).

In Exhibit 6.5 a price drop that began with the hanging man found a floor with the harami of November 4 and 5. The second real body of this harami was so small that I viewed it as a doji.

EXHIBIT 6.3. Harami Cross

EXHIBIT 6.4. S&P—Daily (Harami)

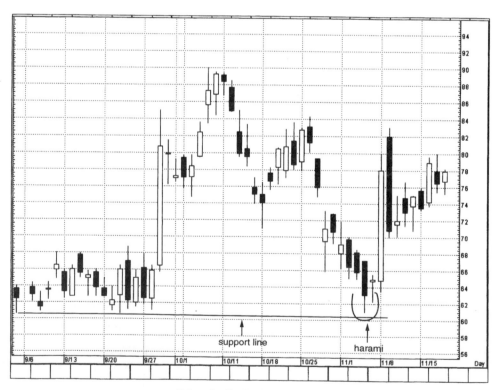

EXHIBIT 6.5. Amazon—Daily (Harami Cross)

As such, this is a harami cross. What was especially significant about the emergence of this pattern was that it helped clearly confirm a defined support near $61 (shown by the horizontal support line). If this were a bar chart, we would have the same support based on the action from early to late September. Although we're using a candle chart, we can and should use traditional bar chart support or resistance areas. Thus, there was an Eastern signal (harami) confirming a traditional Western signal (support line).

There was an earlier harami cross pattern on September 29 and 30. With this harami the short-term trend changed up to lateral. This pattern highlights an important point—one that was addressed in the introduction to Chapter 4: When a trend changes it doesn't necessarily mean that prices will go from, say, up to down. In both harami in this exhibit the former uptrend did change after the appearance of the harami. In the November harami, the trend shifted from down to up and in the September harami from up to neutral. As such, both harami correctly forecasted a change of trend.

We are all detectives in the market as we pick up the small visual clues the market continually sends out. As these clues unravel, we may have to adjust our market stance. Exhibit 6.6 is an example of this. On April 19 this stock pushed above resistance with an extended white candle. With this bullish breakout, the signs pointed north. The next day, the texture of the market had changed with the harami. While this harami doesn't immediately convert the short-term trend from up to down, it was a visual alarm. As such, longs can be scaled back, protective stops moved higher, etc. The doji after the harami (on April 24) helped reinforce that the trend had moved from up to more neutral since the doji represents a time where the bulls and bears are in equilibrium. The descent from this harami continued until a bullish engulfing pattern (the first session of this pattern was a hammer). The rally from the bullish engulfing pattern got clogged on May 9 at the doji. The candle lines marked 1 and 2 were also harami patterns, with line 2, since it was a doji, forming a harami cross.

Exhibit 6.7 is an example of the ease with which we can meld candle charting and Western charting tools. A rising resistance line connects the highs of March 15 and April 12. As will be

© CQG Inc. Used by permission.

EXHIBIT 6.6. Pharmacia—Daily (Harami)

© Aspen Graphics. Used by permission.

EXHIBIT 6.7. Chris-Craft Industries—Daily (Harami)

detailed in Part 2 of this book (where the focus is on Western charting tools), a rising resistance line can be an area of supply. When price intersected this line on May 13 we received visual confirmation that supply was overcoming demand with that candle's bearish upper shadow and then completing a harami. Observe also how the prior price peak on April 12 and 13 was also a harami. Hammers at 1 and 2 gave signs of stabilization.

TWEEZERS TOPS AND BOTTOMS

Tweezers are two or more candle lines with matching highs or lows. They are called *tweezers tops* and *tweezers bottoms* because they are compared to the two prongs of a tweezers. In a rising market, a tweezers top is formed when the two or more consecutive highs match. In a falling market, a tweezers bottom is made when two or more successive lows are the same. The tweezers could be composed of real bodies, shadows, and/or doji. Ideally the tweezers should have a long first candle and a small real body as the next session. This shows that whatever force the market had on the first session (bullish force with a long white candle and bearish force with a long black candle), it was dissolving with the following small real body with the same high (for a tweezers top) or same low (for a tweezers bottom). If there is a bearish (for a top reversal) or a bullish (for a bottom reversal) candle signal that is also a tweezers top, it adds more importance to the pattern.

Let's look at Exhibits 6.8 to 6.13 in detail:

- Exhibit 6.8 shows how, during an ascent, a long white line is followed by a doji. This two-candle pattern, a harami cross with the same high, can be a significant warning.

- Exhibit 6.9 illustrates a tweezers top formed by a long white candle and a hanging man line. If the market opens, and especially closes, under the hanging man's real body, odds are strong that a top has been reached. This two-line mixture can also be considered a harami. As such, it would be a top reversal pattern during an uptrend.

- Exhibit 6.10 illustrates a tweezers top joined with the second period's bearish shooting star line.

EXHIBIT 6.8. Tweezers Top and Harami Cross

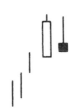

EXHIBIT 6.9. Tweezers Top and Hanging Man

EXHIBIT 6.10. Tweezers Top and Shooting Star

EXHIBIT 6.11. Tweezers Top and Dark-Cloud Cover

EXHIBIT 6.12. Tweezers Bottom and Hammer

EXHIBIT 6.13. Tweezers Bottom and Piercing Pattern

- As mentioned earlier, an ideal tweezers would have as its second session not only the same high, but also a small real body. In Exhibit 6.11 the second candle is not a small real body. However, this second session completes a variation on the dark-cloud cover (the second day opens above the prior day's close instead of above the prior day's high). The black candle session's high also just touches the prior period's high and then falls. Because of this last fact—that is, both sessions have the same highs—it adds more negative impact to this variation of the dark-cloud cover.

- Exhibit 6.12 shows a hammer session that successfully tests the prior long black candlestick's lows. The hammer, and the successful test of support, proves that the sellers are losing control of the market. This two-line combination is also a harami. This would be another reason to view this action as support.

- Exhibit 6.13, while it doesn't have a small real body for the second candle, does complete a variation on the bullish piercing line. (A true piercing line would open under the prior day's low. Here it opened under the prior day's close.) Because of this I view it also as a tweezers bottom.

These examples of tweezers are not inclusive. They are representative of how top and bottom tweezers should be confirmed by other candlestick indications so as to be valuable forecasting tools.

Tweezers should be viewed differently for daily, intraday, and weekly or long charts. This is because there is nothing potent about having the same highs or lows for two daily or intraday sessions. It's only if these sessions also meet the specific criteria for a tweezers (the first long, the second short, or a candle pattern with the same highs or same lows) does it warrant attention. As such, the main aspect to keep in mind with tweezers on a daily or intraday chart is that it takes a special combination of candle lines to warrant acting upon tweezers.

For those who want a longer time perspective, tweezers tops and bottoms on the weekly and monthly candlestick charts made by consecutive candlesticks could be important reversal patterns. This would be true even without other candle confirmation because, on a weekly or monthly chart, for example, a weekly low this week that successfully holds last week's lows could be a base for a rally. The same can't be said of daily or intraday lows.

Exhibit 6.14 shows the tweezers bottom. Note that the second real body of this tweezers was not within the first real body and as such was not a harami pattern. The long white candle after this tweezers on June 1 was immediately followed by a small real body with about the same high near $59.50. As such, the June 1 and June 2 combination can be viewed as the tweezers top. But in the context of the overall technical picture, the market was not overextended and, as such, not so vulnerable to a correction as should be the case if we had a tweezers top in an overbought environment. Even if one acted upon the June 1 and June 2 tweezers top (it was also a harami), once the market closed above the high of these two sessions on June 3, any potential bearish implication of the tweezers top was negated.

In Exhibit 6.15 a series of falling gaps (gaps are called "windows" in candle charts; windows are discussed in detail in Chapter 7) at 1, 2, and 3 kept the bearish momentum in force. A tweezers bottom unfolded with the second candle of the tweezers bottom a hammer. A dark-cloud cover in the week of the

© Aspen Graphics. Used by permission.

EXHIBIT 6.14. Caterpillar—Daily (Tweezers Bottom)

EXHIBIT 6.15. Georgia-Pacific—Daily (Tweezers Bottom)

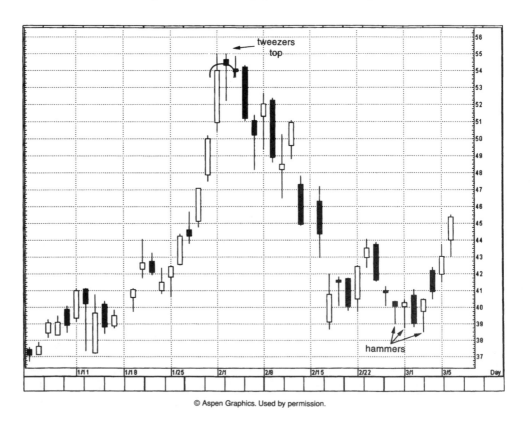

EXHIBIT 6.16. Dell—Daily (Tweezers Top)

18th showed that the upward power of the market was dissipating.

Exhibit 6.16 illustrates a tweezers top. Since the small real body on February 2 was not within the prior real body, this would not have been a harami pattern, but it was a tweezers because of the same high at $55. In addition, the small real body on February 2 was a hanging man line (the upper shadow is small enough to keep this as a hanging man line). Of course, this (like any hanging man line) required bearish confirmation by a close under the hanging man's real body. This occurred the next session.

Dell descended from this tweezers top until a series of hammers in late February–early March showed an area of stabilization. The first two hammers on February 26 and March 1 were not a classic tweezers bottom. Why? While they certainly have the same lows, the duel hammers did not meet one of the normal criterion for a tweezers bottom—having the first candle of the tweezers bottom a long real body. While the dual hammers on February 26 and March 1 were not classified as a tweezers bottom, I certainly would emphasize their importance since

© CQG Inc. Used by permission.

EXHIBIT 6.17. Commerce Bancorp—Daily (Tweezers Top)

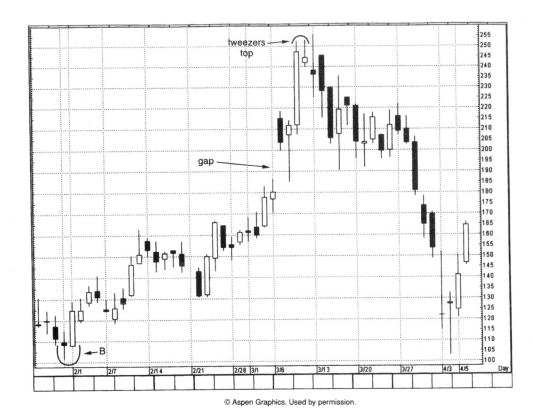

EXHIBIT 6.18. Network Solutions—Daily (Tweezers Top)

they underscored how the market was rejecting lower prices at $39 with bullish long lower shadows. As such, I would view the pattern on February 26 and 27 as a variation of a tweezers bottom.

While the two candle lines on December 22 and 23 in Exhibit 6.17 did not form a dark-cloud cover (since the black candle wasn't even near the middle of the long white candle), they did form a tweezers top. While I would view a dark-cloud cover as more ominous than a tweezers top (since the regular dark-cloud cover closes well into the white candle), this tweezers top could certainly be viewed as a cautionary signal. This was echoed the next week with the small real bodies and doji reflecting that the market had gone from a bullish bias to more neutral.

A bullish engulfing pattern at B in Exhibit 6.18 lays the foundation in early February for a rally that continued via a gap on March 6. As discussed in Chapter 7, the bottom of a rising gap can become support. The support at the bottom of this gap near $185 held very well, as attested by the long lower shadow candle of March 8.

On March 10, near $250, a small real body produced a harami pattern. Since the two candle lines of the harami had the same highs, it was also a tweezers top.

BELT-HOLD LINES

The belt-hold is an individual candle line. The *bullish belt-hold* is a strong white candle that opens on the low of the session (or with a very small lower shadow) and closes at, or near, the session highs (see Exhibit 6.19). The bullish belt-hold line is also called a white opening shaven bottom. If it is at a low price area and a long bullish belt-hold appears, it forecasts a rally.

The *bearish belt-hold* (see Exhibit 6.20) is a long black candle that opens on the high of the session (or within a few ticks of the high) and continues lower through the session. If prices are high, the appearance of a bearish belt-hold is a top reversal. The bearish belt-hold line is sometimes called a black opening shaven head.

The longer the height of the belt-hold candle line, the more significant it becomes. The actual Japanese name for the belt-hold is a sumo wrestling term, *yorikiri*, which means "pushing your opponent out of the ring while holding onto his belt."

A close above a black bearish belt-hold line should mean a resumption of the uptrend. A close under the white bullish belt-hold line implies a renewal of selling pressure.

Belt-hold lines are more important if they confirm resistance or other belt-hold lines or if they have not appeared for a while. In Exhibit 6.21 a bearish engulfing pattern at B indicate potential trouble. The double bearish belt-hold lines came near the same area as this bearish engulfing pattern and as such helped further establish this as an area of supply. Although there were many bearish signals in this short span (the bearish engulfing pattern and the two bearish belt-hold lines), it does not necessarily forecast the free fall that occurred after the second belt-hold. This convergence of candle signals increased the likelihood of a turn, but not the extent of the following action.

A rising gap in early June soon became a support zone as evidenced by its successful defense through the first half of June. The June 13 candle was a bullish belt-hold. On the next retest of the window in late July–early August, another series of bullish belt-hold lines formed. These last two bullish belt-hold lines

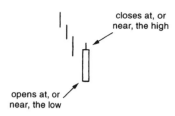

EXHIBIT 6.19. Bullish Belt-Hold Line

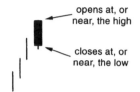

EXHIBIT 6.20. Bearish Belt-Hold Line

EXHIBIT 6.21. Juniper Networks—5 Minutes (Bearish Belt-Hold)

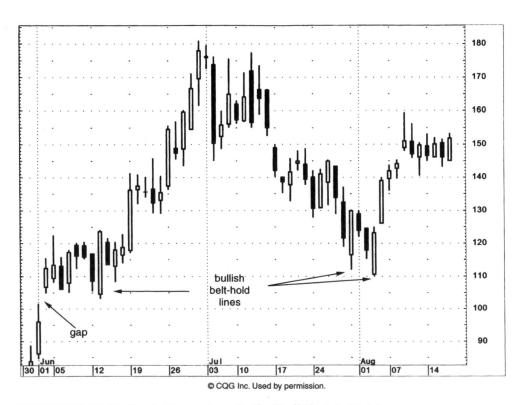

EXHIBIT 6.22. Redback Networks—Daily (Bullish Belt-Hold)

also served to complete back-to-back piercing patterns. The rally from the early August lows stopped at the August 9 shooting star.

UPSIDE-GAP TWO CROWS

An *upside-gap two crows* (what a mouthful!) is illustrated in Exhibit 6.23. It is very rare. The upside-gap refers to the gap between the real body of the small black real body and the real body preceding it. (The real body that precedes the first black candle is usually a long white one.) The two black candles are the "crows" in this pattern. They are analogous to black crows peering down ominously from a tree branch. Based on this portentous comparison, it is obviously a bearish pattern. An ideal upside-gap two crows has the second black real body opening above the first black real body's open. It then closes under the first black candle's close.

The rationale for the bearish aspect of this pattern is as follows: The market is in an uptrend and gaps higher on the open.

EXHIBIT 6.23. Upside-Gap Two Crows

© CQG Inc. Used by permission.

EXHIBIT 6.24. Deutsche Mark—Daily (Upside-Gap Two Crows)

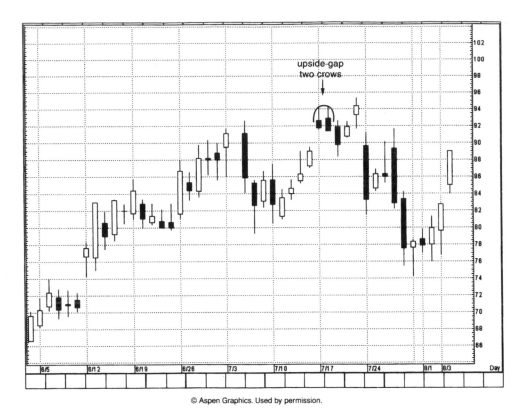

EXHIBIT 6.25. Corning—Daily (Upside-Gap Two Crows)

The new highs fail to hold and the market forms a black candle. But the bulls can take some succor, at least, because the close on this black candle session still holds above the prior day's close. The third session paints a more bearish portrait with another new high and another failure to hold these highs into the close. More negative, however, is that this session closes under the prior day's close. If the market is so strong, why did the new highs fail to hold and why did the market close lower? Those are the questions that the bulls are probably nervously asking themselves. The answers might be that the market may not be so strong as they would like. If prices fail to regain high ground the next day (that is, the fourth session), then expect lower prices.

Exhibit 6.24 has an example of the upside-gap two crows. The very small falling gap after this pattern highlighted the bears had taken control. The rally on the week of February 20 stalled at this gap's resistance.

Exhibit 6.25 illustrates the significance of viewing a candle pattern to its immediate surroundings. Although there was an upside-gap two crows in mid July, this would not have been a signal to sell. This is because, as will be discussed in detail in Chapter 7, the stock gapped higher on July 7. A gap up is normally a bullish sign—whether with candles or bar charts. Thus, while the upside-gap two crows sends out a warning, I would view it as less bearish than would be the case in which there was no gap, such as in Exhibit 6.24.

EXHIBIT 6.26. Three Black Crows

THREE BLACK CROWS

The upside-gap two crows consists of two black candles. If there are three declining consecutive black candles, it is called *three black crows pattern* (see Exhibit 6.26). The three black crows presage lower prices if they appear at high price levels or after a mature advance. Three crows are also sometimes called three-winged crows. The Japanese have an expression, "Bad news has wings." This is an appropriate saying for the three-winged crow pattern. The three crows are, as the name implies, three black candles. Likened to the image of a group of crows sitting ominously in a tall dead tree, the three crows have bearish implications. The three lines should close at, or near, their lows. Ideally, each of the openings should also be within the prior session's real body.

Exhibit 6.27 illustrates three black crows started April 15. The descent from the three black crows continued virtually unhindered until the piercing pattern at P. The second and third black candles of the three black crows (April 16 and 17) opened under the prior real bodies. While the normal three black crows has an opening within the prior real body, and these openings were not in the black real bodies, they could be viewed as more bearish. This is because the second and third black candles opened under the prior day's close and failed to gain substantial ground throughout the remainder of the session.

The three black crows would likely be useful for longer-term traders. This is because this pattern is completed on the third black candle. Obviously, by the time this occurs the market has already corrected substantially. For example, these three black crows started at $70.75. Since we needed the third black candle to finish the pattern, we got the signal when the stock was at $67.87.

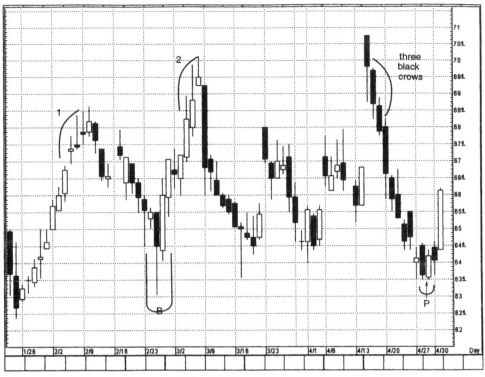

EXHIBIT 6.27. Pennzoil—Daily (Three Black Crows)

However, in this case we received an inkling of trouble on the first black candle session of the three black crows. The reason is that the stock opens above the prior March high of $70, but by session's close the bulls were unable to sustain the new highs as it closed back under $70. As you will see in Part 2 of this book, if the market makes a new high and fails to sustain, it could have bearish implications. This is what unfolded here.

Let's also look at the prior highs at areas 1 and 2. During time frame 1 in early February, Pennzoil was ascending to new highs for the move, but the candles gave us a strong visual warning flare that all was not well. Specifically, during the latter part of the week of February 2, although the stock was making higher highs, higher lows, and higher closes—it did so with small real bodies and long upper shadows. This certainly showed that the action was not one-sided in favor of the bulls. The price retreat ended at the bullish engulfing pattern at B. A rally from there pushed prices up until the week of March 2, shown as area 2 on this chart. The rally at 2 was similar to the rally at area 1 insofar as area 2 had higher highs, higher lows, and higher closes, and as such would look healthy if this were a bar chart. However, from a candlestick perspective, this price ascent on March 4, 5, and 6 had long upper shadows. This proved the rallying strength was being dissipated. The candle line on March 6 was a shooting star.

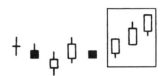

EXHIBIT 6.28. Three White Soldiers

THREE ADVANCING WHITE SOLIDERS

The opposite of the three black crows is *three advancing white soldiers* or, more commonly, *three white soldiers* (Exhibit 6.28). Like much of the candle terminology, this pattern has a military association. It is a group of three long white candles with consecutively higher closes. If this pattern appears at a low price area or after a period of stable prices, then it is a sign of strength ahead.

EXHIBIT 6.29. Advance Block

The three white soldiers are a gradual and steady rise with each white line opening within or near the prior session's white real body. Each of the white candles should close at, or near, its highs. It is a healthy method for the market to rise (although if the white candles are very extended, one should be cautious about an overbought market).

If the second and third or just the third candle shows signs of weakening, it is an *advance block pattern* (see Exhibit 6.29). This means the rally is running into trouble and longs should protect themselves. Be especially cautious about this pattern during a mature uptrend. Signs of weakening could be progressively smaller white real bodies or relatively long upper shadows.

EXHIBIT 6.30. Stalled Pattern

If the last two candles are long white ones that make a new high followed by a small white candle, it is called a *stalled pattern* (see Exhibit 6.30). It is also sometimes called a *deliberation pattern*. The bulls' strength has been at least temporarily exhausted after this formation. This last small white candle can either gap away from the long white body (in which case it becomes a star) or it can be, as the Japanese express it, "riding on the shoulder" of the long white real body (that is, be at the upper end of the prior long white real body). The small real body discloses a deterioration of the bulls' power.

Although the advance block and stalled patterns are not normally top reversal patterns, they can sometimes precede a price decline. The advance block and stalled patterns should be used to liquidate or protect longs, but usually not to short. They are generally more consequential at higher price levels.

As shown in Exhibits 6.28 through 6.30, these patterns can be at a low price area or during a rally.

There is not much difference between the advance block and stalled pattern. The main factor to consider with three white soldiers is that it is most constructive for each of the three candles to close at or near its highs. If the latter two white candles show signs of hesitation, either with small real bodies or upper shadows, then it is a clue that the rally is losing force.

Exhibit 6.31 illustrates almost a classic three white soldiers since each candle, especially the last two, were relatively strong, opening near their lows and closing at, or near, their highs. A sign of hesitation came with the doji on April 23 since it formed a harami cross.

Exhibit 6.32 has a good example of the three white soldiers. Each of the three candle lines closed very near to the highs of the session and each white candle opened within or above the prior white candle. An aspect to consider is by the time the three white soldiers is completed, the market could be well off its lows. In this case, Microsoft was almost $4 from its lows, a high percentage move. Consequently, unless one is longer-term bullish, buying at the completion of these three white soldiers may not present an attractive risk/reward.

I have found that on corrections, the first or second white candle that started the three white soldiers is often support. In this example, the stock consolidated after three white soldiers and slowly pulled back until a hammer was formed. That tended to confirm support within the second white candle of the three soldiers.

In Exhibit 6.33 a base was forming from mid to late June and early July near $36.50. Then three white soldiers emerged (although they had very small upper shadows). After the third white soldier, the stock hesitated and corrected to the first white solider of July 11. This chart again illustrates that the market may sometimes correct after the three white soldiers. We should expect support as the stock gets to the second, or especially the first, white soldier.

An advance block pattern is illustrated in Exhibit 6.34. Although there were three relatively tall white candles, the last

EXHIBIT 6.31. Intel—Daily (Three White Soldiers)

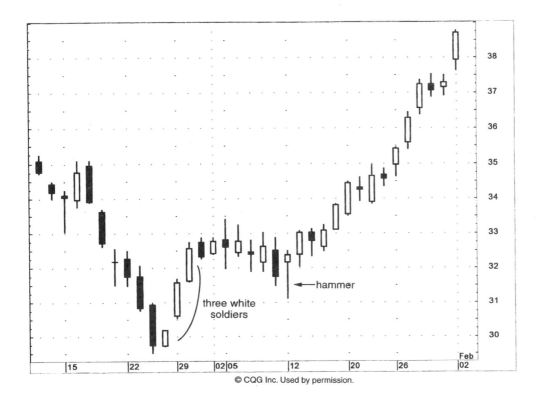

EXHIBIT 6.32. Microsoft—Daily (Three White Soldiers)

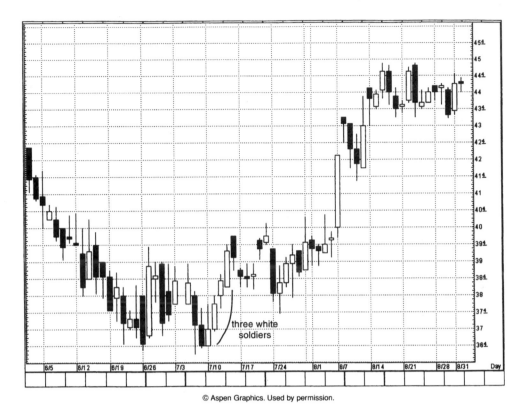

EXHIBIT 6.33. Praxair—Daily (Three White Soldiers)

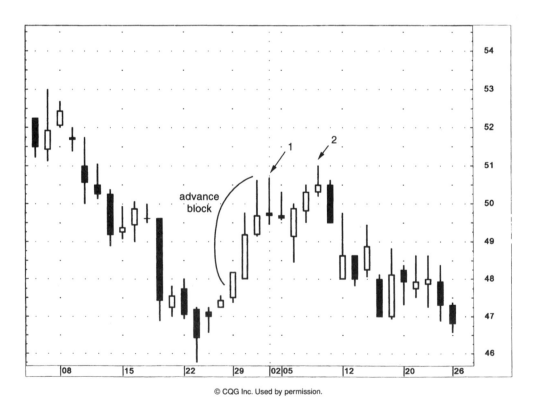

EXHIBIT 6.34. United Health—Daily (Advance Block)

two had bearish upper shadows. This reflected a stalling of the rally. Indeed, a series of more upper shadows, labeled as 1 and 2, highlighted this resistance near $51. The long upper shadow candle at 2 was a shooting star and the next day completed a bearish engulfing pattern.

THREE MOUNTAINS AND THREE RIVERS

There is a group of longer-term topping and bottoming patterns that includes the three mountains, the three rivers, the three Buddha tops, inverted three Buddha, dumpling tops, frypan bottoms, and tower tops and bottoms.

Similar to the Western triple top, the Japanese have a *three mountain top* (see Exhibit 6.35). It is supposed to represent a major top. If the market backs off from a high three times or makes three attempts at a high, it is deemed a three mountain top. The high point of the final mountain ideally should be confirmed with a bearish candle indicator (for example, a doji or dark-cloud cover). If the central mountain of a three mountain top is the highest mountain, it is a special type of three mountain called a *three Buddha top* (see Exhibit 6.36). The reason for this name is because, in Buddhist temples, there is a large central Buddha with smaller Buddhas (that is, saints) on both sides. This is the same pattern as the West's head and shoulders top.

EXHIBIT 6.35. Three Mountain Top

EXHIBIT 6.36. Three Buddha Top

EXHIBIT 6.37. Three River Bottom

EXHIBIT 6.38. Inverted Three Buddha

Although the three Buddha top is analogous to the Western head and shoulders pattern, the theory about the Japanese three Buddha pattern was used over a hundred years before the head and shoulders was known in America. (The earliest I have seen a reference to a head and shoulders pattern in the United States was by Richard Schabacker in the 1930s. For those who are familiar with the Edwards and Magee classic book, *Technical Analysis of Stock Trends*, much of the material in that book is based on Schabacker's work. Schabacker was Edwards's father-in-law.)

It is intriguing how market observers from both the West and the East have come up with this same pattern. Market psychology is the same around the world, or, as a Japanese proverb expresses, "The tone of a bird's song is the same everywhere." The *three river bottom* pattern (see Exhibit 6.37) is the opposite of the three mountain top. This occurs when the market tests a bottom level three times. The peak of the troughs should be exceeded to confirm a bottom. The equivalent of the Western inverted head and shoulders bottom is called, not surprisingly, an *inverted three Buddha* (see Exhibit 6.38).

Area A in Exhibit 6.39 shows hesitation near $124, especially with the bearish engulfing pattern made in the last two weeks in November. The retreat from this bearish engulfing pattern

THE IMPORTANCE OF THE NUMBER THREE IN CANDLESTICK ANALYSIS

Many of the Japanese techniques are based on the number three. This reflects the importance of the number three in the Japanese culture. In premodern Japan, the number three had almost mystical associations. The saying "three times lucky" expresses this belief. Other examples of three in candle charts include the three white soldiers, the ominous three black crows, the aforementioned three mountain top and bottom and their variations, the three Buddha patterns, the rising and falling three methods, and the three candle patterns of the morning and evening stars. (Some of these patterns are discussed later.)

Parenthetically, while the number three is regarded as lucky, the number four is viewed as a foreboding figure. The reason for this belief is easy to ascertain—the Japanese word for four is *shi*, which has the same sound as the word for death. Seat number 4 in a plane of Japanese Airlines, room 304 of a hotel—these can hardly ever be found (still less in a hospital!). Simply because of the number in "Renault 4," the Japanese launch of this car failed miserably.[1]

© Aspen Graphics. Used by permission.

EXHIBIT 6.39. Yen/Dollar—Weekly (Three Mountain Top)

found stabilization at a bullish engulfing pattern. The ascent from this bullish engulfing pattern stopped, not surprisingly at the aforementioned bearish engulfing pattern's resistance near $124 at B. B was another bearish engulfing pattern. The next rally in mid May and the subsequent bearish engulfing pattern at C put a three mountain top in place.

In Exhibit 6.39, the peaks of each mountain were almost the same. This is not necessary. It is still considered a three mountain top if the three price peaks are not exactly at the same highs. In Exhibit 6.40, price crested at A, B, and C, with B and C at slightly higher levels. This would still be considered a three mountain top. During the last two sessions at C, Intel was rising with two very small real bodies. This was a symptom of uneasiness. The price peak came at $76, a shooting star. The real turning signal, and the confirmation of the three Buddha top, came with the gap down after the late August shooting star.

While a three mountain top has nearly the same highs, the three Buddha top has the middle portion as the highest high. Again we can think of the three Buddha top as comparable to

© Aspen Graphics. Used by permission.

EXHIBIT 6.40. Intel—Weekly (Three Mountain Top)

the head and shoulders top. In Exhibit 6.41 we see a three Buddha, a.k.a head and shoulders top, with the price peaks at 1, 2, and 3 defining the pattern. The rising line shown on the chart in Western terms would be called the neckline of the head and shoulders top. Classically, the neckline of the head and shoulders top once broken should become resistance. This is what unfolded with the break of the neckline on August 19 and then a little rebound on August 21 (and three sessions after that), stopping at the neckline's new resistance as confirmed by the bearish upper shadows.

Exhibit 6.42 is another example of the three Buddha top. Since this pattern is the same as the head and shoulders top, we can shift into the Western technicals based on the concept of the head and shoulders neckline discussed in the previous exhibit.

Specifically, once the neckline was broken, it became resistance. The market tried to stabilize with a little bullish engulfing pattern around 13:00, but the failure to push this index above the neckline resistant kept the bears in control. This reflects how critical it is to think about where a candle pattern

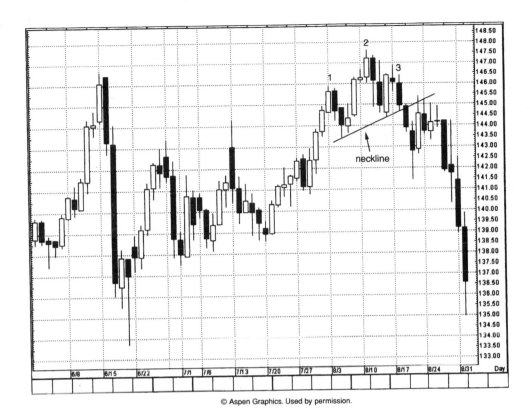

EXHIBIT 6.41. Yen/Dollar—Daily (Three Buddha Top)

is formed. In this instance the bullish engulfing pattern is a potential bottoming signal, but wouldn't it make sense to let the market close over the neckline's resistance before buying— even with the bullish engulfing pattern? It does pay to wait, since such a close over the neckline would help reinforce that the bulls have more control.

Our Western inverted head and shoulders is the same as the Japanese inverted three Buddha. That is, there are three lows made with the middle low as the lowest. This is shown in Exhibit 6.43 at lows at A, B, and C. Since the low at B was under the low at A or C, it formed an inverted three Buddha. Note how once the bulls pushed the pound above 163 with the tall white candle in early January, that prior resistance around 163 became support. This concept of a former resistance area being converted into new support is a powerful trading technique that is discussed in Chapter 11.

Exhibit 6.44 has an inverted three Buddha. Notice once again how a former resistance area from March near $52 to $52.50 once penetrated became a support zone for most of April.

EXHIBIT 6.42. NASDAQ-100 Trust—15 Minutes (Three Buddha Top)

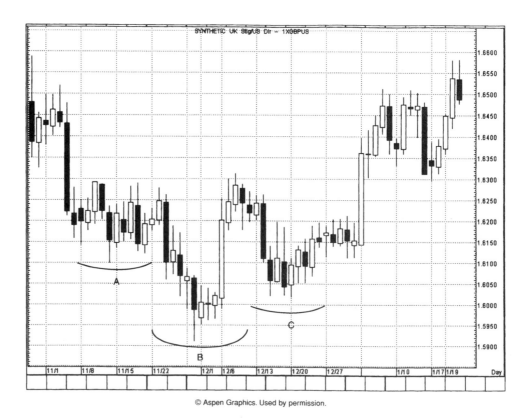

EXHIBIT 6.43. British Pound/Dollar—Daily (Inverted Three Buddha)

© CQG Inc. Used by permission.

EXHIBIT 6.44. Sealed Air—Daily (Inverted Three Buddha)

COUNTERATTACK LINES

Counterattack lines are formed when opposite colored candles have the same close. The best way to describe this pattern is by discussing the illustrations in Exhibits 6.45 and 6.46.

Exhibit 6.45 is an example of a *bullish counterattack line*. This pattern occurs during a decline. The first candle of this pattern is usually a long black candle. The next session opens sharply lower. At this point, the bears are feeling confident. The bulls then stage their counterattack as they push prices back up to unchanged from the prior close. The prior downtrend has then been bridled.

The bullish counterattack is comparable to the bullish piercing line. If you remember, the piercing line has the same two-candle configuration as that shown for the bullish counterattack pattern. The main difference is that the bullish counterattack line does not move into the prior session's white real body. It just gets back to the prior session's close. The piercing pattern's second line pushes well into the black real body.

EXHIBIT 6.45. Bullish Counterattack Line

EXHIBIT 6.46. Bearish Counterattack Line

Consequently, the piercing pattern is a more significant bottom reversal than is this bullish counterattack line. Nonetheless, as shown in some examples below, the bullish counterattack line should be respected, since it proves that there is a change in the flow of direction of the market.

Exhibit 6.46 illustrates the *bearish counterattack line*. The first candle, a long white one, keeps the bullish momentum going. The next session's opening gaps higher. The longs are happy—then the bears come out fighting and pull prices to the prior day's close. The bulls' tide of optimism on the second day's opening probably turned to apprehension by the close.

As the bullish counterattack line is related to the piercing line, so the bearish counterattack line is related to the dark-cloud cover. The bearish counterattack, like the dark-cloud cover, should ideally open above the prior day's high. Unlike the dark-cloud cover, though, the close does not go into the prior day's white candle. Thus, the dark-cloud cover sends a stronger top reversal signal than does the bearish counterattack line.

An important consideration of counterattack lines is if that second session should open robustly higher (in the case of the bearish counterattack) or sharply lower (for the bullish counterattack). The idea is that on the opening of the second day of this pattern, the market has moved strongly in the direction of the original trend. Then, surprise! By the close, it moves back to unchanged from the prior session. In doing so, it changes the market's texture in one day.

In Exhibit 6.47 on March 10, the stock surged one dollar higher on the opening than the prior day's close. By session's end the whole bullish hue of the stock had changed since the bears dragged down prices to the prior close of March 7. This bearish counterattack line of March 10 was the first of three black candles that completed the three black crows.

As mentioned in the section of three black crows, because we need to wait for three black candles for the completion of that signal, much of the move may be lost by the time the third candle of the three black crows unfolds. In this case, however, with the first black candle's counterattack line, we would have received an early turning signal in one session that was further confirmed with the three black crows.

EXHIBIT 6.47. Bank One—Daily (Bearish Counterattack Lines)

Exhibit 6.48 illustrates a bearish counterattack line emerging October 15. We can see that the counterattack did not close exactly at the prior white candle's close but marginally below the prior close. With the counterattack lines, as is true with most candlestick signals, there is room for flexibility in the definition of the pattern. For example, on December 6 there was a bullish counterattack line. On that session, the stock gapped sharply lower on the opening and, by session's end, closed almost, but not exactly, at the prior day's close. I would still view this as a bullish counterattack pattern, although the stock did not close exactly the same as the prior close, but certainly was close enough. The main criterion in this bullish counterattack was the impressive rebound on the white candle from its weak opening.

In Exhibit 6.49 a bearish counterattack pattern helped confirm July's significant resistance near $138–$139. Again, the two closes were not exactly equal, but close enough to validate this pattern. This chart highlights how easy it is to use candles to get extra confirmation of resistance. While this $138–$139 resis-

© CQG Inc. Used by permission.

EXHIBIT 6.48. Gillette—Daily (Bearish and Bullish Counterattack Lines)

© Aspen Graphics. Used by permission.

EXHIBIT 6.49. IBM—Daily (Bearish Counterattack Line)

tance would be available on a bar chart, there is no such thing as a "counterattack" concept with bar charts. Thus, by substituting candle charts for bar charts, a trader gets all the bar chart signals (such as resistance areas) with the bonus of the unique candle indicators.

A bullish counterattack line is shown in Exhibit 6.50 at the January 12 lows. This helped confirm a support area in place since mid December between $25.50 and $27.

This chart also highlights what I call a "cluster of candles." By this I mean a convergence, or grouping, of candle signals that reinforce a specific resistance or support area. With this in mind, let's look at how a cluster of candle signals, denoted by 1–4, reinforced resistance.

1. A shooting star. The next day completed a bearish engulfing pattern.

2. The black real body that intruded well into the prior white real body formed a dark-cloud cover.

3. Another dark-cloud cover.

4. A bearish engulfing pattern.

© Aspen Graphics. Used by permission.

EXHIBIT 6.50. Applied Material—Daily (Bullish Counterattack Line)

After the clues at 1–4 above, would one think there is resistance between $38 and $39.50? As my 11-year-old son would say, "Duh." This technique of a cluster of candles underscores the importance of having a group of signals, whether candles signals or Western signals, converging at one area to increase the importance of that specific area. Convergence is the focus of Part 2 of this book.

DUMPLING TOPS AND FRYPAN BOTTOMS

Dumpling tops and frypan bottoms. Someone must have been hungry when they thought of these names!

The *dumpling top* (Exhibit 6.51) is a top reversal that usually has small real bodies as the market forms a convex pattern. Confirmation of the dumpling top is when the market gaps down. This pattern is the same as the Western rounded top. The only difference is that the dumpling top has the extra bearish kicker of a gap lower. (A gap down is called a "falling window" in candle terminology. See Chapter 7.)

The *frypan bottom* (Exhibit 6.52) reflects a market that is bottoming and whose price action forms a concave design and then opens a gap to the upside (i.e., a rising window). It has the same appearance as a Western rounded bottom, but the Japanese frypan bottom must have a gap higher to confirm this pattern.

I like the concept behind these patterns. With the frypan bottom, the market goes from lower lows to the same lows and then higher lows. This pictorially proves that the bears are losing a foothold. Then, when you add a rising gap to this scenario, it gives even more proof that the bears have lost control of the market.

The Japanese will say that with a frypan bottom the market becomes "immune to bad news." As such, if a market builds a

EXHIBIT 6.51. Dumpling Top

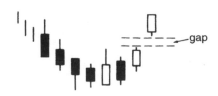

EXHIBIT 6.52. Frypan Bottom

frypan bottom—especially in spite of bearish news—it would be very impressive. As Bernard Baruch stated, "What is important are not the events themselves, but the human reaction to these events."

The same is true with the dumpling top, but in reverse. That is, the market is ascending with higher highs and goes into a period where the highs are the same, and then goes to lower highs. As such, the pace of the rally is slackening. Then when you have a gap down to complete the dumpling top, it just puts another nail in the bulls' coffin.

Exhibit 6.53 illustrates the dumpling top where the stock is making a series of higher highs early on August 24. A few 60-minute sessions of long upper shadows and the dark-cloud cover at noon on that day gave a minor clue of some hesitation near $93.50. The final confirmation came with the lower highs made on the two sessions after the dark-cloud cover and then the gap down, which completed the dumpling top.

Exhibit 6.54 illustrates how IBM started stalling the week of July 12 as it went from mostly white real bodies the preceding week to black real bodies that were making mostly lower highs. The gap down completed the dumpling top.

EXHIBIT 6.53. Micron—60 Minutes (Dumpling Top)

dumpling
top

© CQG Inc. Used by permission.

EXHIBIT 6.54. IBM—Daily (Dumpling Top)

In mid July in Exhibit 6.55 the stock was holding its highs near $55. But look at how these highs were being maintained—through a series of small real bodies and even a long-legged doji on July 16. These spinning tops and doji showed just how confused this stock really was. The gap down on the week of the 20th completed a classic dumpling top. As will be discussed in Chapter 7, when there is a gap down, that gap often becomes resistance. Note how the gap of this dumpling top (made on July 24) became an upside barrier a few days later.

In Exhibit 6.56 the July 7 long black candle reflected how hard this stock was hit. The only mitigating factor was that session's lower shadow. But one session's long lower shadow doesn't change the trend from down to more positive. During the next few days, a series of long lower shadows echoed support near $13.50. The appearance of a white candle on July 10 was a successful defense of those lower shadows' support area that also completed a bullish piercing pattern. With the next

EXHIBIT 6.55. Catalina Marketing—Daily (Dumpling Top)

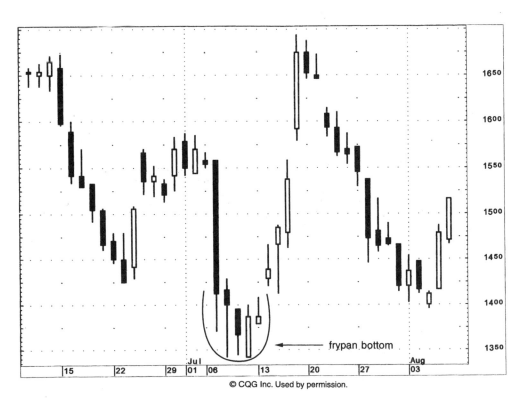

EXHIBIT 6.56. General Motors—Daily (Frypan Bottom)

118   *Part 1* • *The Basics*

session's higher low, and the gap higher on July 13, this stock had built a frypan bottom.

In Exhibit 6.57 a series of consecutive black candles during the week of July 19 kept the stock under pressure. Some diminutive real bodies and doji the next couple of weeks hinted that the stock was stabilizing. Final bullish proof of the breakout from this base came with a very small gap (shown at the arrow) made between August 5 and 6. As this chart illustrates, even if the gap is very small (i.e., a few cents) it is still considered a gap and thus validates this frypan bottom. The same would be true with the dumpling top. That is, even if there were a small gap to the downside, no matter how small, it would still confirm a dumpling top.

Exhibit 6.58 nicely illustrates the difference between the Western rounding bottom and the Eastern frypan bottom. From September 1 through the week of September 14, the stock was building a rounding bottom (since it was going from lower lows to the same lows and then higher lows). However, since this rounding bottom did not have a rising gap, it was not a frypan bottom. Remember, a frypan bottom is the same as a

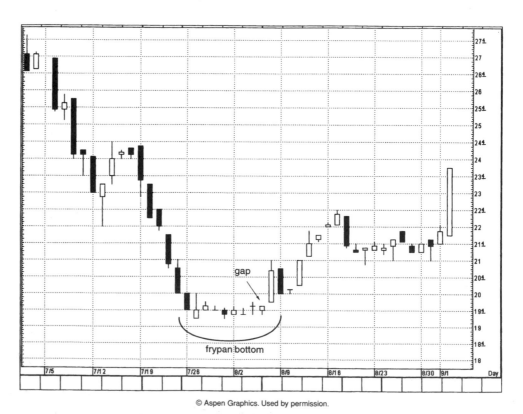

© Aspen Graphics. Used by permission.

EXHIBIT 6.57. Tele Nort—Daily (Frypan Bottom)

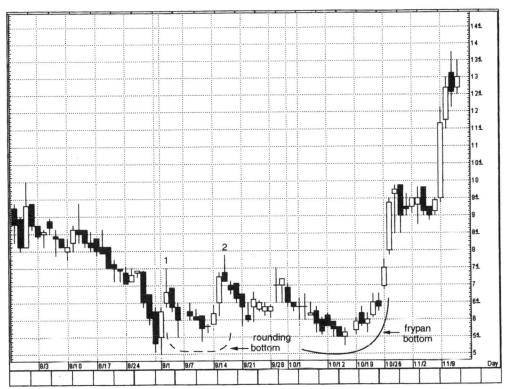

EXHIBIT 6.58. Earthshell—Daily (Frypan Bottom)

rounding bottom of the West, plus it has the extract push of a gap higher. With the aforementioned September's rounding bottom, we get signs of caution at 1 and 2 with their long upper shadows (2 was a shooting star).

Let's now turn our attention to activity from early to the latter part of October. At that time the stock was building a rounding bottom (that is, going from lower lows to higher lows). With the small rising gap on September 26, it became a frypan bottom with all its inherent bullish potential. Because of the rising gap in the frypan bottom (that the classic rounding bottom lacks), I view frypan bottom as more significant than a classic rounding bottom.

TOWER TOPS AND BOTTOMS

The *tower top* unfolds at high price levels. During a rally, there is a short-term lull after one or more white candles. Then one or more large black candles emerge. This creates a top with a

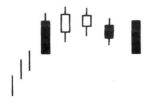

EXHIBIT 6.59. Tower Top

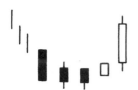

EXHIBIT 6.60. Tower
Bottom

white and black "tower" on either side of the small real bodies (see Exhibit 6.59). That is, long candles on the way down and long candles on the way up.

The *tower bottom* (see Exhibit 6.60) occurs in a descending market in which one or more tall black candles keep the bearish momentum intact. Then some small real bodies lessen the bearish tone and finally a tall white candle finalizes the tower bottom.

The closest Western comparison to the tower top and bottom would be the spike, or V, reversal. In the spike reversal, the market is in a strong trend and then abruptly reverses to a new trend.

The tower top and bottom, like some other candlestick signals such as three black crows, may be most useful for longer-term traders since the tower is often finalized late in the move.

The tower bottom is analogous to the frypan bottom while the tower top is similar to the dumpling top. The main distinction between these two patterns is that long black and white candles are needed for the towers and there is no gap required. The dumpling top and frypan bottom require gaps.

EXHIBIT 6.61. CNB Bancshares—Daily (Tower Top and Dumpling Top)

Exhibit 6.61 highlights the difference between the tower top and the dumpling top. The stock moved up in the first week of October with a series of white real bodies and then started treading water with a series of small real bodies. The gap down on October 15 formed a dumpling top. Shifting our attention to late December, we see a series of extended white candles. Candle line 1 was still healthy, but the small real bodies following 1 illustrated that this stock had a poor chance of rising. The long black candle at 2 was the second "tower" needed to complete the tower top.

In Exhibit 6.62, a hammer in late December hinted of stabilization. The rally from the hammer continued with a tall white candle on December 29. However, as the stock got within shooting distance of a resistance area from early December near $35.75, a group of small real bodies arose. The December 30th candle made a harami pattern. The harami pattern and the spinning tops signaled caution. The trend turned more ominous with the emergence of the January 5 long black real body that completed the tower top.

© Aspen Graphics. Used by permission.

EXHIBIT 6.62. Ducommun—Daily (Tower Top)

As discussed earlier, sometimes tower tops send out a signal late in the move (since we have to wait for a black candle). In this case, however, the reversal signal à la the harami came early. Indeed, the December 30 candle was so tiny that it could be viewed as a harami cross.

A classic tower bottom is shown in Exhibit 6.63. The first tower consists of an extended black real body on July 28. The next day's doji makes a harami cross. (Observe another harami cross at H on July 24 and July 25. Once the index broke under that pattern, any bullish applications of that particular harami cross were voided.) The ascent from the late July harami cross began with a couple of small white real bodies with the longer-term turning signal arising with the tall white candle on August 3, since this completed a tower bottom. The rally continued from this tower bottom until late August when the S&P staled at the resistance area set by the July 17 shooting star.

In Exhibit 6.64 a hammer on April 1 hinted that the market was groping for a bottom. The long black candle the next day, with a marginal close under the hammer's support area (the

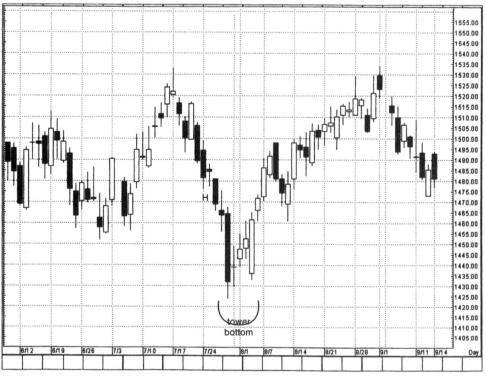

EXHIBIT 6.63. S&P—Daily (Tower Bottom)

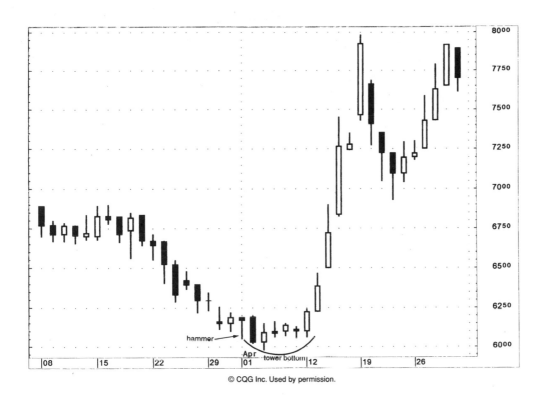

EXHIBIT 6.64. Illinois Tool Works—Daily (Tower Bottom)

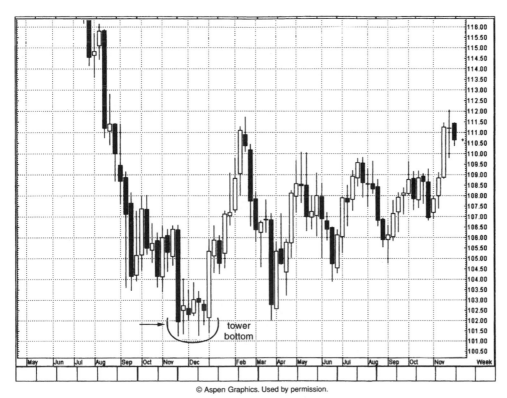

EXHIBIT 6.65. Yen/Dollar—Weekly (Tower Bottom)

low of the hammer's lower shadow), puts the trend back down. A series of small real bodies emerged immediately after this black candle. This mitigates much of the bearish implications of the aforementioned black candle. The stock's health further improved with the April 12 long white candle. This was the second tower of the tower bottom (with the April 2 black candle being the first tower).

Although the stock was propelled sharply higher after the tower bottom, remember that this tower bottom had nothing to do with the extent of the move. As was discussed before, and I want to emphasize again, candles are potent turning signals, but don't give price targets.

An arrow in Exhibit 6.65 points to a long black real body that propelled the market to a new low for the move. A small white real body followed this bearish candle, forming a harami pattern. An extended white body followed six weeks of consolidation and thus completed a tower bottom.

Note

1. Ifrah, Georges. *The Universal History of Numbers* (New York: John Wiley and Sons, 2000, p. 276).

CHAPTER 7

CONTINUATION PATTERNS

運は勇者を助く

Fate aids the courageous.

All of the candle signals we've seen so far have been rever-sals. In fact, most candle signals are trend reversals. There are, however, a group of candle patterns that are continuation indicators. A continuation pattern is one in which the market should continue the same trend as that in force before the con-tinuation pattern. For instance, a continuation pattern follow-ing a rally means that the trend remains up and we should expect the rally to remain in force. (This, however, does not pre-clude a correction after the continuation pattern before the rally, hopefully, unfolds.)

As the Japanese express it, "There are times to buy, times to sell, and times to rest." Many of these continuation patterns imply a time of rest, a breather, before the market resumes its prior trend. The continuation formations reviewed in this chapter are windows (and patterns that include windows), the rising and falling three methods, separating lines, and three white soldiers.

WINDOWS

The Japanese refer to what we call in the West a gap as a *window*. Whereas the Western expression is "filling in the gap," the Japanese would say, "closing the window." In this section I will explain the basic concepts of windows and then explore other patterns containing windows. Throughout my seminars and in this book I often use the terms "windows" and "gaps" interchangeably.

There are two kinds of windows, one bullish and the other bearish. A *rising window* (see Exhibit 7.1) is a bullish signal. There is a price vacuum between the prior session's high (that is, the top of the upper shadow) and the current session's low (e.g., the bottom of the lower shadow).

Exhibit 7.2 displays a *falling window*. This is a bearish signal in which there is a gap between the prior session's low and the current session's high.

It is said by Japanese technicians to "go in the direction of the window." This is because windows are continuation signals. Consequently, with the emergence of a rising window, one should look to buy on dips, and with a falling window to sell on bounces.

It is also said by the Japanese that "corrections stop at the window." This means windows can become support and resistance areas. Thus, a rising window (as we'll see soon, this means the entire window) should also be a zone of support on pullbacks. If the pullback closes under the bottom of the window, the prior uptrend is voided. Note that in Exhibit 7.1, the market got under the bottom of the window, but since it didn't close under this area, the rising windows support remains intact.

Likewise, a falling window implies still lower levels. Any price rebounds should run into resistance at this falling window (the entire window). If the bulls have enough force to close

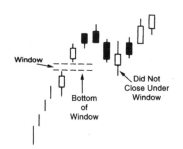

EXHIBIT 7.1. Rising Window

EXHIBIT 7.2. Falling Window

the market above the top of the falling window, the downtrend is done.

There is a belief in the West that a gap is always filled. I don't know if this is true, but using the concept that corrections stop at a window, once prices try to fill a gap we can then consider buying (in a rising window) or selling (in a falling window).

Based on questions from my public and institutional seminars, the most common misunderstanding with windows is that some will view a pattern as a window if the real bodies don't touch. For instance, candle lines A and B in Exhibit 7.3 have a large space between their real bodies. However, because the shadows of A and B overlapped, this was not a window. A window, as shown in Exhibits 7.1 and 7.2, must have no overlap between the shadows. No matter how large the "gap" between the real bodies, it is not a window unless there is a space between the shadows.

In Exhibit 7.3 we see a small rising window of only 4 cents between the high of July 22 and the next day's low. No matter how tiny a rising window, that window should be potential support. The same is true with a falling window as resistance.

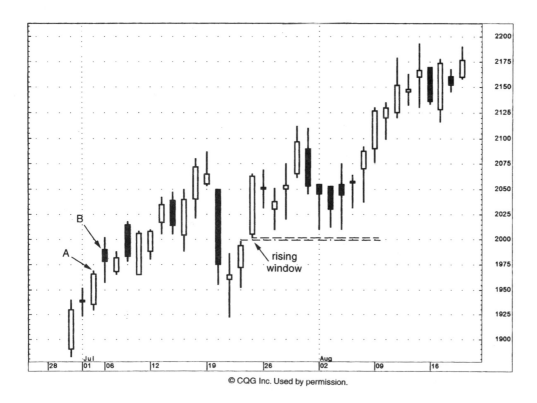

© CQG Inc. Used by permission.

EXHIBIT 7.3. Crude Light—Daily (Rising Window)

Size doesn't matter with windows. The long lower shadows as it descended toward the rising window's support in Exhibit 7.3, underscored the demand near that window. Although the rising window is a potential support zone, as this chart shows, the market may not get down to exactly (or even near) the window's support zone before bouncing. Therefore, if you are aggressively bullish as a market approaches the rising window, you can consider buying even if it gets close to the top of the window and not within the window. How one uses a window is dependent on trading style and aggressiveness. There should be a stop (mental or otherwise) if the market closes under the bottom of the rising window.

In Exhibit 7.3 we saw how a tiny rising window became support. In Exhibit 7.4 there is a very large rising window between $20.50 and $22.50. This gives a $2 zone of support (from the top of the window at $22.50 to the bottom at $20.50).

As previously discussed, the entire rising window becomes a potential support zone. The disadvantage with a large window is that the whole zone is potential support. Consequently, we don't have so tight a support (with a rising window) or resis-

EXHIBIT 7.4. Novell—Daily (Rising Window)

tance (with a falling window) as one would have with a very small window.

In instances in which there are relatively large windows, remember that the key support area for a rising window is the bottom of the window (for a falling window, the critical resistance is the top of the window). Consequently, the "last gasp" of support with a rising window is at the bottom of that window shown by the dashed line. In this chart the market touched the window's low near $20.50 and bounced via a hammer on April 20.

Let's look at the two other rising windows labeled 1 and 2. Window 1 held well as support for the next three weeks before the April 6 candle broke its support. The support at window 2 was broken the day after this window opened. After window 2 was breached, the window at 1 became support. This is how I sometimes use windows. If, for example, a window's support is broken, I will look for another window under the one that was broken as my next support area. In this case, once the window at 2 was broken, my next support was at window 1.

Exhibit 7.5 shows an example of the importance of considering the overall technical picture before reacting to a single candle signal. The first candle line on March 1 was a bullish hammer. But more significantly, look at how that hammer unfolded—with a falling window. While this hammer immediately became a support level, we should remember that because of the falling window, there is now resistance within that entire window. The bounce from the hammer ran out of steam at the top of the falling window.

Note how the window in Exhibit 7.5 was made between the last candle line of February 28 and the first candle of the next day (March 1). This is illustrative of a concept with windows on intraday charts; windows are mostly formed between the last candle line on the prior day and the first line of the current day. This is not surprising since it will be unusual, say on a 5-minute chart, to have a gap from one 5-minute session to the immediate next 5-minute session.

As shown in Exhibit 7.6, there was a dynamic two-day rally in late June. The harami cross told us that the stock was separating from its prior uptrend. (The July 1 second candle within prior tall white real body was so diminutive that it could for all intents and purposes be considered a harami cross.) The ideal

EXHIBIT 7.5. Amazon—5 Minutes (Falling Window)

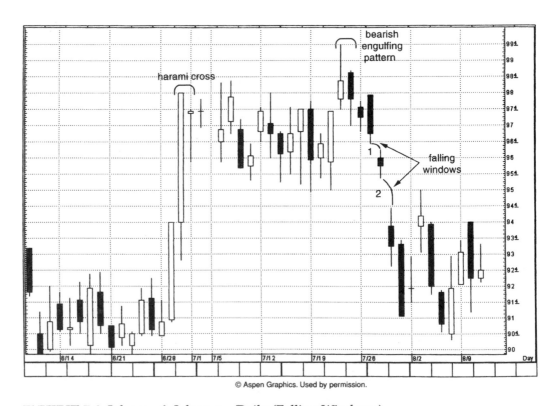

EXHIBIT 7.6. Johnson & Johnson—Daily (Falling Windows)

doji the next day (July 2) echoed what was hinted at the candle line before, to wit, that the market was separating from its trend (i.e. up) near $98. A bearish engulfing pattern in mid July was more proof of trouble overhead.

A small falling window opened between July 27 and 28 (shown as 1) and then another falling window (at 2) on the 29th. This second falling window did the most damage, since it also gapped under a support area near $95 that had been in place through the first half of July (this is called a "breakaway gap" in Western parlance). Not surprisingly, this window, near $95, became pivotal resistance.

One of the major factors for the remarkable appeal of candles is that they will often provide signals not available with bar charts. Exhibit 7.7 shows how we can use windows to get a resistance area not available with bar charts. A hammer emerged on October 8. This was a potentially bullish sign, but the day of the hammer was also a falling window. Therefore, one should wait for a close back over the top of the falling window to corroborate the potentially positive indications of the hammer.

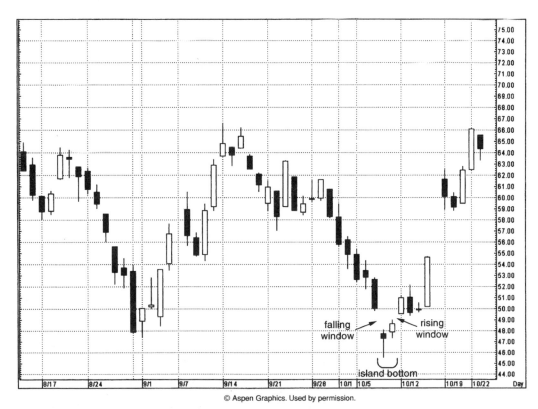

© Aspen Graphics. Used by permission.

EXHIBIT 7.7. Oil Service Index—Daily (Windows)

Two days after the hammer, the bulls proved their mettle by closing above the top of the falling window, and did so with a bullish rising window. In doing this, the Oil Service Index built what in the West is called an island bottom. (This is when the market gaps down, and then within one or a few sessions, gaps up. The name "island bottom" is derived because one or few sessions are like an island surrounded by the water on either side [i.e., the gaps].) While the low of the island bottom is a natural support area (in this chart it is near 45.50), we can shift to our candle charting technique of windows to get an even earlier support area.

Using the concept that a rising window should be support, once the island bottom is completed on October 12 (with the rising window), our first support is not 45.50 (the low of the island bottom), but near 49.00 because of the rising window. This window's support is where the index stabilized for the next few days before exploding with a long white real body. This is yet another example of how candle charting techniques will help get a jump on those who use only bar charting tools, since those using bar charts would use the bottom of the island bottom (at 45.50) as first support, rather than the candle's rising window at 49.00. Of course, if the market had breached the window's support area, we would look for next support toward 45.50 (the low of the island bottom and the hammer).

Traditional Japanese technical analysis posits that after three up or down windows, the chances are that the market is too overbought to continue ascending (in the case of three rising windows) or too oversold to keep the downtrend in force (with three falling windows). This probably has to do with the importance of the number three to the Japanese. However, I have fine-tuned this concept since the first edition of this book.

Windows are so dominant that I have found that no matter how many windows there are, the trend is still intact until the last window is closed. There could be any number of rising windows. The trend is still up until voided by the market closing under the top window. An example of this is illustrated in Exhibit 7.8. Here we see a rally that started with the bullish engulfing pattern at B in mid August. Ultimately this rally opened six rising windows. We got an early clue that the bonds were losing their breath with the October 5 and 6 harami pat-

© CQG Inc. Used by permission.

EXHIBIT 7.8. Bond Futures—Daily (Rising Windows)

tern. But it took the close under the sixth rising window to confirm the rally was over. This reversal turned out to be a major high in bond futures as the market slid for years after.

Exhibit 7.9 is another instance of how a rally can continue even if there are three rising windows. The rising windows are shown at 1, 2, 3, and 4. Each of these held as support. The falling window at A gave an indication of some trouble with that window acting as resistance at $46. The descent from that falling window continued until the first week in May.

On May 4 a black real body punctured the bottom of window 4's support at $42.50. This breaking of window 4's support had potentially further bearish implications for Microsoft. However, the next day, May 5, a powerful white candle (a bullish belt-hold line that opened on its low and closed to near its high) formed a classic piercing pattern. This negated some of the prior day's bearish implications.

This chart is an example of the importance of adapting to the changing market environment as we went from a bearish out-

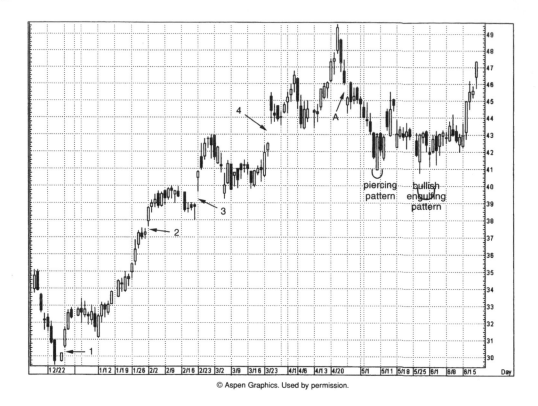

© Aspen Graphics. Used by permission.

EXHIBIT 7.9. Microsoft—Daily (Rising Windows)

look with May 4's breaking of support to a less bearish view the next day because of the piercing pattern.

In the next two trading sessions, on May 11 and May 12, a similar scenario unfolded with a black real body followed by a white real body. If further proof of major support near $41 was needed, it came on May 26 and 27 with a bullish engulfing pattern. Indeed, if one looks at the three candle lines on May 29 through June 2, it could be viewed as a morning star pattern (although classically we like a morning star to come after a downtrend and not as part of the trading range as it was here). Nonetheless, this pattern did confirm the solidity of support near $41.

TASUKI

As shown in Exhibits 7.10 and 7.11 the tasuki are a specific combination of two candle lines that gap higher or lower. The *upward gapping tasuki* in Exhibit 7.10 is made of a rising window formed by a white candle and then a black candle. The black candle opens within the white real body and closes under the white candle's real body. The close on the black candle day is the fight point. If the market closes under the bottom of the window, the bullish outlook of the upward gap tasuki is voided. The same concept is true in reverse for a *downward gapping tasuki* (see Exhibit 7.11). The market opens a falling window with a black candle followed by a white candle. The two candles of the tasuki should be about the same size. Both types of tasuki are rare.

Based on my extra twelve years of experience since the first edition of this book, I have recommended at my seminars that there is little reason to waste brain cells on remembering the tasuki. The window is so overwhelmingly important that, in my opinion, it really doesn't matter the color or combination of candle lines after the rising window. It is the window itself that is critical. All one needs to remember is that if there is a rising window (such as the upward tasuki), it is a bullish signal and the window should be support. A close under this support would turn the trend down. The same is true in reverse for the downward tasuki. That is, since the downward gapping tasuki

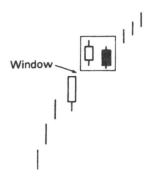

EXHIBIT 7.10. Upward Gapping Tasuki

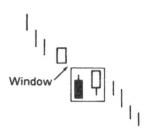

EXHIBIT 7.11. Downward Gapping Tasuki

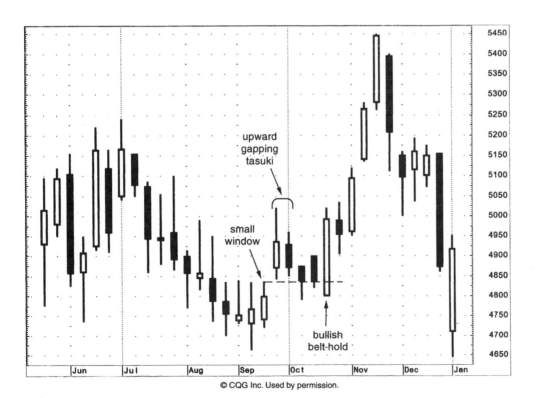

© CQG Inc. Used by permission.

EXHIBIT 7.12. Platinum—Weekly (Upward Gapping Tasuki)

has a falling window, the window should be resistance. A close over the top of the falling window would void the bearish implications of the downward gapping tasuki.

In Exhibit 7.12 a diminutive rising window opened late September. The two candles after this rising window formed the upward gapping tasuki. It's a tasuki because of the white candle followed by the black after the rising window. However, as mentioned above, in my opinion it doesn't matter what the candle lines look like after the rising window. My main concern is looking at that rising window as support based on the close. As shown with the dashed line, that support managed to hold based on the close. Then, significantly in late October, a bullish belt-hold line that wrapped around three black real bodies gave final confirmation of that window's support.

High-Price and Low-Price Gapping Plays

It is normal after a sharp advance for the market to consolidate the gains. Sometimes this consolidation is by a series of small real bodies. A group of small real bodies after a strong white session tells us that the market is undecided. These small real bodies, while changing the trend from up to neutral, are in a sense healthy since, by treading water, the market is then relieving its overbought condition. If there is a rising window from these small real bodies, it is a bullish signal. This is the *high-price gapping play* pattern (see Exhibit 7.13). It is called this because prices hover near their recent highs and then gap to the upside.

A *low-price gapping play* is, not surprisingly, the bearish counterpart of the high-price gapping play. The low-price gapping play (see Exhibit 7.14) is a downside window from a low-price congestion band. This congestion band (a series of small real bodies) initially stabilized a steep decline. At first, this group of small candles gives the appearance that a base is forming. The break to the downside via a window dashes these bullish hopes.

In Exhibit 7.15 a hammer on July 31 proved to be the low of the move as the market ascended into the early part of August with a rising window. A long black real body during the week of August 7 made a dark-cloud cover, putting a temporary damper on the rally.

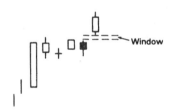

EXHIBIT 7.13. High-Price Gapping Play

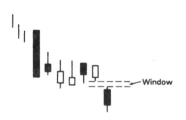

EXHIBIT 7.14. Low-Price Gapping Play

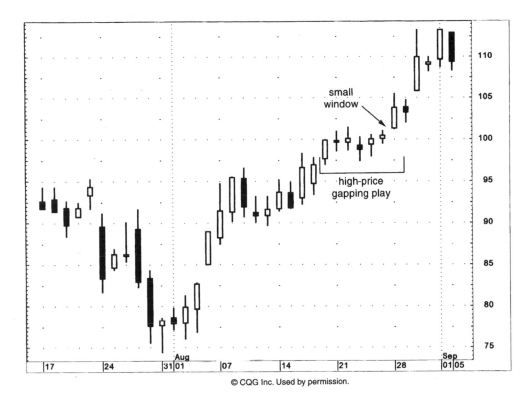

EXHIBIT 7.15. Corning—Daily (High-Price Gapping Play)

During the week of August 21, a series of small real bodies following a tall white candle showed us that the stock had reached a lull. The small rising window on August 28 proved that the bulls had taken full control as the market completed a high-price gapping play.

The bullish implications of this gapping play, or any high-price gapping play, would be voided if the market closed under the rising window that completes the gapping play. The reverse would be true for a low-price gapping play.

In Exhibit 7.16 we see a tall white candle on June 29. The doji on June 30 following the tall white candle showed that the stock had gone from up to more neutral since these two candle lines made a harami cross. The small real bodies following this doji just echoed this outlook. Note how at the bottom of the chart, the tight trading range echoed by the four small real bodies resulted in the oscillator going from an overbought condition at 1 to a neutral reading at 2. This is an aspect discussed in the introduction to this section on gapping plays, namely the small real bodies of the gapping play helped relieve an overbought

© Aspen Graphics. Used by permission.

EXHIBIT 7.16. 99 Cents Only Stores—Daily (High-Price Gapping Play)

© CQG Inc. Used by permission.

EXHIBIT 7.17. Sugar—Daily (Low-Price Gapping Play)

reading. With the stock not overbought at 2, it made it easier for the market to rally. Once the stock opened a small window on July 7, it formed a high-price gapping play. A dumpling top unfolded in mid July.

A harami pattern in early April in Exhibit 7.17 helped short-circuit a rally. The descent from this pattern picked up steam, especially with the extended black real body of April 15. The next two sessions' spinning tops gave a clue that the stock was trying to stabilize. However, the new low close on April 17, and then the low-price gapping play completing the next session, showed the bears had regained complete control.

Observe how a small falling window in early May became resistance. This resistance area was important to keep in mind because there were bottoming signals with a hammer at 1 and the bullish engulfing pattern at 2. A trader should be cautious about buying on either these bullish signals because of the limited profit potential based on the window's resistance.

Gapping Side-by-Side White Lines

In a rally, an upward-gapping white candle followed the next session by another similar-sized white candle with about the same opening is a bullish continuation pattern. This two-candle pattern is referred to as *upgap side-by-side white lines* (see Exhibit 7.18).

There are rarer side-by-side white lines that gap lower. These are called *downgap side-by-side white lines* (see Exhibit 7.19). In spite of the dual white candles, it is still considered a bearish signal because of the falling window. These white lines are viewed as short covering. Once this short covering evaporates, prices should move lower. The reason the downgap side-by-side white line pattern is especially rare is because black candles, not white candles, are more natural in a declining price environment.

Although I have examples of these patterns in the following exhibits, the candle lines that make the gapping side-by-side white candles are not critical to remember. What is important is the rising and falling windows that are part of these patterns. As discussed in the tasuki pattern earlier in this chapter, I view it as of minor consequence if there are two white candles (as with the side-by-side patterns) or a black and white candle (as

EXHIBIT 7.18. Upgap Side-by-Side White Lines in an Uptrend

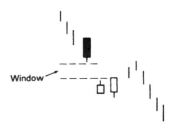

EXHIBIT 7.19. Downgap Side-by-Side White Lines in a Downtrend

with the tasuki) after the window. It is the window itself that gives us the trend and the support or resistance area.

For example, in the downgap side-by-side white candles, it is not surprising that this is a bearish signal in spite of the two white candles. This is because it is the falling window of that pattern that defines the trend (in this case, down). It would take a close over the top of the falling window to negate the bearish outlook of the downgap side-by-side white lines.

The moral of this story: It is not necessary to worry about remembering the esoteric tasuki and gapping side-by-side white lines. *It is the window that is critical.* The combination and colors of the candle lines after a rising or falling window patterns aren't important. A falling window puts the trend down and a rising window puts the trend up with the window as support or resistance.

Exhibit 7.20 shows an upgap side-by-side white lines the first two days in May. As discussed earlier, it's not so much the color of these white lines in the upgap side-by-side lines that make this positive as much as the rising window that opened on May 1.

© CQG Inc. Used by permission.

EXHIBIT 7.20. Platinum—Daily (Upgap Side-by-Side White Lines)

Because this chart has many examples of windows, I will discuss them individually.

1. A falling window at 1 keeps the trend down. This is in spite of the fact that it was a hammer on March 26. Usually, between the window and another pattern, I go with the window. In this case, it was between a bullish hammer and a bearish falling window. The bearish outlook engendered by the falling window takes precedence over the hammer. It would take a close above the window to have the bullish outlook hinted at by the hammer to be validated.

2. The small rising window at 2 became support on the minor retracement from the dark-cloud cover of April 4 and 5. The doji on April 10 (at the window's support) showed two things. The first was that the window at 2 held as support. The second was that the stock was separating from its prior downtrend that was evidenced by the three consecutive black real bodies before the doji.

3. The rally that started with the successful defense of window 2 on April 10 stalled on April 23 as Platinum got to the resistance area at $495 defined by the top of falling window 1. The decline from this resistance opened a falling window at 3. The long black real body on April 25 followed by a small real body inside that black real body formed a harami pattern. This showed that the bears were losing their momentum.

4. The rising window on May 1 followed by the two small white real bodies. (This formed the aforementioned upward gapping side-by-side white candle line pattern.)

   After the upgap side-by-side white lines, it became a battle of windows with the falling window at 3 as resistance (near $488) and rising window at 4 near $475 as support. We can see that for over a week the aforementioned support and resistance areas held intact until April 17 when the demand was strong enough to push the market over the falling window 3's resistance on a close. (On April 14 the market pushed over the window intraday but did not close above it—thus keeping the window's resistance intact.) From the break of that resistance, the market ascended briskly until a harami pattern on May 18 and 21 called an end to that rally.

EXHIBIT 7.21. Rising Three Methods

EXHIBIT 7.22. Falling Three Methods

RISING AND FALLING THREE METHODS

The three methods include the bullish rising three methods and a bearish falling three methods. (Note how the number three again makes an appearance.) These are both continuation patterns. That is, the trend before the bullish rising three methods should continue higher once the bullish three methods is completed. Likewise, a bear trend remains in effect after the bearish falling three methods.

The *rising three methods* (see Exhibit 7.21) is composed of:

1. A long white candle.

2. The white candle is followed by a group of falling or lateral small real body candles. The ideal number of small candles is three but two or more than three are also acceptable if they hold within the long white candle's high–low range. Think of the small candles as forming a pattern similar to a three-day harami pattern since they hold within the first session's range. (For this pattern, that would include holding within the shadows; for a true harami they would have to hold with the real body.) The small candles can be either color, but black is most ideal for this pattern.

3. The final day should be a strong white real body session with a close above the first day's close. The final candle line should ideally also open above the close of the previous session.

This pattern resembles the Western bull flag or pennant formation. Yet the concept behind the rising three methods is from the 1700s. The three methods pattern is considered a rest from trading and a rest from battle. In more modern terms, the market is, with the group of small candles, "taking a breather."

The *falling three methods* pattern (see Exhibit 7.22) is the bearish counterpart of the rising three methods pattern. For this pattern, the market should be in a downtrend. A long black candle is followed by about three small rising candles whose real bodies hold within the first candle's range (including shadows). The final session should open under the prior close and then close under the first black candle's close. This pattern resembles a bear flag or bear pennant formation.

The ideal version of this pattern has the small real bodies as the opposite color of the first long real body. That is, for a bullish rising three methods, there should be small black real bodies; and for the bearish falling three methods, three small white real bodies. Nonetheless, from my experience, two and up to five small real bodies work fine. Also, the small real bodies can be any color.

The ideal rising three methods has three small black real bodies within the entire trading range of a white real body. In Exhibit 7.23 we see a bullish belt-hold on August 13. This is followed by four small black real bodies and doji within the August 13 high–low range. The close on August 21 completes the rising three methods pattern.

The challenge we have with a rising three methods is from a risk/reward aspect. By the time the rising three methods is completed, a stock might be far from its most recent lows. In such a scenario, buying on the completion of the three methods may not offer an attractive trade. As such, one should think of the potential profit once the rising three methods is completed com-

EXHIBIT 7.23. Intel—Daily (Rising Three Methods)

pared to its risk (the risk being the low of the white candle that started the rising three methods).

As shown in Exhibit 7.24 an extended black candle pushed orange juice to a new low in the first week of October. The next session, as orange juice got back above 69 cents, it showed that the new lows made the prior week could not hold. As will be seen in Chapter 11, when a market breaks a significant support area (as this market did when it broke beneath the August–September lows) and then fails to hold the new lows, it often has bullish implications.

The tall white candle in the second week of November and the following week's small real bodies demonstrate hesitation at resistance area from May toward 85 to 87 cents. A group of small real bodies held within the range set by the second tall white candle in November. With the tall white candle in December, we had a rising three methods. (Remember, it is acceptable for the shadows to get outside of the white candles' trading range as long as the real small bodies remain in the white candles' trading range).

After this rising three methods, the market moved laterally for the remainder of December until an extended white candle

© Aspen Graphics. Used by permission.

EXHIBIT 7.24. Orange Juice—Weekly (Rising Three Methods)

after the doji (shown as 4) put the bulls back in charge. Some may have noticed that area A on the chart looks very similar to rising three methods since the real bodies at 1 to 4 held within the white candle. Because the rising three methods should have small real bodies, the long real body at 3 meant this was not viewed as a rising three methods pattern.

In Exhibit 7.25 on May 30 and 31 as the stock was descending, it did so with a series of very small, almost doji, real bodies. This makes the trend less negative. The April 1 bullish engulfing pattern showed that the bulls had now taken control. Some consolidation in the next four days with alternating black and white small real bodies and the April 10 candle finalized the rising three methods pattern.

Let's look at an example of volume in conjunction with the rising three methods. Ideally, with a rising three methods, the first and last candles, i.e., the long white, have the strongest volume of all the sessions that make up the rising three methods. This would confirm that on each of the white candle days the bulls had more control of the market. In Exhibit 7.26 the June 17 tall white candle had relatively strong volume.

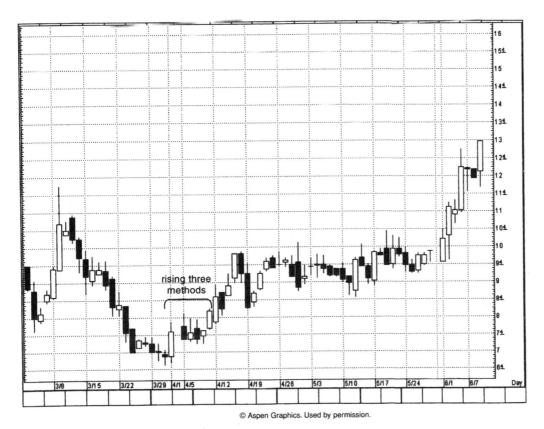

EXHIBIT 7.25. Asyst Tech—Daily (Rising Three Methods)

Additionally, this candle in conjunction with the prior two days formed a morning doji star.

The series of small real bodies that drifted lower after the June 17 white real body were on declining volume. The push higher with a higher volume lofty white candle on June 24 completed the rising three methods. This chart is a classic example of combining volume with a candlestick indicator that can reinforce the likelihood of the candlestick indicator being successful.

After the June 24 white candle, a black real body formed a little dark-cloud cover and caused some temporary hesitation before the rally resumed. Note also the high volume window opened July 8. This high volume reinforced the likelihood that the window, especially the bottom of the window, would become a support area. (Volume is addressed in Chapter 15.)

In most instances, the rising three methods occur during an uptrend or lateral trend. Sometimes, however, this pattern helps define a turning point from a sell-off. Another example of this pattern is shown in Exhibit 7.27. A rising three methods in early September helped to underscore the solidity of support

EXHIBIT 7.26. Citigroup—Daily (Rising Three Methods and Volume)

near 7500. The market did not immediately rally after that rising three methods. While candle signals will often give market turns, they do not necessarily mean that the market will ascend (in the case of a rising three methods) immediately from that signal. Instead, many candle patterns, such as this one, can reinforce a support area. This is what unfolded with the Dow near 7500 as support. Additional confirmation of that support came with the piercing pattern in mid September and early October and a hammer on October 4.

Where a candle pattern or line appears within the market picture is often more important than the individual candle pattern. For example, if there were a bullish engulfing pattern that is completed near a resistance area, from a risk/reward perspective it would not be attractive to purchase on that pattern since one would be buying at resistance.

An example of the overall technical picture and a rising three methods pattern is highlighted in Exhibit 7.28. A small window between December 14 and 15 was support during the latter part of that week. A rally that began on December 20 ran into some problems near $60 with a harami pattern of December 23 and 27. On the close of December 29, the stock formed a rising

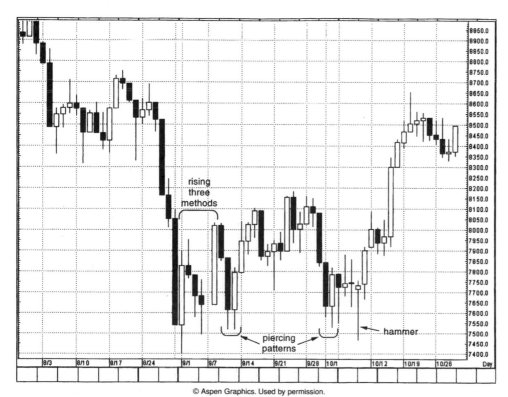

© Aspen Graphics. Used by permission.

EXHIBIT 7.27. Dow Jones Industrials—Daily (Rising Three Methods)

three methods pattern (it had two small real bodies instead of the classic three small real bodies). But look where this pattern was completed, at the $60 area—which was resistance since December 7. Consequently, while the rising three methods is considered a bullish signal, one should keep in mind that since it emerged at a resistance area, it would not be an effective buying opportunity. It took the close above this $60 resistance area on January 11 to get this market going on the upside.

Exhibit 7.29 shows a falling three methods pattern. Notice that the first small real body of this pattern on May 18 was outside the real body of the prior long black real body. This does not negate the falling three methods pattern since a requisite is that the small real bodies should then be within the entire trading range of a long black candle, not necessarily in the black candle's real body.

The black real body on May 21, which closed under the close of the May 17 black real body, fulfilled the conditions for the falling three methods. A very impressive bounce on May 25 in which the stock opened sharply lower and then closed about unchanged from the prior session was almost a counterattack pattern. Although the white candle's close did not get exactly to

EXHIBIT 7.28. Schlumberger—Daily (Rising Three Methods and Resistance)

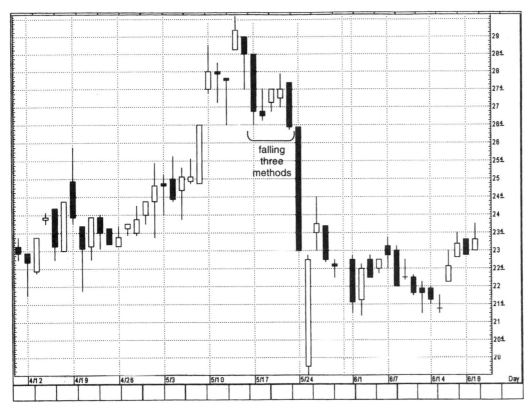

© Aspen Graphics. Used by permission.

EXHIBIT 7.29. Unibanco Uniao de Bancos Brasileros—Daily (Falling Three Methods)

© CQG Inc. Used by permission.

EXHIBIT 7.30. WorldCom—Weekly (Falling Three Methods)

the May 24 close, the intense bounce from the opening to closing on the 25 would have the same implications as a classic counterattack.

In Exhibit 7.30, WorldCom broke a multimonth support area near $38 in the first week of August. A minor rally in early August managed to put the stock back to the prior support area of $38. From there it failed. (In Chapter 11, I examine this technique of old support becoming new resistance.) The price activity in September formed a falling three methods pattern.

SEPARATING LINES

We examined the counterattack line in Chapter 6. This is a white/black or black/white combination of candle lines with the same close as the previous close. Whereas the counterattack line has the same close, the *separating lines* in Exhibit 7.31 have the same open as the previous opposite color candle.

The separating line is a continuation pattern. It is easy to see why. During a market rise, a black real body (especially a relatively long one) would be a bull's cause for concern. The bears might be gaining control. However, if the next session's opening gaps high enough to open at the previous black session's opening price, it impressively proves that the bears have lost control of the market—especially if that session closes as a white candle. This is the scenario that unfolds with the bullish separating line as shown in Exhibit 7.31. The white line ideally should also be a bullish belt-hold (that is, open on the low of the session and close at, or near, the high of the session). The opposite would be true with a bearish separating line in Exhibit 7.31. This is viewed as a bearish continuation signal. Separating lines are rare.

While most of us would like to see an ideal version of a particular candle pattern, even variations of these patterns can also prove useful. Exhibit 7.32 illustrates this. A bearish engulfing pattern in mid August (at B) presaged a decline that culminated with a bullish engulfing pattern completed on August 3. The two lines following the August 3 white candle was almost a bullish separating line. This is because the open on August 7 was almost the same as the prior day's open, but not exactly. Nonetheless, considering the stock closed at $46.25 on August

EXHIBIT 7.31. Bullish and Bearish Separating Lines

4 and then gapped sharply higher to open almost the same as the August 4 opening was, undoubtedly, very impressive. If one needed more bullish proof than this that demand had overwhelmed supply, it came with the August 9 rising window.

In Exhibit 7.33 bearish separating lines occurred in the second week of August. After these bearish separating lines, the stock stabilized near the early August support area of $29. Confirmation of a bearish down leg came with the falling window of August 15.

There were bullish separating lines on September 13 and 14. These failed to correctly signal a continuation of the rally. However, this should not be too surprising considering that the white candle of the bullish separating lines came at $28. This was a resistance area in place during the week of August 21, as shown by the dashed line. Once again this underscores that where one gets a candle signal is a major factor in deciding if one buys or sells on that signal. In this example, if someone bought on the completion of the bullish separating lines, that trader would have purchased the stock at resistance. In such a

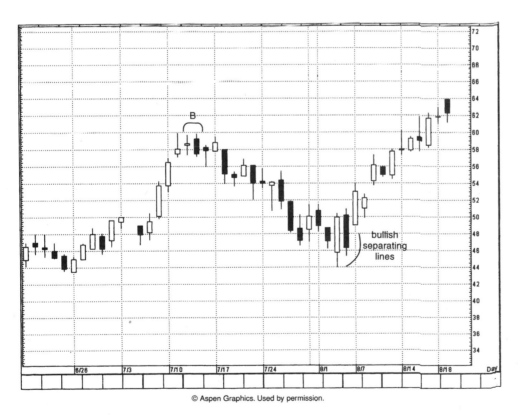

EXHIBIT 7.32. Jabil Circuit—Daily (Bullish Separating Lines)

© CQG Inc. Used by permission.

EXHIBIT 7.33. Target—Daily (Bearish and Bullish Separating Lines)

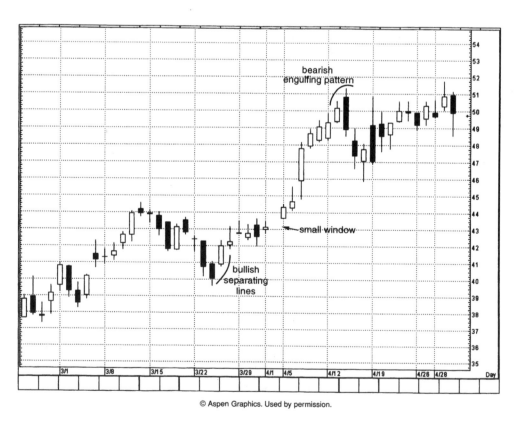

© Aspen Graphics. Used by permission.

EXHIBIT 7.34. Citicorp—Daily (Bullish Separating Lines)

scenario it might be more prudent waiting for the stock to close above $28 for further bullish confirmation.

Although the bullish separating lines are rare, they normally appear during a rally. There are a few instances, however, where a bullish separating line can help signal a bottom. In Exhibit 7.34 a bullish separating line arose on March 24 and 25. After this pattern the stock hesitated near $43.50. This market's hesitation came to an end on April 5 as the stock opened a small rising window above this $43.50 resistance.

Interestingly, the candle lines from March 25 to the afore-mentioned gap on April 5 formed a high-price gapping play. The April rally continued until the bearish engulfing pattern on April 14 and 15.

CHAPTER 8

THE MAGIC DOJI

窓から槍

A sudden danger.

As described in Chapter 3, a doji is a candle session where the opening and closing prices are the same. Examples of doji lines are shown in Exhibits 8.1 through 8.6. The doji is such a significant reversal indicator that this chapter is devoted to its manifestations. In prior chapters, we have seen the power of a doji as a component of some patterns. These included the doji star (see Chapter 5) and the harami cross (see Chapter 6).

The doji is a distinct trend change signal, especially during rallies. The likelihood of a reversal with the emergence of a doji increases if:

1. Subsequent candles confirm the doji's reversal potential.

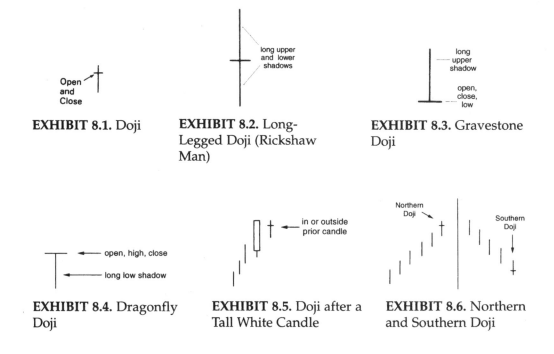

EXHIBIT 8.1. Doji

EXHIBIT 8.2. Long-Legged Doji (Rickshaw Man)

EXHIBIT 8.3. Gravestone Doji

EXHIBIT 8.4. Dragonfly Doji

EXHIBIT 8.5. Doji after a Tall White Candle

EXHIBIT 8.6. Northern and Southern Doji

2. The market is overbought or oversold.

3. The market doesn't have many doji (the plural of doji is doji). If there are numerous doji on a particular chart, one should not view the emergence of a new doji as a meaningful development.

The ideal doji session has the same opening and closing price, yet there is some flexibility to this rule. If the opening and closing prices are within a few ticks of each other (for example, a few cents in stocks or a few thirty-seconds in bonds, and so on), the line could still be viewed as a doji. How do you decide whether a near-doji day (that is, where the open and close are very close, but not exact) should be considered a doji? This is subjective and there are no rigid rules. Here are some techniques I have found useful for saying that a doji-like session would be reacted upon like a classic doji:

1. Compare a near-doji day in relation to recent action. If there were a series of very small real bodies, the near-doji day would not be viewed as significant since so many other recent periods had small real bodies. If, however, a doji-like session emerges among tall candles, then we can say that such a session could have the same implications as a doji

since this session is displaying there is something very different on that session from the preceding action.

2. If the market is at an important market junction.

3. If the market is extremely overbought or oversold.

4. If there are other technical signals sending out an alert.

Since a doji can be a significant warning, it is better to attend to a false warning than to ignore a real one.

This chapter will address doji at tops, doji as resistance, specific types of doji, doji and trend, and the tri-star.

Doji are valued for their ability to call market tops. This is especially true after a long white candle in an uptrend (see Exhibit 8.5). The reason for the doji's potential negative implications in uptrends is because a doji represents indecision. Indecision, uncertainty, or vacillation by buyers will not maintain a rally. It takes the conviction of buyers to sustain a rally. If the market has had an extended rally, and/or is overbought, and then a doji surfaces (read "indecision"), it could mean the scaffolding of buyers' support will give way.

A caveat, from my experience, is that as successful as doji are at calling tops, they tend to lose some reversal potential in downtrends. The reason may be that a doji reflects a balance between buying and selling forces. With ambivalent market participants, the market could fall, as the market saying goes, "fall of its own weight." This is similar to the idea that strong volume is more important to confirm an upside breakout than volume confirmation for a downside breakout.

Thus, a doji in a rally could signal an exhausted market. But with a doji during a price descent, the market may continue its fall. Because of this, doji need more confirmation to signal a bottom than they do a top. For example, a doji that confirms support should be heeded although it comes during a decline.

To separate a doji during a rally from doji during declines, I call the former *Northern doji* and the latter *Southern doji* (see Exhibit 8.6). This section will focus on Northern doji. Southern doji (doji in a falling market) are addressed later in this chapter.

Keep in mind that doji not working so effectively at signaling bottoms as tops is based on my experiences. The Japanese say, "The market is like a person's face; never are two alike." Consequently, for your markets, doji may work well at calling bottoms. This brings out a pivotal point about candle charts in general. All of the candle lines or patterns may be effective in your markets, or only some. Seeing which work well comes with experience.

THE NORTHERN DOJI (DOJI DURING RALLIES)

The Japanese say that with a doji after a tall white candle, or a doji in an overbought environment, that the market is "tired." That is a wonderfully apt way to view doji. A doji may not mean an immediate price reversal. The doji shows us the market is vulnerable, and may be at a transition point.

I received a letter from an attendee at one of my on-site institutional seminars. The attendee wrote, "You're right about a little knowledge being dangerous. We are all running around shouting 'doji, doji, doji!'" This comment is not surprising since doji are so easy to spot. Traders may get so excited about seeing a doji that they jump on it as a trading signal. But don't make more of the doji than it is meant to show. A doji means the trend may be in the process of changing.

For example, in my advisory service, I provide short-term trend. When a doji arises, I don't change the market's short-term trend from up to down, but from up to up/neutral. If this doji also confirms another technical signal, then I would change the trend from up to neutral or neutral/down. (This idea of one technical indicator confirming another is the focus of Part 2.) It is rare that with a doji itself I would change the short-term trend from up to down.

In Exhibit 8.7 the spinning tops at A and B were clues that the trends before these candles were stalling. While such small real bodies represent a tug-of-war between the buyers and sellers, a doji is a session in which the bulls and bears are in complete balance.

During the ascent from B a series of long white real bodies echoed a vibrant market. The doji, in a single session, shows that the market is separating from its trend. The doji indicates that there is something very different on that day (in which the open and close are the same) from the preceding white candle lines where the closes were well above the openings.

In this example, after the doji, the index went from up to lateral and then down. However, the appearance of the doji doesn't necessarily mean the market will descend. Yet, the doji, especially in such an overbought market, would be reason for caution. Liquidating some long positions, selling calls, and moving up stops are all examples of what could be done with this doji session.

In Exhibit 8.8 the stock retreated from a bearish engulfing pattern (at B). A few sessions later a lengthy white candle showed that the bulls have taken control since that line closed over the bearish engulfing pattern's $58.50 resistance area. But the next session's doji changed the outlook. The market went from one where the bulls were in charge to one where, as shown by the doji, the forces of supply and demand were in equilibrium.

Observe how the stock stalled a couple of sessions after the doji neared $58.62. This brings out a useful technique I use frequently with a doji following a tall white candle. Specifically, I

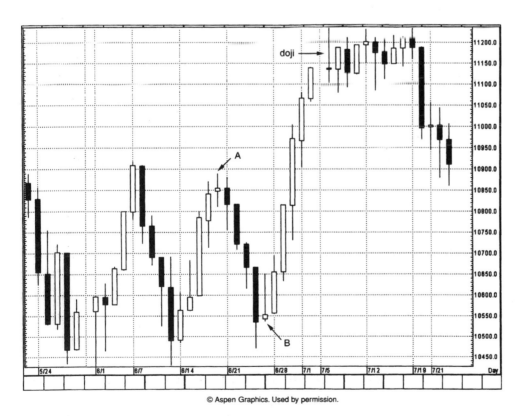

EXHIBIT 8.7. Dow Jones Industrials—Daily (Doji after a Tall White Candle)

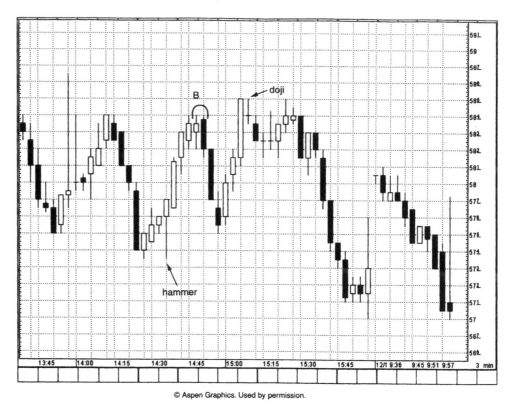

EXHIBIT 8.8. Microsoft—3 Minutes (Doji after a Tall White Candle)

will take the highest high between the doji session and the tall white candle (that is, the highest upper shadow). That level should be resistance based on the close. In this example, the high of the doji session and the long white candle were both $58.62. At such, that becomes our resistance area.

In Exhibit 8.9 sessions 1 through 6 had higher highs, higher lows, and higher closes. Session 7 was the first lower high, lower close, and lower low since candle line 1. Normally this is not of great consequence, but since candle 7 was also a doji, it adds more importance to this aspect. Sometimes the small clues add up to signal an important market juncture. As the Japanese proverb says, "The water of even a great ocean comes one drop at a time." So it is in the markets, where small clues that are not meaningful by themselves take on more weight when combined with other technical clues.

The dashed line on the chart is our resistance area once the doji emerged. As explained in Exhibit 8.8, if we have a doji after a tall white candle, we take the highest high between those two lines and make that resistance based on the close. In

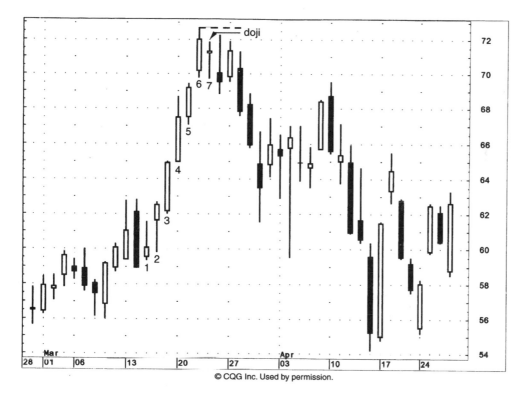

EXHIBIT 8.9. Intel—Daily (Doji after a Tall White Candle)

this chart, since the white candle line had a higher high than the doji's high, that becomes our prime resistance area (shown by the dashed line). With the appearance of the doji, Intel had become "tired." If Intel had closed over that resistance line, we would say that the market is refreshed and it would be a bullish breakout.

THE LONG-LEGGED DOJI (RICKSHAW MAN), THE GRAVESTONE DOJI, AND THE DRAGONFLY DOJI

As shown in Exhibits 8.2 to 8.4, some doji have nicknames depending on if the open/close (i.e., the horizontal component of the doji) is at the low or high of the session or if there are unusually long upper and lower shadows on the doji.

A candle line with long upper and lower shadows and a small real body is called a high-wave candle.[1] If such a candle line is a doji instead of a small real body, then it is called a *long-legged doji* (see Exhibit 8.2). It also has the nickname *rickshaw man*.

The doji portion of the long-legged doji shows the market is at a transition point. The long upper shadow shows the market had rallied during the session, but by session's end had backed off from these highs. The extended lower shadow visually depicts a market that had sold off during the session; by session's end it had been able, by the close, to recoup some of its lost ground. In other words, the market rallies, sells off, rallies, etc. It is a confused market. These long shadows hint, as the Japanese say, "The market has lost its sense of direction." As such, a long-legged doji is an indication of a market separating from its trend.

The *gravestone doji* (see Exhibit 8.3) is another distinctive doji. It develops when the open, low, and close are at the low of the day. This line is an example of how visually intuitive candles are. Even if you never saw an explanation of the gravestone doji, just by looking at it, would you think it was a bullish or bearish signal? Of course, the answer is bearish. With its extended upper shadow and close at the low of the session, we can graphically see that at some time during the session the stock had rallied and by session's end the bears dragged this stock down to the lows at the close. It can be viewed as the ultimate shooting star. The shooting star has a long upper shadow and small real body. If the shooting star's real body becomes a doji, then we have a gravestone doji.

The gravestone's forte is in calling tops. The shape of the gravestone doji makes its name appropriate. As we have discussed, many of the Japanese technical terms are based on military analogies. In Japanese candlestick literature it is said that the gravestone doji represents the gravestone of the bulls that have died defending their territory.

The *dragonfly doji* is the bullish counterpart of the gravestone doji. The dragonfly has the open/close at the highs of the session. This means the market had touched much lower lows during the session, but had impressively managed to close at, or very close to, the highs. This is like the hammer, but the hammer has a small real body where the dragonfly doji has no real body since it is a doji.

In Exhibit 8.10 a long-legged doji appeared on October 23. By using the highest high between the doji and the prior white candle, we immediately obtain resistance near $88. The index

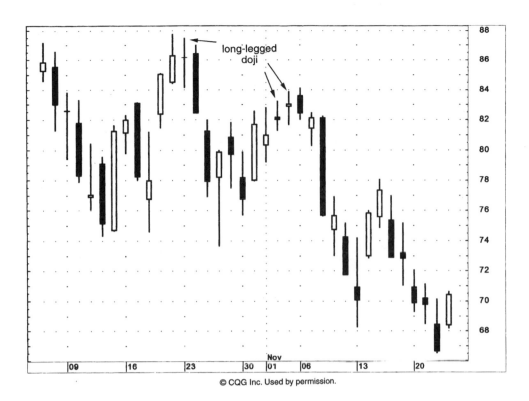

long-legged doji

EXHIBIT 8.10. NASDAQ-100 Trust—Daily (Long-Legged Doji)

descended from this long-legged doji until the hammer three days later. In early November the market was ascending, but the two long-legged doji put a damper on any bullish outlook. A further sign of trouble emerged with the November 6 and 7 bearish engulfing pattern. Note how in the early part of October the stock was falling with doji during this descent. As previously discussed, doji, based on my experience, work better at calling tops reversals than bottom reversals.

An example of a gravestone doji is shown in Exhibit 8.11. Since the doji's high was the same as the prior session, it is also a tweezers top. As ominous as "gravestone" sounds, please don't make the mistake of thinking it implies a large move lower. While the gravestone doji, because of its extended upper shadow and close at the session low, does increase the chances for a turn, it doesn't forecast the extent of a potential decline. Candle signals are unexcelled for spotting the early reversals, not to predict the extent of a move. Don't make more out of candles than they are designed to provide. As the Japanese adage goes, "Don't climb a tree to catch a fish."

EXHIBIT 8.11. Inktomi—15 Minutes (Gravestone Doji)

Although that doji was a reason for caution, I would not have turned outright bearish on that gravestone doji. Why? Notice how the close of that doji was still over the late March 22 resistance area near $224. It would take the close on the session after the gravestone to turn the trend south. That session, with its close back under $224, proved what the doji had hinted at—that the new highs couldn't hold.

In Exhibit 8.12 some long-legged doji in mid April signaled that the prior downtrend was losing momentum near $6.75. The rally in early May made a rising window. But there was a problem on the day of the rising window on May 9: It was another long-legged doji. This signified that the bulls were not in complete control. The window's support was broken the day after this long-legged doji. This confirmed the potential for another down draft. When the stock got near the aforementioned $6.75 support area from mid April on May 23, it successfully defended it with a hammer. The rally from this hammer made two windows at 1 and 2. The stock corrected from the bearish engulfing pattern at B. The decline from this bear-

Saturday, December 02, 2000 02:49PM (Ver: 5.250.0)
© CQG Inc. Used by permission.

EXHIBIT 8.12. 3Com—Daily (Dragonfly Doji)

ish engulfing pattern found stabilization near $8.75 to $8.25 with a series of dragonfly doji. Since the third dragonfly didn't have the open/close at the high, but near it, I view it as a variation of the dragonfly doji. These dragonfly doji confirmed support at the windows at 1 and 2. Final confirmation of the support came with the June 28 hammer.

The general concept with doji (and for all candle signals) is that one should look at what happened before the signal. For instance, a doji in a rally is a potential reversal. Therefore, there needs to be a rally to reverse. This means that doji have little forecasting implications if they are in a trading range environment since there is no trend to reverse. The Japanese aptly call a market that is locked within a range a "box."

The doji in Exhibit 8.13 is reflecting on a micro scale what the trading range environment on a more macro aspect is showing: The market is undecided. With no trend to change, the doji in Exhibit 8.13 has no forecasting implications, except for the fact that it is confirming a trendless environment. An exception to this is if a doji, while still in a trading range, is at the top or bot-

$+$

EXHIBIT 8.13. Doji in a Box Range

tom end of a range. As such, it is confirming resistance or support and could be a useful signal.

In Exhibit 8.14 let's look at three doji in relation to their preceding trend. Doji 1 is in the middle of a box range. Consequently, this doji doesn't have any forecasting implications since there's no trend to reverse. The same scenario is true with the dragonfly doji at 2. The doji at 3 is very different because of where it appears. This doji comes after a rally that placed the stock into an overbought condition. As such it has reversal implications. The two doji following doji 3 are echoing what the first doji at 3 told us—that the stock was running out of bullish force. To recap: Where the doji is in relation to its preceding trend is of pivotal importance.

Exhibit 8.15 illustrates a point alluded to previously in this chapter: Doji during descents (what I call Southern doji) often do not work well as bottom turning signals. In this chart doji, or doji-like lines A to F, appeared during a market decline. But these Southern doji did not signal any reversals. The first sign of a turn came with the tall white candle on March 3 wrapping around the two previous doji lines at F. This formed a bullish engulfing pat-

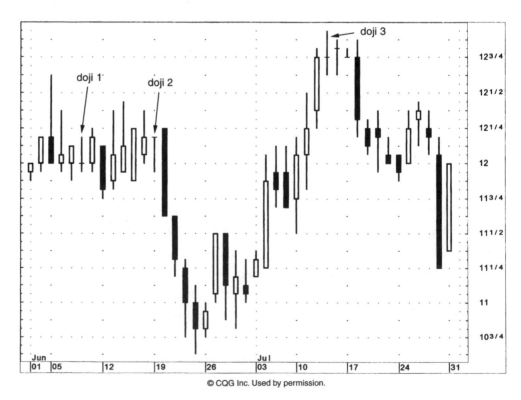

EXHIBIT 8.14. Longview Fiber—Daily (Doji in a Box)

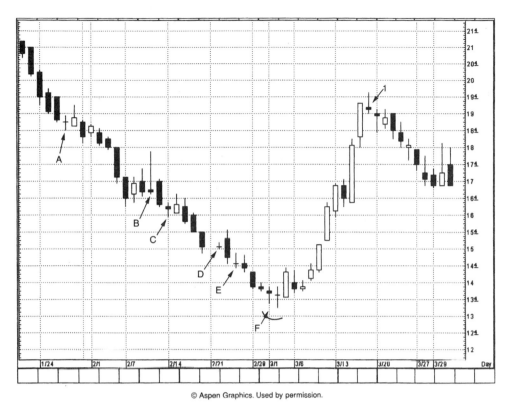

EXHIBIT 8.15. Owens Illinois—Daily (Southern and Northern Doji)

tern that held as support. (There was also a small bullish engulf-ing pattern at time frame C, but once the black candle closed under the low of that pattern, the hopes for a bottom were negat-ed.) An indication that the rally from the bullish engulfing pat-tern at F was stalling came with the doji like line at 1.

In Exhibit 8.16, I have a series of doji illustrating how differ-ent market surroundings influence a doji's importance. Let's look at each individually.

- *Doji 1.* "An earthquake of magnitude 8" is how the Japanese would describe the action preceding doji 1. Two forceful black real bodies are followed by equally intense long white candles that made up all the lost ground of those black can-dles. The doji at 1 showed the stock was separating from its trend (in this case the trend was up because of the two long white candles). As is the case for a doji and tall white candle, we use the highest high of these two sessions (in this exam-ple, it is the high of the white candle at 3745) as resistance. This resistance held on the next session.

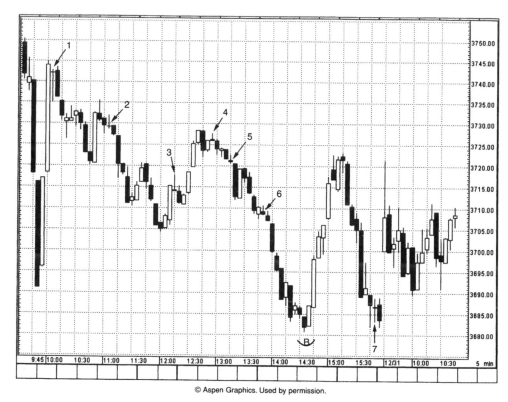

EXHIBIT 8.16. NASDAQ Composite—5 Minutes (Doji)

© Aspen Graphics. Used by permission.

- *Doji 2.* This doji came after a short-term decline. (Even if there are a few down sessions before the doji, I still view the immediately preceding trend as down.) Therefore, as a doji in a downtrend, it warrants less attention as a turning signal.

- *Doji 3.* This doji came after a tall white candle. As such, it does hint the rally that started from 3705 could be losing its steam. However, is the stock overbought when this doji arose? In my opinion, it wasn't (compare this to doji 1 that came after an intense vertical rally). Consequently, this doji has less meaning than it would in an overbought environment. Once the market closed over the doji, it negated any of its potentially bearish implications.

- *Doji 4.* Doji 4 arose within a lateral price environment. Since there was no preceding trend to reverse (the doji was in a box range), it has less significance as a turning signal. One useful aspect of this doji was that it helped reinforce the resistance area defined by the bearish engulfing pattern built a few sessions earlier.

- *Doji 5.* A Southern doji. Since it did not confirm any other bottoming signals, it is not important.
- *Doji 6.* Same as doji 5.
- *Doji 7.* This doji shows how candle lines and patterns must be viewed in the context of the price activity before that pattern. This doji came after a downtrend. Normally, as detailed with doji 2, 5, and 6, I would not view a southern doji as a visual warning of a bottom. However, in the context of the overall market picture, this doji takes on more significance since it was confirming support. There was a bullish engulfing pattern at B at 3680 and the hammer on the session before doji 7 told us the market was building a base near 3680–3682. That is why this Southern doji at 7 takes on extra consequence, even though it comes after a decline. It was confirming the dual support area at the bullish engulfing pattern and hammer.

Let's look at Exhibit 8.17 to understand why doji should not be viewed in isolation. This doji following a tall white candle

EXHIBIT 8.17. AT&T—Daily (Doji at New High Close)

was also a new high close for the move. Doji or not, a new high close is a plus. Many traders use "line charts" that are based solely on the close. The media will say that the stock closed at a new high. Many Western indicators (moving averages, oscillators, etc.) are keyed on the close. As such, a new high close keeps the trend up. With this in mind, I normally suggest that if there is a doji, that is also a new high close for the move to wait for bearish confirmation of the doji. This confirmation would be a close the next session under the doji's close. In this example, we got that bearish confirmation with the next session's close. That black candle day was also a failure at our resistance area defined by the doji's resistance area near $45.50.

THE TRI-STAR

The tri-star is a very rare reversal pattern. As shown in Exhibit 8.18, the tri-star is formed by three doji lines at a new high for the move. For my candle-charting research, I followed a rule before revealing a pattern or signal: It had to be corroborated by at least two independent sources. This helped confirm the tried-and-true techniques and helped avoid the hundreds of possible patterns that anyone can think of. (This is why I warn traders to be careful about other sources of candle-charting information.)

This tri-star is an exception to my rule of corroboration. I got this from a single source. It came from a Japanese trader who used candle charts all his professional career. More important, he told me his father had found this particular pattern decades ago and successfully used it. My feeling is that a pattern with this much history deserved to be included.

The ideal tri-star top has three doji (remember that the plural of doji is also doji) with the middle doji higher than the first and second doji. (This is reminiscent of the Western head and shoulders top, where the head is higher than the left and right shoulders.) In Exhibit 8.19, there are dual hammers during the week of January 3. This built a foundation for a rally that gave a hint that it was exhausting itself via the doji on January 10. After this doji, Honeywell settled into a mostly lateral range, but in doing so formed a tri-star top. Although this stock fell steeply after the tri-star top, it should be remembered that candle charts do

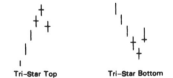

Tri-Star Top   Tri-Star Bottom

EXHIBIT 8.18. Tri-Star Top and Bottom

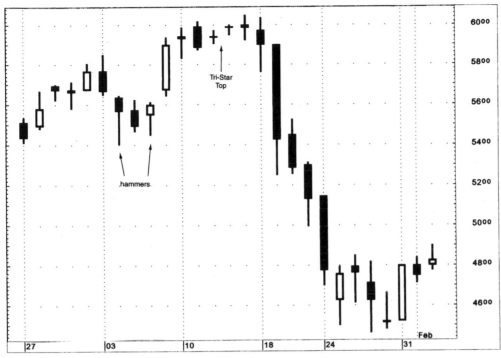

EXHIBIT 8.19. Honeywell—Daily (Tri-Star Top)

not predict moves. As such, while this pattern greatly increased the chances for a top reversal, it did not forecast the extent of the potential decline. Note also the tri-star top in Exhibit 8.14 in mid August.

Note

1. These are addressed in detail in my book, *Beyond Candlesticks* (New York: John Wiley, 1994).

CHAPTER 9

PUTTING IT ALL TOGETHER

ちりも積もれば山となる

The water of even a great ocean comes one drop at a time.

In Part 1 of this book, I examined many candle lines and formations. This chapter is a visual summary. The following chart has numbered lines and patterns. All are candle indicators that have been discussed previously. How would you interpret them? If necessary, use the visual Japanese candle glossary at the back of the book to help you with your interpretations.

Remember, the following interpretations are subjective. You may see different indicators from those I did, or some that I did not. As with any charting technique, different experiences will give different perspectives. There are no concrete rules, just general guidelines. For example, what if a hammer-like line had a lower shadow only one and one-half times the height of the real body instead of the more ideal version with a lower shadow twice—or even three times—the height of the real body? A purist might say this was not a hammer and ignore it. Others may cover shorts on such a line. Still others might wait for the next session to see what unfolds.

"To hear it told is not equal to experience" is a Japanese proverb. I can relay basic candle charting techniques, but it will be only through your experience with these tools, in your markets, that you will unravel the candles' full potential.

Exhibit 9.1 illustrates the following patterns and lines.

1. A long upper shadow candle. This is a very small clue of the bulls' hesitation since one session's long upper shadow doesn't change the directional bias of the market. There is also not enough history yet to see if the market is overbought.

2. The shooting star is now confirming potential resistance at the aforementioned long upper shadow candle at 1.

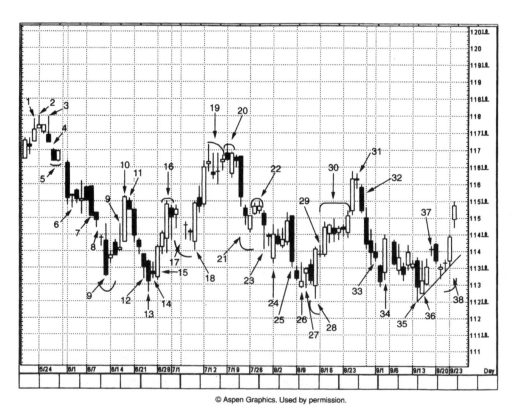

Exhibit 9.1. Bond Futures—Daily (All Together)

3. Yet another long upper shadow candle. Three days of bearish upper shadows from the same highs is certainly enough reason to stand up and take notice. The candle has the same shape as a shooting star (that is, a long upper shadow and small real body at the bottom end of the trading range); however, a shooting star should come after an ascending market. Here the market was trading laterally. As such, while I would not view this as a shooting star, the candle's long upper shadow is cause for concern since it is confirming trouble at the shooting star at 2.

4. A falling window further reinforces the bearishness hinted at by the long upper shadows at 1, 2, and 3.

5. A small piercing pattern may be some cause for optimism. However, in the context of the overall technical picture, the piercing pattern was completed at a resistance area as defined by the falling window in 4. As such, if one buys because of this piercing pattern, the trader is buying at resistance. An extended black real body after this piercing pattern puts the bears back in domination.

6. A hammer at 6 hints that the bears' momentum may be slackening. For the next few days the market was stabilizing as the low of the hammer held as support—that is, until:

7. The long black real body that closed under the low of the hammer. This turned the trend southward again. This also completed a bearish falling three methods pattern.

8. A falling window added more bearish momentum. The doji on June 10, which opened this window, gave a minor suggestion that the bears are losing some momentum. But doji normally don't work satisfactorily in downtrends as they do in rallies. Additionally, the market now has the hurdle of the falling window as resistance with which to contend.

9. Another long black real body whose upper shadow validated the falling windows resistance from the prior day. On June 14, the market very impressively gapped higher on the open (compared with the prior session's close) and managed to hold these higher levels into the close of the session. The two sessions on June 11 and June 14 were a harami pattern. This neutralized some of the bearish force from the June 11 candle. However, the falling window from 8 is still in force as illustrated by a long upper shadow session on June 16 whose high was within the window's resistance near 114³/₄.

10. The June 17 tall white candle finally pushed this market above the window's resistance. This turned the trend more positive. Note also how each session since the June 11 long black candle had higher highs and higher lows.

11. A small black real body was the first lower high in many sessions. Additionally, the diminutive black real body, inside the prior extended white candle, completed a harami pattern. This hinted that the bulls were losing their breath. The market descended steadily from there.

12. The lower shadow of this candle was holding support at the June 11 low near 113.25 and as such provided a small hope that the market was trying to stabilize.

13. Unfortunately (or fortunately, depending on whether you're long or short), this candle line made a new low for the move, both on an intraday and closing basis. It looked like bears were in control until:

14. A doji that was a double plus. First, as a doji within the prior black real body, it formed a harami cross. More important, the close back above 113.25 showed that the lows made the prior day could not be maintained. This would likely lead shorts to second-guess themselves and give encouragement to those looking to buy.

15. This white candle gave further bullish impetus to this market because, by wrapping around the prior small real body, it formed a bullish engulfing pattern.

16. The rally from 15 continued unchecked until the small real body on July 1 made a harami pattern. Interestingly, this harami pattern, with its extended long white candle and small black real body, emerged at the same area and looked similar to the harami pattern a few weeks before at candle lines 10 and 11.

17. The descent from the harami at 16 visually depicted that the bears did not have complete control since the minor decline came with a series of bullish long lower shadow candles. These candles also had small real bodies.

18. Another long white candle (a.k.a bullish belt-hold line) at the same area where another tall white candle appeared on June 30 gave a foundation for rally. There was another small black real body the session after this tall white candle. This small black real body following a tall white real body was reminiscent of what happened with candle lines 10 and 11 and with a harami at 16. The difference was that this small black real body (on July 19) was not within the prior tall white candle. As such, it did not form a harami as was the case with candle lines 10, 11, and 16. Also, since the black real body on July 9 did not get deeply into the prior white real body, it was not a dark-cloud cover.

19. During this time frame, the market was hovering near its highs of the move. But these small real bodies and the bearish long upper shadows conveyed a sense that the market was separating from its prior uptrend. This hesitation is not surprising since 117 was a resistance defined by the falling window in late May as previously discussed at 4.

20. The white candle wrapping around the black real body has the correct combination of candle lines to form a bullish engulfing pattern. However, this was not a bullish engulfing pattern because that pattern, as a bottom turning signal, must come after a price decline.

21. The white candle on July 26 opening lower and then closing unchanged from the prior session was a bullish counterattack line. This turned the trend less bearish.

22. The two small white real bodies that gapped slightly higher from the July 26 candle formed an upgap side-by-side white candle lines. This was another positive indicator.

23. The August 2 candle broke support at the small rising window between July 26 and July 27. In spite of the break of the support, this August 2 candle made a hammer. This provided potential support near 114 (the hammer's low), which was confirmed the following day vis-à-vis a dragonfly doji.

24. Although the August 2 candle broke the hammer's support intraday, by session's end it had managed to close above the support area and formed a bullish engulfing pattern.

25. An extended black real body took steam out of the market, but it managed to maintain the support from the low of the bullish engulfing pattern at 24. The following session, August 19, this support was broken. However, the market was now approaching the major support set in the latter part of June in the 113–112.75 area. As such, the trend is down. The market is near support, but there are no turning signals yet.

26. An inverted hammer gives a very tentative clue that the support near 113 might hold. Nonetheless, because of the bearish shape of the inverted hammer, one needs to wait for bullish confirmation the next session with the close over the inverted hammer's real body to become even marginally positive. This confirmation came:

27. With a hammer.

28. The white real body of August 13 completed a bullish engulfing pattern. Consequently, with the inverted hammer at 26, the hammer at 27, and this bullish engulfing pattern, we got strong visual reinforcement that June's support near 113 was rock solid.

29. The doji after the tall white candle would be a sign for a bit of caution. But, as addressed in Chapter 8, a prime consideration with a doji after a tall white candle (or for any candle signal) is whether the market is overbought or oversold. Obviously, with this doji marginally off the recent lows, I would not view this market as being overbought. Hence, this doji has less implication as a sign of turn.

30. The group of spinning tops throughout the latter part of the week of August 16 put the trend from up to neutral. The close via a white candle on August 24 completed a rising three methods pattern. This pattern formed with the candles from August 17 through August 24.

31. This doji (the real body is so small that, to me, it is the same as a classic doji) shows the importance of looking at the overall technical picture. This doji appears in a more overbought environment than the doji at 29. Consequently, the doji at 31 would be viewed as more consequential than the doji at 29.

32. Because the doji at 31 was still hovering near its highs, I would prefer further bearish confirmation to buttress the potential turning signal of this doji. This confirmation came

with this black real body that closed under the doji's close. This black real body formed an evening star pattern.

33. This tiny falling window kept the bearish momentum intact. There was a minor plus, however. This September 2 candle still maintained the pivotal support near 112.75–113 in force since the latter part of June.

34. A tall white candle that opened almost at the same opening as the prior candle. As such, this could be viewed as a separating line. This gave cause for optimism that the support near 113 was continuing to be solidly sustained. However, the next day's black candle and failure to maintain this momentum short-circuited any bullish optimism.

35. A relatively long black real body keeps the bias lower, but the bulls still have hope since the 112.75–113 support area is still being sustained.

36. A small white real body that gets above the close of the prior black real body helps reinforce support near 113. This is not a piercing pattern since that pattern requires the close of the white real body be more than the middle of the prior black real body.

37. The doji on September 16 opened a very small rising window. Because the market was not overextended, we would not view this doji as a cautionary signal, especially since there is potential support at the rising window in the doji session. Next session, however, the support at the rising window was penetrated.

38. Using the lows from some of the candle lines from September 14 to 23, we can now obtain a rising support line. This aspect of combining the power of trend lines on candle charts, as well as integrating many other Western technical signals, is the focus of Part 2.

PART 2

CONVERGENCE

千里の道も一歩から

It is what all eyes see and what all fingers point to.

Candle methods by themselves are a valuable trading tool. But these techniques become even more powerfully significant if they confirm one or more Western technical signals. This is where my principle of "convergence" comes in.

I define convergence as "a cluster of technical signals converging at, or near, the same price." Convergence is a pivotal concept. This is because the more signals that join at a support or resistance area, the more likely a reversal. The area of convergence can be confirmed by a series of candle patterns or Western signals or a combination of both.

Remember when as a kid you grabbed some crayons and went crazy with a coloring book? Each page was a black-and-white sketch of a beach or outer space scene. Your choice of colors gave the picture your own personal touch. Likewise, based on your trading style and personality, you likely have your favorite tools and techniques. But whichever Western tools you use, candles should be a part of your trading arsenal.

While I believe candle charts will replace bar charts as the charts of choice, this does not mean I recommend ignoring the tools used on bar charts such as trend lines, moving averages, oscillators, etc. Indeed, I strongly suggest using classic Western technical tools on candle charts. Here are some reasons:

1. *Candle charting techniques are a tool, not a system:* As such, they should always be used in conjunction with other technical indicators. This is a major advantage of candle charts: Since they use the same data as a bar chart—that is, the open, high, low, and close—you can use all your favorite Western tools on the candle chart. This includes anything as basic as trend lines and moving averages to the more esoteric Elliott Wave. If a candle signal, i.e., a hammer, confirms a Western signal, say a trend line, this convergence of indicators would increase the likelihood of a reversal. As such, candle signals become even more powerfully significant if they confirm a Western technical signal.

2. *Price targets:* Candle charts provide many useful trading signals, especially early reversal signals. They do not, however, provide price targets. This is where measured moves—looking for prior support and resistance areas, retracements, trend lines, and other Western clues—are used.

3. *Be aware of what the competition is using:* Since so many traders and analysts use technical analysis, it often has a major influence on the market. As such, it is important to be alerted to technical signals others may be using, including Western technical indicators.

Chapter 10 illustrates how a "cluster of candles" can dramatically magnify the significance of a support or resistance area. For the remaining chapters in Part 2, the focus will be on Western tools, especially combined with candle charting signals. Chapter 11 addresses the many techniques one can utilize with trend lines. For example, a failure to hold above a broken resistance line or below broken support line can provide important market signals. Chapter 12 looks at retracements and the importance of waiting for confirmation of a retracement level with a candlestick signal. Then, in Chapter 13 we look at the value added of moving averages, especially when combined with candlestick signals. Chapter 14 discusses oscillators including stochastics, the relative strength index, and others, and their usefulness when integrated with candle chart signals. Chapter 15 focuses on what I consider one of the most important weapons in a trader's arsenal (besides candles)—volume. The focus in Chapter 16 is on price targets and measured moves. This is especially important since candle charts, while giving reversal signals, do not provide price targets. Finally, Chapter 17 brings it all together by showing how a plethora of Eastern and Western technical tools converged and sent many warning signals of a reversal in the NASDAQ.

Since the focus of this book isn't Western technicals, but candle charts and using candles to supplement traditional Western technical techniques, I have only touched on the basics of Western technical tools. There are many fine books that provide much more detail on these Western techniques. An excellent source of material can be found at www.TradersLibrary.com.

My quarter-century of experience with Western technicals has been mainly the classic Western indicators. Sentiment indicators such as advance/decline lines, the ARMS/TRIN index, specialist short sales, and so on are not included. This is only because of my limitations in knowledge, not because of limitation of these tools. For example, while I don't cover point and figure charts, traders who specialize in this charting method have told me they use candle charts to get the reversal signals and then shift into point and figure charts to get their price targets. This is an example of using the tools and techniques of candles as a complementary tool, no matter your technical specialty. Western techniques, when joined with candles, can be a powerfully efficient combination.

THE MARKET IS NEVER WRONG

To convey in my Western technical seminars the importance of a disciplined approach to trading, I use the word "DISCIPLINE" as an anagram. For each letter of the word DISCIPLINE I offer a trading rule. For the letter "N," my rule is "Never trade in the belief the market is wrong."[1]

What do I mean by the expression "the market is never wrong"? It means do not try to impose your beliefs on the market. For example, if you are firmly convinced the NASDAQ is going to rally, wait until the trend is heading north before buying. Say the NASDAQ is in a bear market. If you buy in the expectation that a bull market will materialize, you are then trying to impose your hopes and expectations on the market. You are fighting the trend. This could be disastrous. You may ultimately be correct in your bullish viewpoint, but by then it may be too late. As an analogy, imagine you are driving along a one-way street. You notice a steamroller going down this one-way street the wrong way. You stop your car, take out a sign (that you always carry with you) that reads, "Stop! Wrong Way!" and hold it in front of the steamroller. You know the steamroller is going in the wrong direction. But the driver may not see you in time. By the time the steamroller turns around, it could be too late. By then you may be part of the pavement.

So it is with the markets. If you are bucking the trend, your outlook may turn out to be correct—but by then it may be too late. Margin calls in futures may force you out of the position before your expected move occurs. Or, worse, in the end, you may be right, but by then you could be broke.

Do not try to impose your will on the markets. Be a trend follower, not a trend predictor. If you are bullish, jump onto uptrends; if bearish, hop onto downtrends.

A Japanese book I had translated expresses this idea almost poetically: "Buying or selling from the beginning without knowing the character of the market is the same nonsense as a literary man talking about weapons. When faced with a large bull or bear market they are sure to lose the castle; what seems safe is infinitely dangerous. . . . Waiting for just the right moment is virtuous and essential."[2]

Notes

1. The DISCIPLINE rules are:
   <u>D</u>on't forget old support and resistance levels. (Old support becomes new resistance and vice versa.)
   <u>I</u>f. . . then system. (If the market behaves as anticipated, then stay with the trade—otherwise exit.)
   <u>S</u>tops—Always use them.
   <u>C</u>onsider options.
   <u>I</u>ntraday technicals are important even if you are not a day or swing trader.
   <u>P</u>ace trades to market environment. (Change your trading style according to market conditions.)
   <u>L</u>ocals—Never forget them.
   <u>I</u>ndicators—The more the better (convergence of signals).
   <u>N</u>ever trade in the belief the market is wrong.
   <u>E</u>xamine the market's reaction to news.
2. Sakata Goho Wa Furinkazan. *Sakata's Five Rules Are Wind, Forest, Fire, and Mountain* (Tokyo: Nihon Shoken Shimbunsha, 1969, p. 46). This section translated by Richard Solberg.

CHAPTER 10

A CLUSTER OF CANDLES

念には念を入れよ

Add caution to caution.

This chapter explores how a group, or a cluster, of candle lines and/or patterns that converge at the same price area can magnify the importance of that area as support or resistance and increase the likelihood of a market turn.

Exhibit 10.1 illustrates how a group of separate candle signals converged near $75 and, in doing so, underscored the solidity of the support at that area. Let's look at each signal individually:

1. The extremely long white candle on April 17 that wrapped around the prior black real body formed a bullish engulfing pattern. Since the white candle in this bullish engulfing pat-

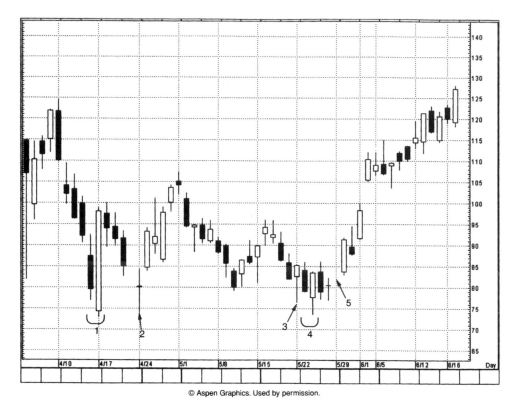

© Aspen Graphics. Used by permission.

EXHIBIT 10.1. JDS Uniphase—Daily (Cluster of Candles)

tern was so large, it meant that by the time the engulfing pattern was completed, the stock was nearly $25 off its lows. As such, while the bullish engulfing pattern gave us a reversal signal, the close of that pattern may not have presented an attractive area to buy based on the risk/reward aspect of such a trade.

2. Remembering the concept that the low of the bullish engulfing pattern can become support, we turn our attention to the lows of this pattern near $73 as potential support. The downdraft that started during the week of April 17 stabilized near this expected support area with this long-legged doji.

3. The May 22 hammer reinforced the aforementioned support area.

4. The two sessions after the hammer at 3 completed a classic piercing pattern with the low of that pattern bouncing off the support area defined by the bullish engulfing pattern at 1.

5. If further proof of a bottom was needed, it came at 5 with the small rising window in late May. Additionally, if one looks at

the action from the week of May 15 through the week of May 29, the stock was building a rounding bottom. By adding the window (at 5) to this rounding bottom, we have a frypan bottom.

Exhibit 10.2 displays how a confluence of candles can help pinpoint support or resistance.

- *A cluster of candles as support:* There was a hammer on December 11. In spite of this hammer's potentially bullish implications, the falling window that opened on the day of the hammer kept the trend down. As the market descended from this hammer, it did so with a series of three long lower shadows. These long lower shadows offset some of the bearishness. The candle line at 1 was also a hammer, but unlike the first hammer, discussed above, during the next two days, December 16 and 17, this hammer successfully held as support. The two candles at 2 made a bullish engulfing pattern.

EXHIBIT 10.2. Brown Forman—Daily (Cluster of Candles)

Another hammer emerged at 3 in early February. This was the support area defined by 1 and 2. The dragonfly doji at 4 was further confirmation of support near $42.

- *A cluster of candles as resistance:* As the stock was ascending during A, it did so via a series of long upper shadows. Because of the higher highs, higher lows, and higher closes, the short-term trend remained up, but the long upper shadows were a warning signal that the bulls did not have a complete foothold on the stock. The last long upper shadow candle on January 6 was a shooting star. A few days later, at B, the stock formed a bearish engulfing pattern. At C the small black real body in the tall white real body formed a harami pattern. As such, the shooting star at A, the bearish engulfing pattern at B, and the harami at C gave us a convergence of candles that underscored the ceiling between $47.50 and $48.

Candle charts are a very efficient form of visual analysis. This is because one can use them to pick up very quick pictorial

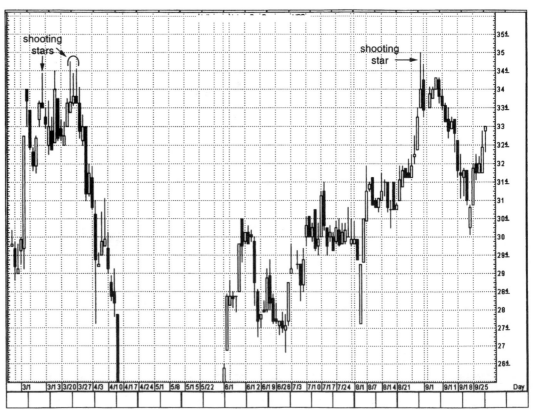

EXHIBIT 10.3. Unibanco Uniao de Bancos Brasileros—Daily (Cluster of Candles)

clues about the market's health, or lack thereof. Simply by look-ing at the shape of the individual candle lines we can rapidly see the demand/supply situation. With this in mind, let's look at Exhibit 10.3.

In mid to late March a series of shooting stars defined resis-tance toward $34.50. Looking at this group of shooting stars, would there be any doubt about the trouble this stock is having near $34.50? Of course not, since the shooting stars are graphi-cally highlighting that each time the stock gets near its session highs, the bears drag down prices to close the stock at or near the lows of the day. In late August, there is another assault at these shooting stars' resistance. Once again, there appears another shooting star overhead on this August rally. Adding to this shooting star's negative indication is the next day's black real body, which completes a bearish engulfing pattern.

CHAPTER 11

CANDLES WITH TREND LINES

備えあれば憂いなし

A prudent man has more than one string to his bow.

This chapter examines candle techniques in conjunction with trend lines, breakouts from trend lines, false breakouts, and uses of penetrated support and resistance areas.

Exhibit 11.1 shows a classic *rising support line*. It is obtained by connecting two, and preferably three, or more reaction lows. When drawing rising support lines on candle charts, I use the bottom of the lower shadows as my connecting points. This ascending line demonstrates that buyers are more aggressive than sellers since demand is stepping in at higher lows. There is a saying that there are more buyers than sellers. Since a trade requires both a buyer and seller, I prefer to think of it as not

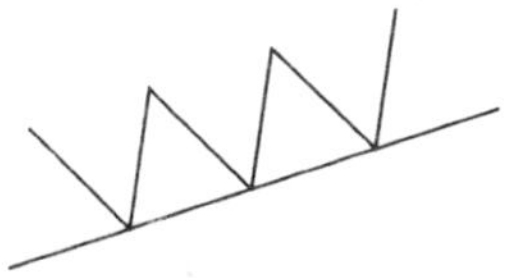

EXHIBIT 11.1. Rising Support Line

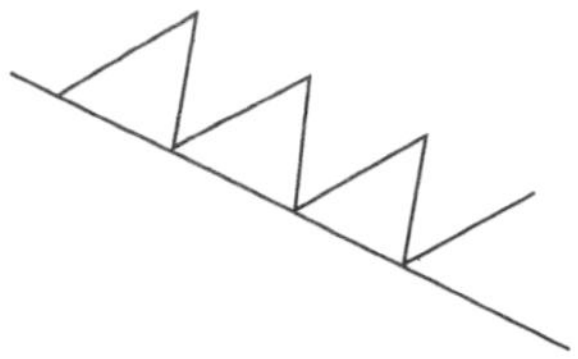

EXHIBIT 11.2. Falling Support Line

more buyers than sellers, but more aggressive buyers than sellers.

Exhibit 11.2 shows a *falling support line*. The traditional support line, as discussed in Exhibit 11.1, is derived by connecting higher lows. The line in Exhibit 11.2 joins lower lows. The falling line's usefulness comes into play because there will be many instances in which prices rebound from this descending line. This line gives us a potential support area when none may exist. A situation where there may be no evident support is when a market makes either a low for the move or an all-time low.

A regular rising support line, since it is ascending, is considered bullish. The falling support line, because the market is making lower lows, can be considered as a bearish support line. As such, bounces from this line are likely to be only marginal and temporary. Yet, it can be an area to consider buying, especially if there is a convergence of technical indicators at that line.

A piercing pattern appears early on the morning of November 22 in Exhibit 11.3. After a minor rally from this piercing pattern, the market retreated to the $62.50 area at around 12:30–13:00. By connecting the lows of the piercing pattern to the lows near $62.50 made a few hours later, we obtain a rising support line. This line intersected late in the session of November 22 where we see a variation of the piercing pattern. (It's a variation because the close of the white candle did not get above the middle of the prior black candle.) This is an example of how a less-than-ideal pattern can still provide a turning signal. Specifically, while this was not an ideal piercing pattern, it helped increase its importance because it came at a rising support line. Further reinforcement that the bulls had taken control came immediately after the successful test of this rising support line via a rising window that became support early on November 24.

Throughout January in Exhibit 11.4, Amazon was in downtrend as gauged by the lower lows. Joining the lows at L1 and L2 provides a tentative support line. Solidifying the importance of this descending support line was another successful defense at L3. The lows at L4 were a successful test of this downward sloping support line and a bullish piercing pattern. The rally

EXHIBIT 11.3. Corning—15 Minutes (Rising Support Line)

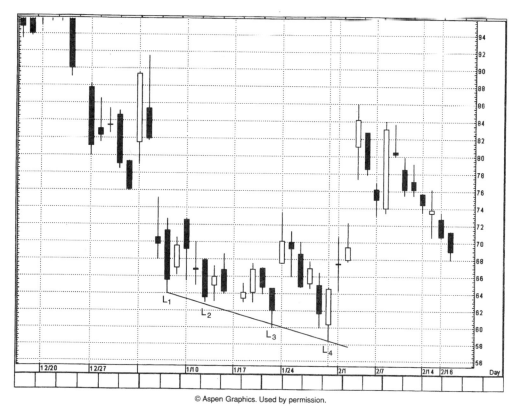

EXHIBIT 11.4. Amazon—Daily (Falling Support Line)

© Aspen Graphics. Used by permission.

EXHIBIT 11.5. Cotton—Weekly (Falling Support Line)

from this piercing pattern opened a rising window on February 2 and 3. While the bottom of this window held as support, the rally was short-circuited with the doji (which was also a shooting star) after the long white candle on February 9.

A descending falling support line in Exhibit 11.5 commenced with the two lows at A and B and then the bullish engulfing pattern at C. The last test of this line came in March at D followed by an inverted hammer. The day after this inverted hammer, a white candle formed a bullish engulfing pattern. Indeed, if the white candle of the bullish engulfing pattern had a higher close, it would have formed a morning star. Nonetheless, the convergence of the inverted hammer, the bullish engulfing pattern, and the falling support line shouted "Cover shorts!"

Exhibit 11.6 displays a typical *falling resistance line*. It is derived by joining at least two reaction highs; three or more would give the line more clout. It shows that sellers are more aggressive than buyers as evidenced by the sellers' willingness

EXHIBIT 11.6. Falling
Resistance Line

to sell at lower highs. This reflects a market that is trending lower. With a resistance line on the candle charts, we connect the tops of the upper shadows.

A regular resistance line is made with a series of lower highs. But what if the market is at an all-time high and there are no former highs from where we can peg a potential resistance area? In this instance I frequently use a *rising resistance line*. As shown in Exhibit 11.7, this is built by linking a series of higher highs (instead of the falling resistance line's lower highs).

In Exhibit 11.8 we join areas 1, 2, and 3 to obtain a classic resistance line. At the bottom of the decline that started from the harami at area 2, silver produced two high-wave candle lines. This was the first indication that the downward power of the market was dissipating. The rising window that opened between March 6 and 7 then turned the trend up. The window immediately became support as evidenced by the following few days' action.

Now that there were turning signals with the candle charts, we can shift to the Western technicals a la the resistance line to get a price target. This becomes the potential resistance area as

EXHIBIT 11.7. Rising Resistance Line

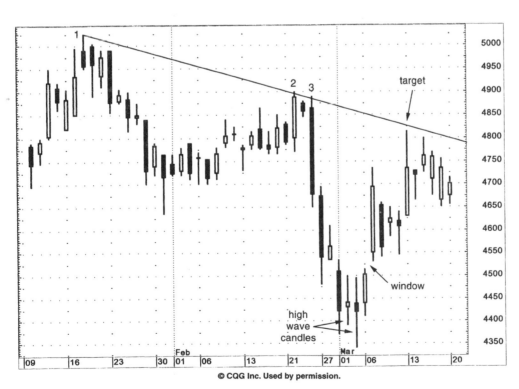

EXHIBIT 11.8. Silver—Daily (Falling Resistance Line)

EXHIBIT 11.9. Chris-Craft—Daily (Rising Resistance Line)

shown by the market stalling there the week of March 13. This chart underscores why one needs Western technical tools, even if the main focus is on candles. The candles can give the earliest turning signals, while the Western tools can give a price objective and stop-out area.

A new high close via a tall white candle in Exhibit 11.9 on April 12 (at 2) keeps the bull trend in force. The next day the whole tone of the market had been transformed as a small black real body which completed the second part of the harami pattern at 2. By connecting the highs at 1 and 2 we get a rising resistance line that intersected near $50 in mid May. Another harami pattern intersected with the rising resistance line at this point of intersection at $50 at area 3. (The fact that the May 13 session's upper shadow exceeded the prior day's range doesn't preclude this from being a harami since that pattern is only concerned with the real bodies.) Thus, the candles give us added proof (via the harami and long upper shadow of the second line of the harami at 3) that the rising resistance line could be an area where defensive actions are warranted.

EXHIBIT 11.10. Crude Oil—Daily (Rising Resistance Line)

Looking at Exhibit 11.10 we see an upward sloping resistance line. The price activity from mid May reflects a market that is creating a series of higher highs. However, a convergence of technical factors on June 30, including a doji-like line (which also formed a harami cross) at the ascending resistance line, gave a signal for longs to take protective measures. Note the large falling window opened the day after the doji-like line between $31 and $30. The market fell until it found support in early July. The rally from this support area stalled at the top of the aforementioned window.

SPRINGS AND UPTHRUSTS

The concept of springs and upthrusts is based on work by Richard Wyckoff, a very successful trader and newsletter publisher of the early twentieth century.

Exhibit 11.11 shows that a *spring* develops when the market breaks under a horizontal support area and then springs back above that previously broken support. In other words, new

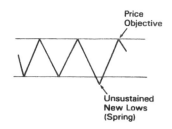

EXHIBIT 11.11. Spring

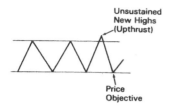

EXHIBIT 11.12. Upthrust

lows could not hold. Once a spring is formed, we can get a stop-out area and a price target. As shown in Exhibit 11.11, when a market gets back above a recently broken support area, one can consider buying. If the market is solid, it should not get back to the most recent lows. That would be a stop level (preferably on a close). The target for the spring is either its high before the spring was made or the top end of its trading range. This will be illustrated in some examples later in this section.

Exhibit 11.12 shows an *upthrust*. This is when there is penetration of a horizontal resistance area and then the bulls fail to sustain these new highs. This is another way of saying a false breakout. To use an upthrust for trading, when the market gets back under its former resistance area, one can consider selling. If the market is indeed weak, it should not return to the most recent highs. A downside target is its most recent low or the bottom of a recent trading range.

Although we will not focus on volume in this section, it will be more bullish for a spring if the break of support is on light volume and the subsequent rebound above the recently broken support is on heavier volume. Similarly, the likelihood of an upthrust successfully working should be increased if the break over the resistance is on low volume and the consequent return move under the old resistance is on high volume.

Why do springs and upthrusts work so well? To answer this, refer to Napoleon's response when asked which troops he considered best. His terse response was, "Those [that] are victorious." We can view the market as a battlefield between two sets of troops—the bulls and the bears. The territory they each claim is especially evident when there is a lateral trading range. The horizontal resistance line is the bears' terrain to defend. The horizontal support line is the bulls' domain to defend. If the bears can't defend the new lows on a break of support or the bulls maintain the new highs on a penetration of resistance, then they are not victorious.

In Exhibit 11.13 resistance is shown at A, B, and C, with the doji at C confirming hesitation in the 1.7100–1.7150 area. At the session after the doji at C, a surge of demand pushed the pound over this resistance as it approached 1.74. However, the bulls' victory was short-lived as the market soon pulled back under

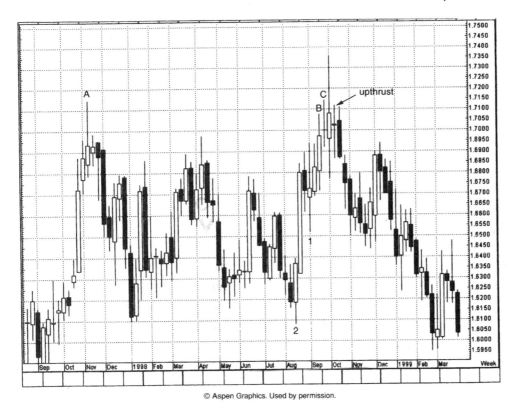

EXHIBIT 11.13. British Pound—Weekly (Upthrust)

what was broken resistance at A, B, and C. This was an upthrust. As such, we have a downside target to the initial area where the rally that took us to the upthrust began. Here is where some subjectivity comes in. In my opinion the rally began at area 1; others may view the leg up that began the rally was the low of the bullish engulfing pattern at 2. In a scenario like this, I suggest using a conservative target (at 1) and a more liberal target (at 2). Interestingly, 1 became an area of temporary stabilization before the more liberal target was obtained.

This steeply descending price action after this upthrust reminds me of an apt Japanese saying, "Let him climb the roof and then take away the ladder."

At times there will be "scouting parties" (this is my term and not a candle expression) sent by big traders, commercial accounts, or even market makers or locals to test the resolve of the opposing troops. For instance, there might be a move by the bulls to try to propel prices over a resistance area. In such a battle, we have to monitor the determination of the bulls. If this bullish scouting party can set up camp in enemy territory (that is, close above resistance and maintain the new highs), then a beachhead is made. New, fresh bullish troops should join the scouting party. The market should move up. As long as the beachhead is maintained (that is, the market holds above resistance), the bulls will have control of the market. But once the market pushes back under the broken resistance, the bulls have lost control.

Let's look at this idea in the context of the upthrust in Exhibit 11.14. In late September there was a resistance zone shown by the two horizontal lines. The extended white candle of October 16 pushed the stock over this resistance. The bulls' "scouting party" had, at least then, gotten a foothold as Juniper made a new high close over an evident resistance area. By the next day the whole texture of the market had changed as the black candle's close proved that the bulls didn't have enough mettle to hold the new highs. As such, an upthrust was created. The highs of this upthrust remained resistance for the next week before the market collapsed after the bearish engulfing pattern that was completed October 23.

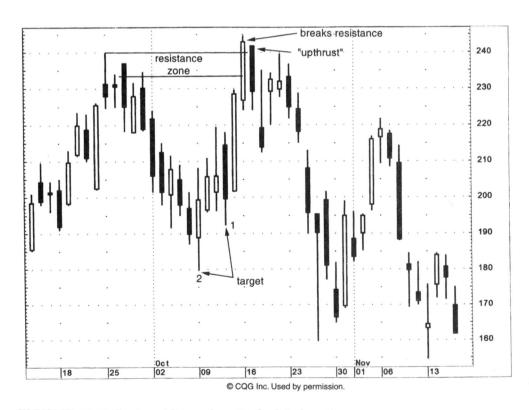

EXHIBIT 11.14. Juniper Networks—Daily (Upthrust)

Our target for the upthrust was the prior low from where the rally that took us to the upthrust began. Some may view this as area 1; others, at area 2. As discussed in Exhibit 11.13 of the British Pound, this is where subjectivity comes in. I would have a conservative target at 1 and a liberal target at 2. This upthrust also shows that it does not have to be an exact resistance area for this technique to work.

In the prior exhibits the market had closed over resistance and then retreated the next session to close back under the previously broken resistance area. Exhibit 11.15 illustrates where an upthrust unfolds in a single session. In early April, at A, small real bodies (including a shooting star) showed hesitation near $30. Another attack on that area at B formed an evening doji star on April 23, 26, and 27. On May 13 a shooting star propelled the stock intraday over this $30 resistance. By session's end the stock showed it was unable to maintain these new highs as it closed back under resistance. In doing so, it had formed an upthrust with a target to the immediately preceding low near $26.25. This objective was reached on May 24 and 25.

© CQG Inc. Used by permission.

EXHIBIT 11.15. Cisco—Daily (Upthrust)

In Exhibit 11.16 candle lines at 1, 2, and 3 are maintaining support near 308.50. On March 1 the bears tried to get a foothold as they made new lows to slightly under 306. By session's end the bears lost control as the index closed above the previously broken support area of 308.50. Thus, the bears could not get a beachhead—and a spring was formed. The day of the spring was also a hammer. Now that we have the spring, we also have a target. Specifically, this was the high before the spring was made near 326. Note how at A and B the index got within a few ticks of this target. This shows how technicals are subjective. Those who waited to sell at the exact target area would have been disappointed since it got very close to this target, but did not touch it.

Exhibit 11.16 showed a spring based on a single session (the market made a new low and then closed above the broken support area by session end). Exhibit 11.17 is an example of a spring formed over a few sessions. A new low close on February 1 broke an evident support level at $20. The next day the bulls came back, as the Japanese would express it, "in a kamikaze attack," and propelled the stock over this broken

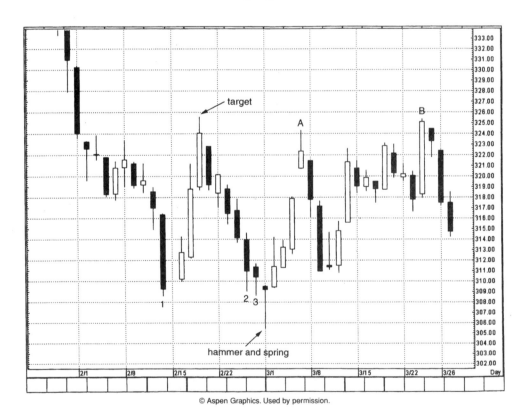

© Aspen Graphics. Used by permission.

EXHIBIT 11.16. Utility Index—Daily (Spring)

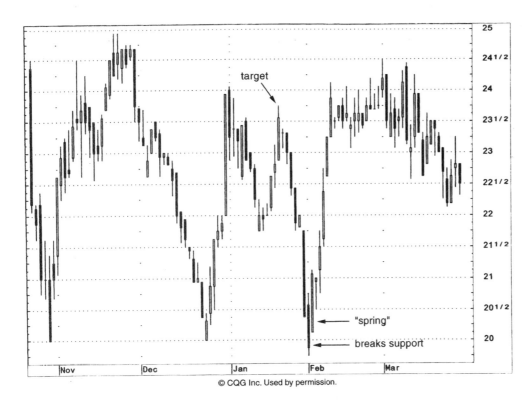

© CQG Inc. Used by permission.

EXHIBIT 11.17. Hon Industries—Daily (Spring)

support area. In doing so, the stock made a spring. The target is the most recent high near $23.75 from late January. This January high was made via a doji following a tall white candle. Interestingly, the stock hesitated there again with a similar combination of tall white real body and doji lines on February 9 and 10.

One of the most powerful aspects of technical analysis is that it helps foster a risk and money management approach to the market. As such there should always be a price that says we are wrong about our forecast. In this example, if after the February 2 spring, the market had pulled under the February 1 low, it would void the target and would be a sign to reconsider long positions.

THE CHANGE OF POLARITY PRINCIPLE

The Japanese have a saying: "A red lacquer dish needs no decoration." This concept of simple beauty is the essence of a technical principle I use frequently. It is as simple as it is powerful:

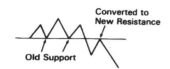

EXHIBIT 11.18 Change of Polarity: Old Support = New Resistance

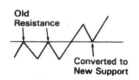

EXHIBIT 11.19. Change of Polarity: Old Resistance = New Support

Old support becomes new resistance and old resistance becomes support. This is what I call the "change of polarity" principle. Exhibit 11.18 shows support converting to resistance. Exhibit 11.19 illustrates prior resistance becoming new support.

The concept behind the change of polarity principle (although not traditionally called that) is an axiom discussed in many books on technical analysis. Yet, it is an underutilized gem. To see how universally well this rule works, let us briefly look at some examples across the various time horizons and markets.

In Exhibit 11.20 a late December sell-off culminated near $5.35 (at A). On another test at or near this level, there are at least three groups who could consider buying.

- *Group 1:* Those who were waiting for the market to stabilize after the prior sell-off and who now have a point at which the market found support—$5.35 (the lows at area A). A few days later, a successful test (at B) of this support probably pulled in new longs.

- *Group 2:* Traders who were previously long but were stopped out during the late December sell-off. On the rally from B to $5.60, in mid

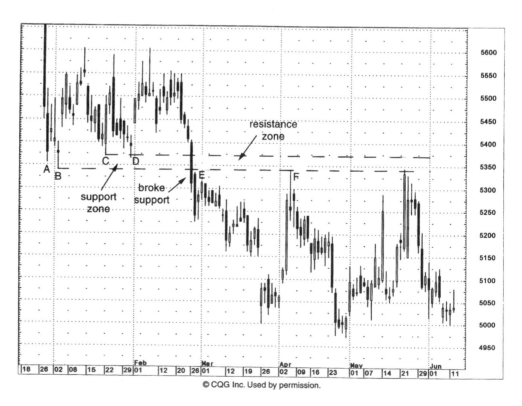

© CQG Inc. Used by permission.

EXHIBIT 11.20. Silver—Daily (Change of Polarity)

January, some of these old longs who were stopped out would say to themselves that they were right about silver being in a bull market. They just timed their original purchase incorrectly. Now is the time to buy. They want to be vindicated in their original view. They wait for a pullback to support at A or B to buy. They again go long at C.

- *Group 3:* Those who bought at points A and B. They also see the rally from B and may want to add to their position if they get a "good price." At area C, they have their good price since the market is at support. Thus, more buyers come in at C. Then, for good measure, another pullback to D draws in more longs.

Then the problems start for the longs. In late February, prices puncture support areas A, B, C, and D. A hammer on February 28 is a reason for some optimism, but anyone who bought at this old support area is now in a losing trade.

What is the most important price in any market? The highs made for move? The lows? Yesterday's close? No. *The most important price on any chart is the price at which you entered the market. People become strongly, keenly, and emotionally attached to the price at which they bought or sold.* These longs from $5.35 probably learn prayers in seven languages to get the market back to breakeven.

Consequently, rallies to anywhere near where the longs bought (around $5.35) will be gratefully used by them to exit their longs. Thus, the original buyers at areas A, B, C, and D may now become sellers. This is the main reason why old support becomes new resistance as shown by the resistance at E and F.

A classic example of convergence of technical factors is highlighted in Exhibit 11.21. A support area from mid September to early October near 1435 was breached in early October. A piercing pattern on October 12 and 13 (in which the white candle was so strong that it was almost a bullish engulfing pattern) signaled a rebound. The rally from this piercing pattern took the S&P to the 1425 area, where we have a series of technical signals converging including:

1. The bearish engulfing pattern of October 23 and 24.

© CQG Inc. Used by permission.

EXHIBIT 11.21. S&P—Daily (Change of Polarity)

2. A falling resistance line obtained by connecting the highs from late September.

3. The resistance area defined by the change of polarity obtained from a former support level near 1435.

In this instance of convergence, we had a candle signal (the bearish engulfing pattern) confirming two Western indicators (a resistance line and change of polarity).

The change of polarity does not necessarily have to be an exact support area; it can be a zone. In Exhibit 11.22 there was a region of support (shown by the two horizontal lines) from $116 to $117.50. Once the lower end of this territory of support was breached late on April 3, we then use the change of polarity principle. This gives us resistance at prior support in the aforementioned $116–$117.50 zone. The stock continued its retreat late on April 3 until a pair of hammers hinted at stabilization. The ascent from these hammers came to an end with the convergence of the dark-cloud cover and change of polarity on the morning of April 4.

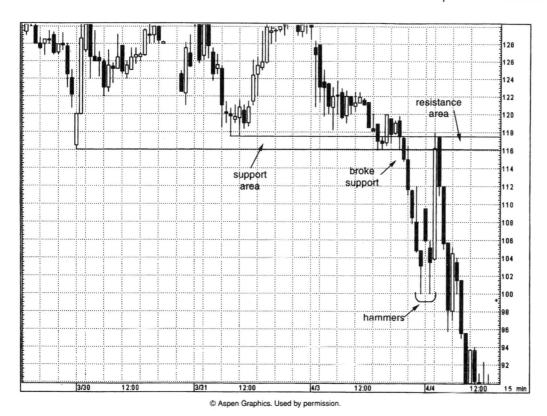

EXHIBIT 11.22. QLogic—15 Minutes (Change of Polarity)

EXHIBIT 11.23. Procter & Gamble—15 Minutes (Change of Polarity)

We see resistance near $111.25 in Exhibit 11.23. Once the bulls propelled Procter & Gamble over this area, we look for that to become potential support. Although the series of small real bodies from noon to late in the session on December 14 kept the trend neutral. Since $111.25 held as support, the outlook remained favorable. The last two long lower shadow candles on December 14 visually confirmed the support near $111.25.

An evident resistance area in Exhibit 11.24 was reinforced by the March 17 doji. Once the index pushed over this resistance, we then convert this multitested resistance near 775 into support. This brings out an aspect about the change of polarity principle: It usually requires that a support or resistance be tested a few times before we can apply this technique.

A resistance line in Exhibit 11.25 was penetrated in early February. On the price dip on the week of February 16, we see a convergence of technical indicators as a hammer on February 20 confirmed a support level based on the change of polarity. Another price descent ended with another hammer at this same

© Aspen Graphics. Used by permission.

EXHIBIT 11.24. Bank Index—Daily (Change of Polarity)

EXHIBIT 11.25. Lee Enterprises—Daily (Change of Polarity)

support area near $29.75. Although the hammer was confirming support, the hammer doesn't provide a price target. This is where the Western technicals come into play. We see a resistance line formed from the highs in early to mid April. Using this line as a potential resistance area, we then have a target if we buy on the hammer near $31.50. This chart illustrated the usefulness and advantage of using Western techniques in combination with candles. The Western technicals can confirm a candle signal (as the hammer confirmed the change of polarity's support) and we can also utilize the Western technicals to obtain a potential target (the falling resistance line).

CHAPTER 12

CANDLES WITH RETRACEMENT LEVELS

待てば海路の日和あり

All things come to those who wait.

Markets usually do not trend straight up, nor do they fall vertically down. They often retrace, or correct, some of their advance, or decline, before resuming the prior trend. Some of the more popular retracement levels are the 50% level and the Fibonacci figures of 38% and 62% (see Exhibits 12.1 and 12.2). Fibonacci was a thirteenth-century mathematician who derived a special sequence of numbers. These ratios include 61.8% (or its inverse of 1.618) and 38.2% (or its inverse of 2.618). This is why the 62% (61.8% rounded off) and the 38% (38.2% rounded off) corrections are so popular. The popular 50% cor-

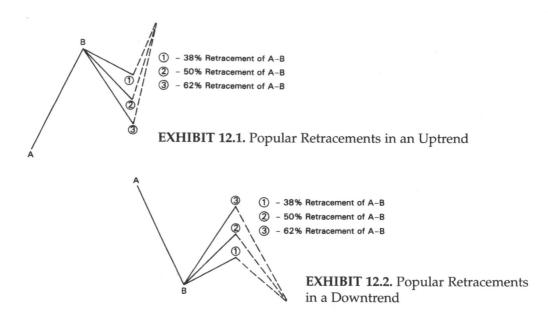

EXHIBIT 12.1. Popular Retracements in an Uptrend

① – 38% Retracement of A–B
② – 50% Retracement of A–B
③ – 62% Retracement of A–B

① – 38% Retracement of A–B
② – 50% Retracement of A–B
③ – 62% Retracement of A–B

EXHIBIT 12.2. Popular Retracements in a Downtrend

rection is also a Fibonacci ratio. The 50% retracement is probably the most widely monitored level. This is because the 50% retracement is by users of Gann, Elliott Wave, or Dow theories.

Let us look at instances where retracements melded with candle techniques to provide important turning signals.

A bullish engulfing pattern at B held as support with the bullish long lower shadows on November 21. The rally from 1 to 2 pushed the stock $8 higher. As such, a 50% correction of this rally is $4 off the highs. This means expected support near $62.50 (50% of the $8 rally = $4; $4 added to $58.50 = $62.50). On the approach to this level on November 22, the stock formed a piercing pattern. As such we got a convergence via a candle pattern at a 50% retracement level. While retracement levels can become support or resistance, I would not suggest buying or selling at a retracement area unless it was confirmed by a candle pattern as it was here.

Exhibit 12.4 shows a rally from 1 to 2 that took the stock from $25 to $33.50. A 50% correction of this rally would give potential support near $29. As the stock was descending from area 2 toward the potential support area, it did so with a series of long lower shadows that hinted the bears were losing control. The $29 level was potential support for another reason. Specifically, if we look at the prior price peaks at A, B, and C, we can use the change of polarity principle since this broken resistance zone

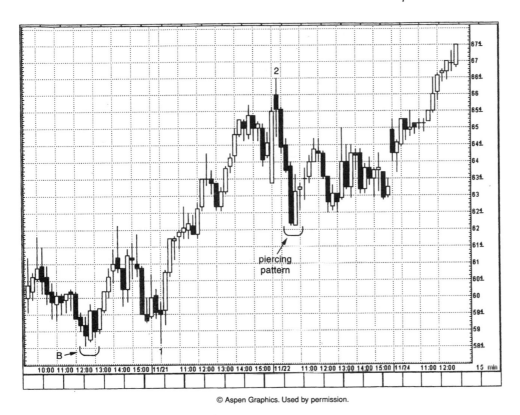

© Aspen Graphics. Used by permission.

EXHIBIT 12.3. Corning—15 Minutes (Retracement)

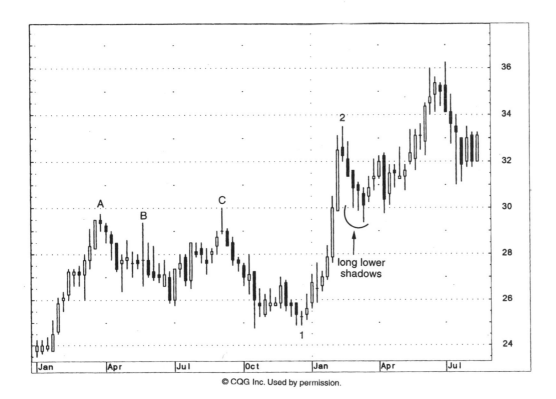

© CQG Inc. Used by permission.

EXHIBIT 12.4. Bemis Inc.—Weekly (Retracement)

from $29 to $30 should become potential support. So, there was a 50% correction in this scenario, along with a change of polarity and converging long lower shadows, thus confirming one another as the stock approached the $29 area.

We see a decline in Exhibit 12.5 from the price peak in January at 1 to a bullish engulfing pattern in mid March at 2. This low of the bullish engulfing pattern confirmed a hammer from late February. The rally from the bullish engulfing pattern stalled with a high-wave candle almost exactly at a 38.2% Fibonacci retracement from the decline from 1 (at $22.65) to 2 (at $22.57). Another reason for resistance in this area was that it was the November and December former support area. Since the support area was broken, it then becomes new resistance based on the change of polarity principle.

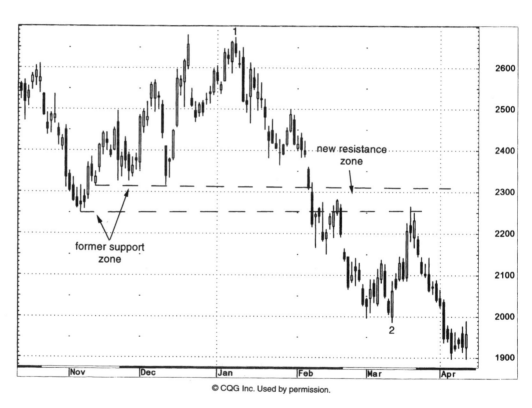

© CQG Inc. Used by permission.

EXHIBIT 12.5. Crude Oil—Daily (Retracement)

CHAPTER 13

CANDLES WITH MOVING AVERAGES

十人十色

Ten men, ten tastes.

The moving average is one of the oldest and most popular tools used by technicians. Its strength is as a trend-following device that offers the trader the ability to catch major moves. Thus, it is utilized most effectively in trending markets.

THE SIMPLE MOVING AVERAGE

The most basic of the moving averages is, as the name implies, the simple moving average. This is the average of all the price points used. For example, let us say that the last five closing prices of a stock were $38, $41, $36, $41, and $38. The 5-day moving average of these closes would be:

$$(\$38 + \$41 + \$36 + \$41 + \$38 = \$194 = \$38.80)$$

The general formula is:

$$\frac{(P1 + P2 + P3 + P4 + P5)}{n}$$

where P1 = the most recent price
P2 = the second most recent price and so on
n = the number of data points

The term "moving" in moving average is applicable because, as the newest data is added to the moving average, the oldest data is dropped. Consequently, the average is always moving as the new data is added.

As seen in the simple moving average example above, each day's stock price contributed 1/5 to the total moving average (since this was a 5-day moving average). A 9-day moving average means that each day will only be 1/9 of the total moving average. Consequently, the longer the moving average, the less effect an individual price will have on it.

The shorter the term of the moving average, the closer it will "hug" prices. This is a plus insofar as it is more sensitive to recent price action. The negative aspect is that it has a greater potential for whipsaws. Longer-term moving averages provide a greater smoothing effect, but are less responsive to recent prices.

Some of the more popular moving averages include the 5-, 9-, 30-, and 50-day moving averages. Probably the most widely monitored is the 200-day moving average.

The spectrum of moving average users runs from the intraday trader, who uses moving averages of real-time trades, to the hedger, who may focus on monthly, or even yearly, moving averages.

Other than the length of the average, another avenue of analysis is based on what price is used to compute the average. Most moving average systems use, as we did in our prior example, closing prices. However, moving averages of highs, lows, and the midpoint of the highs and lows have all been used. Sometimes, even moving averages of moving averages are used.

THE WEIGHTED MOVING AVERAGE

A weighted moving average assigns a different weight to each price used to compute the average. Almost all weighted moving averages are front loaded. That is, the most recent prices are weighted more heavily than older prices. How the data is weighted is a matter of preference.

THE EXPONENTIAL MOVING AVERAGE

The exponential moving average is a special type of weighted moving average. Like the basic weighted moving average, the exponential moving average is front weighted. Unlike other moving averages, though, the exponential moving average incorporates all prior prices used in the data. This type of moving average assigns progressively smaller weights to each of the past prices. Each weight is exponentially smaller than the previous weight, hence, the name exponential moving average. One of the most popular uses of the exponential moving average is for use in the MACD. The MACD is discussed in Chapter 14.

USING MOVING AVERAGES

Moving averages can provide objective strategies with clearly defined trading rules. Many of the computerized technical trading systems are underpinned on moving averages. How can moving averages be used? The answer to this is as varied as there are different trading styles and philosophies. Some of the more prevalent uses of the moving average include:

1. Comparing the price versus the moving averages as a trend indicator. For instance, a good gauge to see if a market is in an intermediate-term uptrend could be that prices have to be above the 65-day moving average. For a longer-term uptrend, prices would have to be higher than the 40-week moving average.
2. Using the moving average as support or resistance levels. A close above the specified moving average would be bullish. A close below the moving average would be bearish.

3. Monitoring the moving average band (also known as envelopes). These bands are a certain percentage above or below the moving average and can serve as support or resistance.

4. Watching the slope of the moving average. For instance, if the moving average levels off or declines after a period of a sustained rise, it may be a bearish signal. Drawing trend lines on the moving averages is a simple method of monitoring their slope.

5. Trading with dual moving averages. One can compare a shorter- and longer-term moving average to each other. If the short-term moving average crosses under the longer-term moving average, it would turn the trend down. In Japan, such a crossover is called a "dead cross." When a shorter-term moving average crosses over a long-term moving average, the Japanese refer to that as a "golden cross" because it is viewed as a potentially bullish signal. Some traders will even take the dual moving averages a step further by saying that for a trend to be higher, not only does the short-term moving average have to be over the long-term moving average, but the slope of both moving averages must be up. Trading with dual moving averages is discussed in Chapter 14.

The following examples use various moving averages. Generally I have found the 30-day and shorter-term 5-day moving averages are good gauges for the equity markets. For futures, the 40- and 65-day moving averages are useful. They are not based on optimum moving averages. An optimum moving average today might not be the optimum one tomorrow. The length of the moving averages used in the following examples are not the important point. What is meaningful is how moving averages can be melded with candles.

In Exhibit 13.1 we see a moving average that became an excellent area of support. There may have been times before August (when this chart begins) in which this moving average was not so effective as it was during this time. However, once we determined that the moving average was valid, as it was in late August and late September, we can then turn our attention to this particular moving average with the idea that retrace-

EXHIBIT 13.1. Agribrands—Daily (Moving Average as Support)

ments should hold the moving average as support. With a downdraft that started with the bearish engulfing pattern the week of October 11, we would view this moving average as potential support. As the stock got to this moving average on October 15, it made a hammer with the white candle after the hammer completed a bullish engulfing pattern. This convergence of factors (moving average as support, the hammer, the bullish engulfing pattern) defined the low of the correction near $48.75. As useful as moving averages are, I would not suggest using a moving average—no matter how often it has successfully been defended—as a sole reason to trade. It is much more important to have a candlestick signal confirming a moving average's support or resistance before initiating, or offsetting, a position.

In Exhibit 13.2 we have a short-term moving average. We can tell it is a short-term moving average because of how closely it hugs prices. This happens to be a 9-period exponential moving average, which is popular among foreign exchange traders. We could see how well this moving average acted as an upside

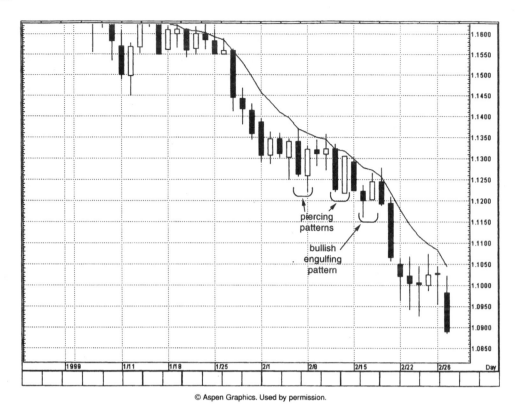

EXHIBIT 13.2. Eurodollar/US—Daily (Moving Average as Resistance)

resistance area during the decline from mid January on. In early February through mid February, there were numerous candlestick bottoming signals including two piercing patterns and a bullish engulfing pattern. Nonetheless, resistance at the moving average remained in force. Consequently, to confirm the potential bullish implication of these candle signals, one should wait for a breakout over the resistance area defined by the moving average. Since this breakout didn't occur, it would keep one from buying.

Exhibit 13.3 displays a short-term moving average that was resistance during the descent beginning in mid August. On August 30 and 31 the stock pushed over this resistance intraday, but failed to close above it—thus keeping the trend down. On September 7 and 8 there was a little whipsaw as the stock closed above this moving average and then failed. Generally, however, this moving average (which is a 5-day moving average) should be respected as resistance because of how well it worked. Starting September 20 the stock built a series of bullish long lower shadows with the last long lower shadow candle on

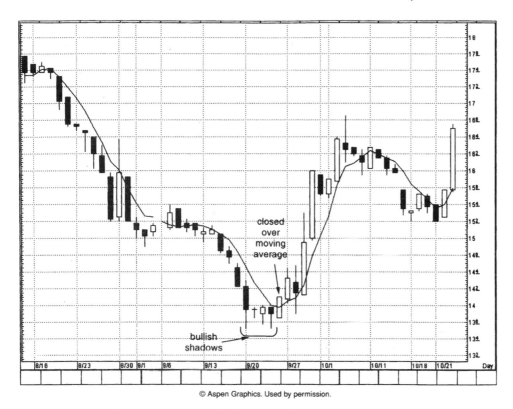

EXHIBIT 13.3. Eaton Vance—Daily (Moving Average as Resistance)

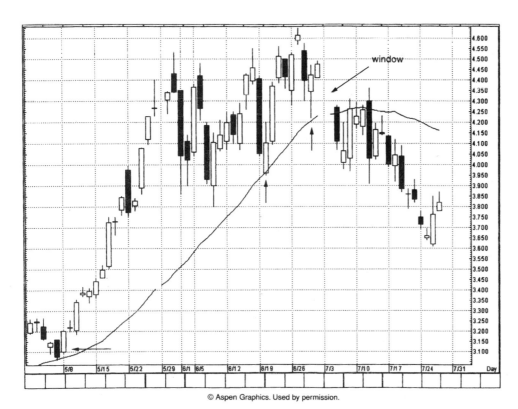

EXHIBIT 13.4. Natural Gas—Daily (Moving Average as Support and Resistance)

September 24 as a hammer. While these candle lines gave a visual clue that the market was groping for a bottom, it took the September 25 close to get final bullish confirmation as this candle completed a bullish engulfing pattern and closed above this moving average. Note how this moving average held as support on the late September rally and as resistance during the early October decline.

Exhibit 13.4 displays how a moving average can become support and resistance. On the initial ascent on the week of May 8, natural gas ascended and maintained this moving average's support (shown at the arrows). On July 5 the moving average's support was penetrated with a falling window. Consequently, we now have two reasons for resistance. The first is the moving average. Since this average worked so well as support, it should be expected to act equally well as resistance. Second, a falling window between $4.29 and $4.41 should also be resistance. In early July, natural gas got to this moving average's resistance but failed to close over it. The early July rally was also a failure of the window's resistance zone.

CHAPTER 14

CANDLES WITH OSCILLATORS

得手に帆をあげよ

Let every bird sing its own note.

Unlike pattern recognition techniques that are subjective (this includes candlestick techniques), oscillators are mathematically derived techniques that offer a more objective means of analyzing the market. They are widely used and are the basis of many computerized trading systems.

Oscillators include such technical tools as the relative strength index, stochastics, and MACD. The three major uses of oscillators are:

1. *As a divergence indicator.* There are two kinds of divergence. A negative, or bearish, divergence occurs when prices are at a new high, but the oscillator is not. This implies the market is internally weak. A positive, or bullish, divergence is when

225

prices are at a new low, but the oscillator does not hit a new low. The implication is that the selling pressure is losing steam.

2. *As overbought/oversold indicators.* This means oscillators can notify the trader if the market has become overextended and, thus, vulnerable to a correction.

3. *As confirmation of the force behind a trend's move.* Oscillators can confirm the market's momentum, measuring the velocity of a price move by comparing price changes. In theory, the velocity should increase as the trend is under way. A flattening of momentum could be an early warning that a price move may be decelerating.

There is a Japanese saying: "All clouds do not rain." I view the oscillator as a rain cloud that has the potential for rain—but the only way to tell it's raining is either seeing or feeling the raindrops. So it is with oscillators. An oscillator is like a storm cloud, but we need a final confirmation with candle signals. Thus, I view an overbought or oversold oscillator as only a warning, a clue, with final confirmation coming with a candlestick pattern.

THE RELATIVE STRENGTH INDEX

The Relative Strength Index (RSI) is one of the most popular oscillators. The RSI oscillator is different from the concept of the relative strength. The relative strength compares the relative strength performance of a stock, or a small group of stocks, with the performance of a sector or a broader market index such as the Dow Jones or the S&P 500.

Computing the RSI

The RSI compares the relative strength of price advances to price declines over a specified period. Nine and 14 days are two of the most popular periods used. The RSI is figured by comparing the gains of up sessions with the losses of the down sessions over a given time frame. The calculations used are dependent only on closing prices. The formula is:

$$RSI = 100 - (100/(1 + RS))$$

$$\text{where } RS = \frac{\text{average up points for period}}{\text{average down points for period}}$$

Thus, computing a 14-day RSI entails adding the total gains made on the up days over the last 14 days (on a close-to-close basis) and dividing by 14. The same would be done for the down days. These figures provide the relative strength (RS). This RS is then put into the RSI formula. This RSI formula converts the RS data so that it becomes an index with a range between 0 and 100.

Using the RSI

The two main uses of RSI are as an overbought/oversold indicator and as a tool to monitor divergence.

- As an overbought/oversold indicator, the RSI implies that the market is overbought if it approaches the upper end of this band (that is, above 70%). At that point, the market may be vulnerable to a pullback or could move into a period of consolidation. Conversely, at the lower end of the RSI range (usually below 30%), it is said to reflect an oversold condition. In such an environment, there is a potential of a short covering move.

- As a divergence tool, RSI calculations can be helpful when prices make a new high for the move and the RSI fails to make a concurrent high. This is called negative divergence and is potentially bearish. Positive divergence occurs when prices make a new low, but the RSI does not. Divergence is more meaningful when RSI oscillator readings are in overbought or oversold regions.

In Exhibit 14.1, through the later part of November there was resistance near $58. Once Albertson's pushed over that level with a tall white candle on December 1, we can then use the change of polarity that converts the prior resistance into new support. There was vacillation the week of December 14, but a series of bullish long lower shadows showed that this stock had a good foundation near $62. The rally resumed on December 21, stalling with a dark-cloud cover. As the stock formed this dark-cloud cover at new highs, the RSI was overbought and also formed a negative divergence signal. That is, the stock's price was higher at 2 than 1, but the RSI was lower at 2 than 1. The aforementioned dark-cloud cover became resistance as confirmed by another dark-cloud cover made on January 10 and 11. A piercing pattern in mid January at P occurred in an oversold environment (as gauged by the RSI).

© Aspen Graphics. Used by permission.

EXHIBIT 14.1. Albertson's—Daily (RSI)

This convergence of bearish divergence and the dark-cloud cover reinforced the potential bearish implications of the dark-cloud cover. Trend lines can also be used on the relative strength index. This is shown by the dashed line on the oscillator. Note that, once this rising support line was penetrated, it became another negative signal.

A key concept with candle charts is that the overall technical picture is more important than a single candle line. One should always view the candle line or candle pattern in the context of its market surroundings.

In Exhibit 14.2 there are two bullish engulfing patterns shown as 1 and 2. (Although the open of the white candle of this pattern was the same as the close of the black candle, this is acceptable as a bullish engulfing pattern since foreign exchange markets' open and close are the same.) Bullish engulfing pattern 2 was more important than bullish engulfing pattern 1 because the second bullish engulfing pattern was confirmed by bullish divergence. In the first bullish engulfing pattern, the RSI was continuing its descent as the stock made new lows. This kept the bearish momentum intact.

EXHIBIT 14.2. British Pound—Daily (RSI)

MOVING AVERAGE OSCILLATOR

Computing the Moving Average Oscillator

This indicator is obtained by subtracting the longer-term moving average from the shorter-term moving average. It has plus or minus values. Thus, a value above 0 means the shorter-term moving average is above the longer-term moving average. A reading under 0 means the shorter-term moving average is less than the longer-term moving average.

Using the Moving Average Oscillator

Since this oscillator uses a short- and long-term moving average, we are comparing the short-term momentum to a longer-term momentum. This is because the short-term moving average is more responsive to recent price activity. If the short-term moving average is relatively far above (or below) the longer-term moving average, the market is said to be overbought (or oversold). As with the other oscillators, the moving average oscillator is also used as a divergence vehicle.

As prices increase, the technician wants to see the short-term moving average increase relative to the longer-term moving average. This would mean increasing positive values for the moving average difference line. If prices advance and the difference between the short- and long-term moving averages narrows, the market is indicating that the shorter-term momentum is running out of steam.

During the first week of May in Exhibit 14.3 the Eurodollar built a bullish engulfing pattern at B. After a small rally from this pattern, the market retreated and found support, as expected, at the lows of the bullish engulfing pattern. Not only was the support area defended with a May 19 hammer, but there was also the bullish divergence as the Eurodollar marginally made a new low while the moving average oscillator made a higher low with the hammer. Once the market pushed above .9200 from the hammer, it confirmed a double bottom made with the dual lows at the bullish engulfing pattern and hammer. As will be discussed in Chapter 16, we can use a breakout from the .350 trading range (i.e., from .8850 to .9200) to give us a target toward .9550 (obtained by adding the .350 trading range onto the breakout point of .9200).

EXHIBIT 14.3. Eurodollar/US—Daily (Moving Average Oscillator)

In Exhibit 14.4 Catalina was ascending along a rising resistance line. During the week of July 13, although the stock was hovering near its current highs, a series of small real bodies showed that the bulls' advance was being constrained by the bears. This hesitation near $56 is not surprising considering that level was resistance in late April.

We now turn our attention to the moving average oscillator. At the time of the aforementioned small real bodies in mid July, there was also bearish convergence. Consequently, we have a classic example of convergence at $56. Specifically: (1) The stock was at a resistance area based on the rising resistance line and the prior April price peak; (2) a series of small real bodies showing a market separating from its bull trend; and (3) the bearish divergence. If we need more proof of a market in trouble, then we would have received this signal with a falling window (at the arrow) that became resistance.

Exhibit 14.5 displays a key use of candles and oscillators. Most equity traders are buyers; relatively few are short sellers. A challenge longs may have is knowing when to exit a position. This is where an oscillator, especially when confirmed with a candles line or pattern, can become useful. As we saw in

EXHIBIT 14.4. Catalina Marketing—Daily (Moving Average Oscillator)

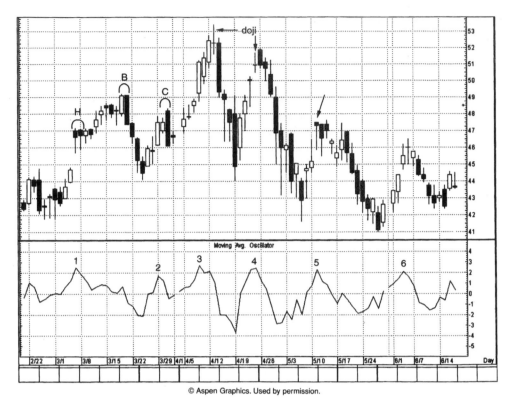

© Aspen Graphics. Used by permission.

EXHIBIT 14.5. Wal-Mart Stores—Daily (Moving Average Oscillator)

Exhibit 14.4, when a stock becomes overextended and there is also a candlestick confirming a turn, it could be a good place to either exit longs or lighten up on long positions. With this in mind, let's look at each overbought occurrence:

1. There were two hanging man lines at H in the first week of March. These appeared during an overbought market (based on the oscillator), but they were not confirmed by a close under their real bodies. Remember, for bearish confirmation of a hanging man, we need a close under the hanging man's real body to confirm a hanging man's potentially bearish implications. Additionally, the market formed a rising window on the first hanging man session. As such, the window became support. So, while the market was overextended, there was no bearish confirmation of a market rate turn at 1 based on the candle lines. The bearish engulfing pattern at B on March 18 and 19 was a turning signal not only because of the bearish engulfing pattern itself, but also because at the time of that pattern the stock had made a new high and the moving average oscillator had made a lower high. This formed bearish or negative divergence.

2. An overbought reading with the oscillator, but no turning signals with the candles since the candle line during the overbought reading was a tall white real body. A few days after this white real body we can see a bearish engulfing pattern (at C) which became resistance for a few sessions.

3. On April 7 Wal-Mart moved above the bearish engulfing pattern discussed above. As such, it could be viewed as a bullish breakout. At area 3 the oscillator was overbought, but there were no turning signals with the candles and we would not look to sell. A cautionary signal would come a few days later with a long-legged doji after a tall white candle.

4. An overbought oscillator with a doji confirming a potential turn. While the stock hesitated at this doji, a small rising window opened between April 22 and 23 as support. Thus, we would need further bearish confirmation by a close under the window. The break of the window's support occurred on April 28.

5. A hanging man at the arrow on May 11 and an overextended oscillator gave us a turning signal. The bearish implications of the hanging man were confirmed by a lower close the next day.

6. A doji confirming hesitation. Similar to 4, there was a rising window that needed to be closed before the trend could be viewed as damaged. The close under the window's support took place on June 8.

STOCHASTICS

The stochastic oscillator is another popular tool. It, like all the other oscillators, provides overbought and oversold readings and signals divergences. It also affords a mechanism to relate a shorter-term trend to a longer-term trend. The stochastic indicator compares the latest closing price with the total range of price action for a specified period. Stochastic values are between 0 and 100. A high stochastic reading would mean the close is near the upper end of the entire range for the period. A low reading means that the close is near the low end of the period's range. The idea behind stochastics is that as the market moves higher, closes tend to be near the highs of the range; as the market moves lower, prices tend to cluster near the lows of the range.

Computing Stochastics

The stochastic indicator is comprised of two lines: the %K and the %D. The %K line, called the raw stochastic or the fast %K, is more sensitive. The formula for the %K line is:

$$\frac{(\text{Close}) - (\text{Low of N})}{(\text{High of N}) - (\text{Low of N})} \times 100 = \%K$$

where Close = current close
Low of N = low of the range during the period used
High of N = high of the range during the period used

The "100" in the equation converts the value into a percentage. Thus, if the close today is the same as the high for the period under observation, the fast %K would be 100%. A period can be in days, weeks, or even intraday (such as hourly). Fourteen, nineteen, and twenty-one periods are some of the more common periods.

Because the fast %K line can be so volatile, this line is usually smoothed by taking a 3-period moving average of the last three %K values. This 3-period moving average of %K is called the slow %K. Most technicians use the slow %K line instead of the choppy fast %K line. This slow %K is then smoothed again using a 3-day moving average of the slow %K to get what is called the %D line. This %D is essentially a moving average of a moving average. One way to think of the difference between the %K and %D lines is too view them as you would two moving averages with the %K line comparable to a short-term moving average, and the %D line comparable to a longer-term moving average.

Using Stochastics

As mentioned previously, stochastics can be used in several ways. The most popular method is as a tool for showing divergence. Most technicians who monitor stochastics use this aspect of divergence in conjunction with overbought/oversold readings.

Some technicians require another rule: to have the slow %K line cross under the %D line for a sell signal, or for the slow %K to move above the %D for a buy signal. This is comparable to the bullish (bearish) signal of a faster moving average crossing over (under) the slower moving average.

Another use is as a gauge for overbought/oversold. Most traders will view an 80% or higher reading as overbought, and

20% or lower as oversold. For instance, to get a buy signal, the market must be oversold (20% or less for %D), there is positive divergence, and the %K line is crossing above the %D line.

Exhibit 14.6 displays a small bearish engulfing pattern at B in the early morning of October 23. Normally such a small bearish engulfing pattern is not significant, but, when combined with stochastics, we see that the stochastic is overextended and there is a bearish crossover (where the faster %K line crosses under the slower %D line). This put more significance on the bearish engulfing pattern. We look for the high of this pattern at $105 to be resistance. This resistance held as a stock got to $104 the following morning from where it then failed.

A large falling window opened October 25. A nicely defined hammer appeared early the next morning (October 26). A few periods before this hammer, we got a tentative clue of bottom with the stochastics. Specifically, early on October 26 the stochastic was in oversold territory (that is, below 20%). We also see a bullish crossover where the faster %K line crossed above the slower %D line. Soon after the stochastic turning signal, we got a bullish candle signal with the aforementioned

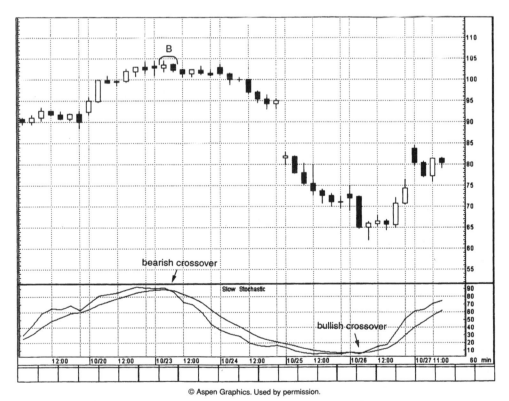

EXHIBIT 14.6. JDS Uniphase—60 Minutes (Stochastics)

hammer. This hammer held as support. If the stock had pulled under the hammer's low then, in spite of the positive stochastic reading, one should consider vacating longs.

Exhibit 14.7 shows a series of long lower shadows emerged in early October. During the week of October 12 we see the stochastic oscillator in oversold readings near 20% with a bullish crossover. This reinforced what the bullish shadows had hinted at, that the stock was stabilizing.

A doji-like line emerged on October 19 following a tall white candle. This converted the trend from up to more neutral since the doji hinted that the market was "tired." The market treaded water after this doji and then pushed higher with the November 2 rising window. This window became support during the week of November 2. A bearish engulfing pattern on November 6 and 9 at B turned the trend less positive. This bearish engulfing pattern had about equally sized real bodies; normally we like to see a black real body of the bearish engulfing pattern much larger than the white real body. This shows the bears have wrested control from the bulls. In this case, however, at the time of the bearish engulfing pattern, there was also a bearish crossover in the stochastic reading. As such, when

EXHIBIT 14.7. Schlumberger—Daily (Stochastics)

combined with the stochastic reading, this bearish engulfing pattern took on extra significance.

MOVING AVERAGE CONVERGENCE–DIVERGENCE

Constructing the MACD

While the Moving Average Convergence–Divergence (MACD) is composed of two lines, it is really a combination of three exponentially smoothed moving averages. The first line is the difference between two exponential moving averages (usually the 26- and 12-period exponential moving averages). The second line of the MACD is made by taking an exponential moving average (usually 9-period) of the difference between the two exponential moving averages used to make the first line. This second line is called the signal line.

Using the MACD

When the faster line crosses above the slower (the signal line), it is viewed as a positive. A bearish crossover is when the faster line moves under the slower line. The MACD can also be used to find areas in which the market is overbought or oversold. Because of the slower nature of MACD, it is not generally used as a short-term trading tool.

In Exhibit 14.8 the tall white candle on March 16 opened a rising window. The next day the small real body inside this white candle formed a harami pattern. The correction from this harami pattern found stabilization at the aforementioned window. A dark-cloud cover on March 30 and April 1 at D gave early evidence that the market, as the Japanese would say, "had a poor chance of rising." This dark-cloud cover became resistance shown by the action the following two days. While the stock pushed over the dark-cloud's resistance intraday, it had failed to close above it, thus keeping the resistance intact.

The week after the emergence of the dark-cloud cover, we get the bearish confirmation via the MACD as the faster line crosses under the slower signal line.

Note how the decline from the dark-cloud cover continued until the market formed a bullish engulfing pattern in mid April. This bullish engulfing pattern confirmed the potential support area at the rising window from March 15 and 16.

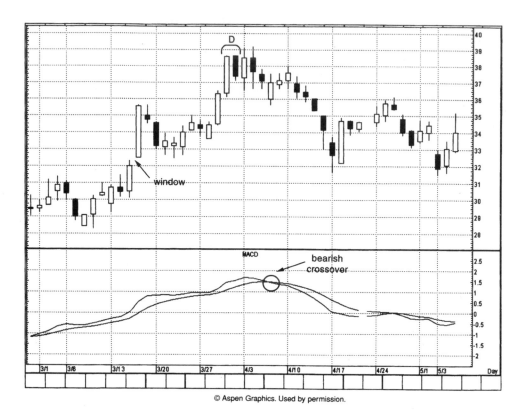

© Aspen Graphics. Used by permission.

EXHIBIT 14.8. Target—Daily (MACD)

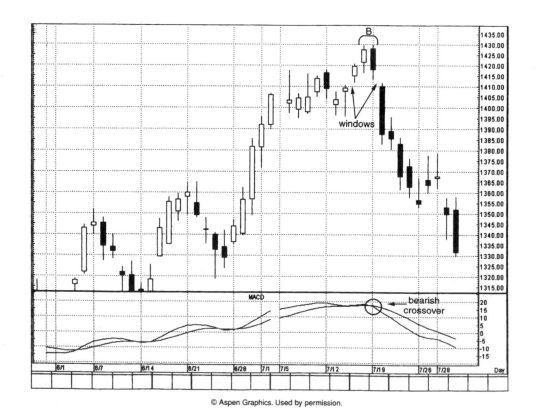

© Aspen Graphics. Used by permission.

EXHIBIT 14.9. S&P 500—Daily (MACD)

This chart is a good example of the value added of candle charts. Very often candles will give a turning signal ahead of traditional Western technicals. In this scenario we saw the dark-cloud cover presaging a top almost a week before the MACD gave its reversal signal.

In Exhibit 14.9 the S&P made a new high in mid July. But indications of trouble came with the bearish engulfing pattern at B. Further dampening the bullish outlook was a bearish clue sent via the MACD as the faster line crossed under the slower line. The session after the bearish engulfing pattern, the market opened a falling window. Because the market had a rising window the prior week, this falling window built an island top. This further reinforced the potentially bearish outlook.

In Exhibit 14.10 a large bullish engulfing pattern was completed on August 3. A few sessions after this, there was a bullish crossover in the MACD (another example of candles giving an earlier clue of a reversal than Western techniques). The ascent from this bullish engulfing pattern continued until the evening star. (The middle part of the pattern was also a high-wave candle.) A day after this evening star pattern, the nail in the coffin was placed with the bearish crossover in the MACD.

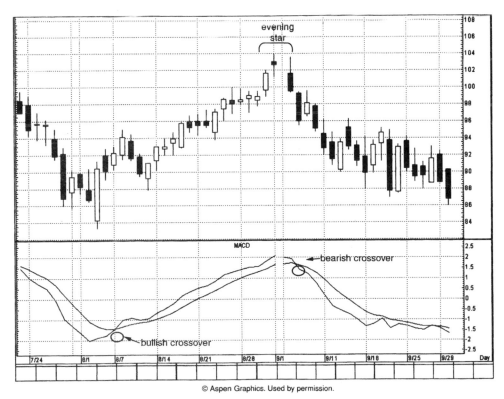

EXHIBIT 14.10. NASDAQ-100 Trust—Daily (MACD)

CHAPTER 15

CANDLES WITH VOLUME

一条の矢は折るべく、十条は折るべからず

A single arrow is easily broken, but not ten in a bundle.

One of the most important clues sent out by the market is volume. Volume is like water pressure in a hose. The greater the water pressure, the more powerful the water flow. Likewise, the stronger the volume, the more the force behind the move.

Volume should increase in the direction of the trend to improve the likelihood that the current trend should continue. If, however, volume declines as a trend progresses, there is less reason to believe the trend will continue. Volume can also be useful for confirming tops and bottoms.

While specific volume measurements, such as On Balance Volume and Open Interest, are not addressed in this chapter,

© Aspen Graphics. Used by permission.

EXHIBIT 15.1. Corning—60 Minutes (Volume with Hammer)

whichever forms of volume analysis you now use will help enhance the effectiveness of candle charts.

I'm frequently asked at my seminars about combining volume with candle charts by changing the width of the candles according to their volume. That is, the higher the volume, the wider the real body. In my opinion, it is just as easy to read volume classically—on the bottom of a chart. The disadvantage to adjusting the thickness of the candle line with volume is that if there are many high-volume sessions, there will be fewer candle charts that can fit on the screen. Volume is so important that however you choose to display it is not important. What is important is that if it is available, you should use it.

Because volume numbers are different from market to market, I don't look at an absolute volume figure, but at relative volume. In other words, in one stock 50,000 shares could be an extraordinarily high-volume session—while, in another, 10 million shares might be light volume. As such, I look for relative volume spikes in a market.

In Exhibit 15.1 we can see how this stock had a volume spurt late on May 3. We see that compared with preceding sessions, this was an abnormal volume. As such, we should pay attention to it. This high-volume session was also a hammer. This is what we like to see—volume confirming price.

This chart brings out another aspect. A very long lower shadow hammer means that by the time the hammer is confirmed (we need to wait for a close to confirm the hammer), the market could be well off its lows. Buying at the close of such a hammer may not present an attractive risk/reward since the market may retrace back to the lows of the hammer before, potentially, resuming an upward course. A high-volume hammer, such as in this chart, decreases the chance for a correction to the hammer's low. Therefore, one may be more aggressive about buying on the hammer's close if it is a usually high-volume hammer than one would if the volume didn't give the same forceful confirmation.

In Exhibit 15.2 in early November a precipitous decline with a group of long black real bodies visually reinforced the bears'

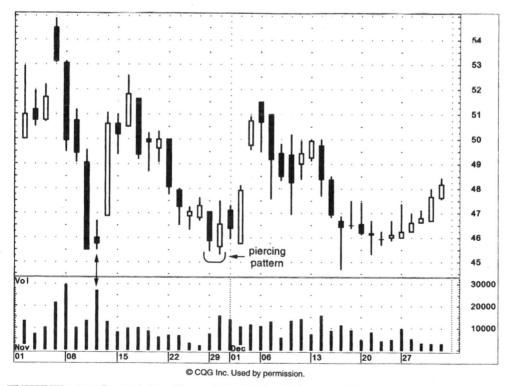

© CQG Inc. Used by permission.

EXHIBIT 15.2. Capital One Financial—Daily (Volume with a Harami and Piercing Pattern)

momentum. A single session, on November 11, changed the technical picture. That session's spinning top completed the second session of the harami pattern. However, of greater consequence was that spinning top's strong volume. This showed that as heavy as the supply was (and we know there was heavy supply because of the high volume), the demand was strong enough to keep the bears in check—hence, the small real body.

The market rallied from this harami. On the next sell-off later in November, the stock stabilized with a piercing pattern. With the piercing pattern, we would like to see lighter volume on the black candle and heavier volume on the white candle. This would serve to reinforce that the bears are losing force and the bulls are gaining a stronger foothold. This scenario of lighter volume black and heavier volume white is what unfolded in Capital One. This volume scenario also increases the odds that the piercing pattern will hold. In this example, the piercing pattern's support was well defended with the December 15 hammer.

This concept of volume confirming the candle pattern can be used for any candle signals. For instance, this would mean that a bearish engulfing pattern should have a lighter volume on the first candle (the white) and a heavier volume on the second candle (the black) to increase the bearish engulfing pattern's significance.

Adding the insights of volume to the power of a falling or rising window is, as the Japanese proverb says, "Like the right hand helping the left." In Exhibit 15.3, the market formed a bullish harami cross the week of May 8. A few sessions later a tiny rising window opened between May 13 and 15. This diminutive window was support throughout the week of May 15. On May 22 an expanded rising window opened. This window also had the bullish kicker of extra heavy volume. While a rising window is viewed as potential support, a high-volume window enhances its effectiveness as support (or, in the case of a falling window, as resistance). A bullish long lower shadow on June 1 was confirmation of the bulls' force as the stock held the $30 support area on a close (as defined by the bottom of the May 22 window).

While a small real body is a clue that a decline or advance may be exhausting itself, if we add high volume to a small real

© Aspen Graphics. Used by permission.

EXHIBIT 15.3. General Motors—Daily (Volume with a Window)

body, we get more substantiation of a turn. Let's look at Exhibit 15.4 to describe why this is so. In this chart of Dell I circled a high-volume day (at 1) on August 18, which was also a rising window. As examined in Exhibit 15.3, a high-volume rising window should be a solid support area. This was the case with Dell as shown by the action a few days after the rising window.

Another unusually large volume session occurred October 19 (at 2). The day was also a doji. This high-volume doji was significant insofar as it came after a steep decline that took Dell to a support area at the early August bullish engulfing pattern (that had a hammer as the first candle line). As discussed in Chapter 8, I usually pay less attention to doji in declines than advances. However, since this doji corroborated a support area and had large volume, I certainly would stand up and take notice of it. What this high-volume doji evidenced was that there was heavy supply (as proven by the high volume); but with the stock forming a doji, it proved that the demand was strong enough to absorb the supply. On October 19 we thus

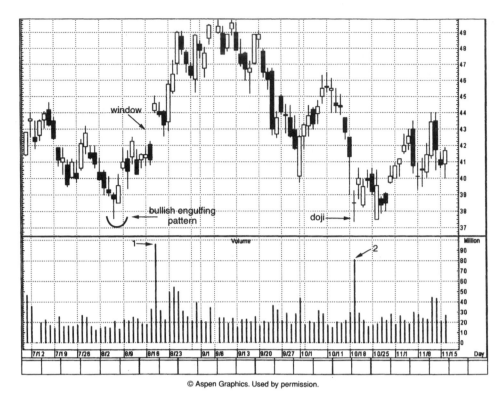

© Aspen Graphics. Used by permission.

EXHIBIT 15.4. Dell—Daily (Volume with a Doji and Window)

have a convergence of technical factors underscoring the importance of $37.25 as support:

1. A support area based on the lows of the August bullish engulfing pattern.
2. The doji.
3. The expansive volume on the doji displaying all the heavy supply was being absorbed.

Note how this support was again successfully defended the week after the doji with a tall white candle.

The same theory about a high-volume doji during a decline increasing the chance of a turn compared with a regular volume session is true even if the candle is a small real body. (We saw a high-volume spinning top in Exhibit 15.2.) To summarize integrating high volume with spinning tops or doji:

1. An unusually high-volume doji or spinning top after an extended advance illustrates that the bulls' drive is being

met with enough supply to stall the rally. This is a possible top reversal.

2. A very heavy-volume doji or small real body during a steep decline shows that heavy supply is being taken by the equally aggressive demand.

Whether there is a single candle line or a group of candles forming a pattern, the chances of a turnaround are increased if volume confirms what the candle pattern is showing. Exhibit 15.5 shows a bullish engulfing pattern late on October 5. The first part of the bullish engulfing pattern was a spinning top that hinted the previous downdraft was losing some steam. The next session's long white candle showed the bulls had grabbed control. Adding to the bullish impetus of this bullish engulfing pattern was that the first part of this pattern was lighter volume as compared with the long white candle's volume. This convergence of volume and bullish engulfing pattern reinforced one another and increased the likelihood of a turn. The ascent from the bullish engulfing pattern stalled early on October 7 with a bearish engulfing pattern and a series of can-

© Aspen Graphics. Used by permission.

EXHIBIT 15.5. Home Depot—30 Minutes (Volume Confirming a Bullish Engulfing Pattern)

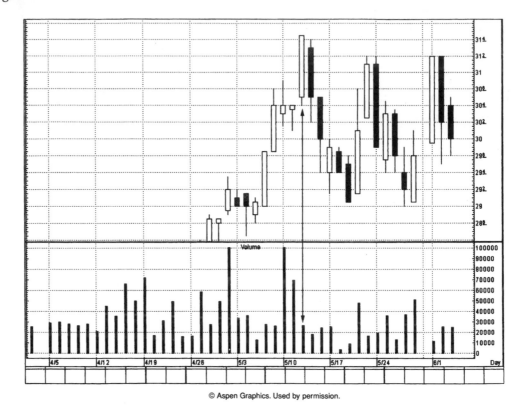

EXHIBIT 15.6. Technitrol (Volume Confirmation of a Breakout)

dles with bearish upper shadows at $72.50. This confirmed resistance from the prior session's long upper shadow at the same level.

As a general rule we can say that the longer the white candle, the more probable a continuation of a rally. But volume adds another important dimension to this. As illustrated in Exhibit 15.6, an extended white candle line on May 12 pushed the stock to a new high. However, mitigating some of this bullishness is this candle's light volume. When a market creates a new high, we would like to see that confirmed by a push in volume. In this case, volume didn't corroborate the breakout. Although lack of volume on an upside breakout wouldn't convert me from a bull to a bear, it is a reason to be more circumspect. This is because such a low-volume rally increases the chances that it will not be sustained. In this stock, the candle after the May 12 low-volume tall white candle was a long black one and, as such, reinforced the lack of the bulls' control.

CHAPTER 16

MEASURED MOVES

鬼の留守に洗濯

Make use of your opportunities.

Candle charts, because they provide an x-ray into the demand/supply situation, are potent in calling early turning signals. Assuming one enters a trade with a candle signal (preferably with confirmation with other candle or Western signals), the challenge becomes knowing when to exit.

My firm, candlecharts.com, utilizes different exit strategies, depending on the client's trading style. One method we use is forecasting price objectives from classic Western patterns. There is another reason for incorporating measured targets. No matter how ideal a candle pattern or how many reversal signals converge at one area, it doesn't predict the extent of the reversal. This is where we shift to Western technicals for price objectives.

The measuring techniques in this chapter will illustrate a few of these many patterns, including breakouts from a box range, swing targets, flags and pennants, and ascending and descending triangles.

Price targets are not synonymous with support or resistance. For example, if there is an upside objective of $42, this does not mean the rally will stop at $42 (of course, it may not even get to $42). In my opinion, one should not look at a price objective to initiate a new position, but to offset an outstanding position. In the example discussed above, I would use a rally to the $42 area to liquidate longs, but not to initiate a new short position. Of course, if there were a bearish candle signal or a convergence of other technical signals, hinting that $42 was an area of resistance, one could then be more aggressive about considering a sale.

BREAKOUTS FROM BOXES

Most of the time, the markets are not in a trending mode but rather in a lateral range, what the Japanese call a *box range*. On such occasions, the market is in a relative state of harmony with neither the bulls nor the bears in charge. The Japanese word for tranquility and calm is "wa." I like to think of markets that are bounded in a box range as being in a state of "wa."

When a market is in a box, it is like a coiled spring ready to unwind when the surrounding pressure is released. We can use this potential pent-up energy. When a breakout from box range unfolds, the market has good potential continuing in the direction of the breakout.

As shown in Exhibit 16.1, a move outside the box implies a move at least equal to the vertical height of the box. Specifically, on a push above the top end of the box (bullish breakout), one takes the vertical measurement from the bottom end of the box (the support area) to the top end of the box range (the previous resistance). This distance is shown as A–B. We derive a target by adding this A–B range onto the prior resistance area. As an example, an upside breakout from a $50–$53 box range would give a $56 target.

The opposite would be a penetration of a box range's support (shown as a bearish breakout in Exhibit 16.1). If we used

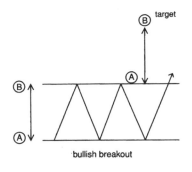
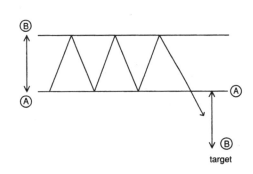

EXHIBIT 16.1. Breakout from Boxes

the same $50–$53 box range, a bearish break of this support at $50 would provide a $47 target.

In Exhibit 16.2 there's a box range environment with the top end at areas 1 and 2. The bottom end of the box (the support zone) is delineated by the two horizontal lines between 3600 and 3500 (we will discuss area A in a moment).

The top at 1 did not have any candlestick reversals. This illustrates that not all reversals are signaled with candles. The top at 2 was an ideal version of an evening star since none of the three real bodies that comprise this pattern touched. Additionally, the high point of 2 was a hanging man line that was confirmed the next session.

Once the NASDAQ failed from area 2, we can say that as a failure from the prior high at 1, it could retreat to the low made between the highs at 1 and 2. This low was the bullish engulfing pattern at A. As such, we have a price target toward 3600–3500. This area held in the latter part of September via a couple of tall white candles near 3600.

The early October rupturing of this support did double damage. First, the long black real body of October 2 punctured the bottom end of the bullish engulfing pattern at A and thus broke a support area. Perhaps of more consequence was that once the bottom end of the large box range of 4250 to 3500 was broken, it gave us a target toward 2750. This measurement was obtained by taking the 750 points (from the high to low of the box range) from the bottom end of the box near 3500. This target was met a few months later.

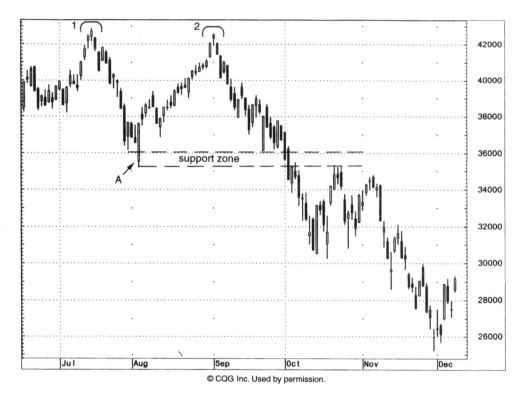

© CQG Inc. Used by permission.

EXHIBIT 16.2. NASDAQ Composite Index—Daily (Downside Breakout from a Box)

We can see by the move under this target of 2750 that price targets do not necessarily mean a support area. This is a very important point to consider. Just because the NASDAQ got to 2750 does not mean that one should buy because it got to a target.

This chart also highlights a reason I like box breakouts. Once a support area is penetrated, we can then use the change of polarity principle (see Chapter 11) to define what should become resistance. Based on this technique, the prior support (in this example, 3600–3500) should be converted into resistance. That is what unfolded here. If the index had closed back above 3600, it would have voided my downside target of 2750.

Exhibit 16.3 shows a clearly defined lateral range from $66.25 to $67.75. The candle line at A breaches this support line, but since it did not close below it, the support was still intact. At B the market closed under its box range. This was the bearish signal. We got earlier clues of a stock in trouble before the break at B with the downward sloping resistance line shown on the chart. This increased the likelihood that the support level at $66.25 would eventually break.

© Aspen Graphics. Used by permission.

EXHIBIT 16.3. JDS Uniphase—5 Minutes (Downside Breakout from a Box)

Once support gave way with candle line B, we know (from the change of polarity) that this old support, $66.25, converts into resistance. So, now we have a resistance area, but what is our downside potential? For this we use the vertical distance of the $66.25–$67.75 box range and subtract that $1.50 from the bottom end of the trading range, giving us a target toward $64.75.

The S&P, as shown in Exhibit 16.4, was in a trading range between the 1090 area (at B) and 1140 (at A). The bulls propelled this index above the 1140 resistance on June 24. Adding this A–B (50-point) span onto 1140 gave us a price projection of 1190. This target was exceeded marginally as the stock ascended along a rising resistance line (see Chapter 11). There are a couple of high-wave candles near 1200. (A high-wave candle has extended upper and lower shadows and a small real body. It is related to a long-legged doji, except that a long-legged doji has a doji instead of the small real body, as described in Chapter 8.) These high-wave candles gave a sense that the market was losing its sense of direction (which heretofore was up).

© CQG Inc. Used by permission.

EXHIBIT 16.4. S&P—Daily (Upside Breakout from a Box)

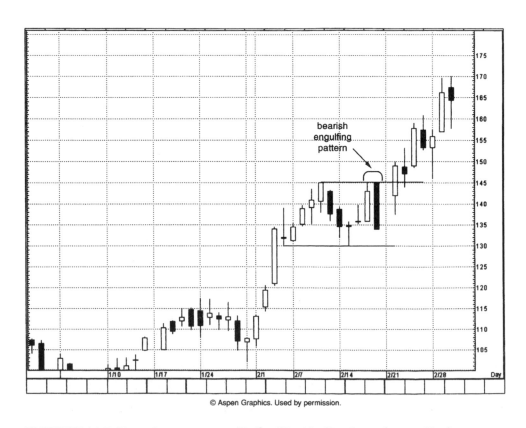

© Aspen Graphics. Used by permission.

EXHIBIT 16.5. Texas Instruments—Daily (Upside Breakout from a Box)

Exhibit 16.5 shows that Texas Instruments was locked in a $130–$145 box. When it approached the top end of this range on February 17 and 18, it formed a bearish engulfing pattern. This pattern should be resistance. However, the next session (February 22) got above this resistance. This was a bullish breakout pushed over the bearish engulfing pattern's resistance and also penetrated the top end of a box. This implied a price target toward $160 (based on the previous $15 range).

What would tell us we were wrong about this target? If, once the market got above $145, as it did on September 22, it got back down under $145 on a close, such a scenario would negate this target. In other words, once the market makes a new high, it is important for the bulls to show they have control by sustaining the new highs.

SWING TARGETS, FLAGS, AND PENNANTS

Swing targets, flags, and pennants are comprised of three segments:

1. An initial cleanly defined brisk move.

2. A correction of the move.

3. A resumption of the move in the same direction as the initial move.

We will look at swing targets first and then flags and pennants.

The theory behind the swing target (see Exhibit 16.6) is that if the market advances, or declines, vigorously, and then there is a retracement of this move, the next leg of the move should be at least equal to the move of the previous channel.

This is shown in Exhibit 16.6 where the height of the first leg is a rally from A to B. There is then a correction to C. Once the market ascends from C, we would "swing" the initial channel height of A to B onto the correction low at C. Hence, the name "swing target."

Swing targets are very similar in concept to flags and pennants. The major difference is that corrections in a swing target are more substantial than flags or pennants. As shown in Exhibit 16.7, flags are lateral, or small countertrend, moves after

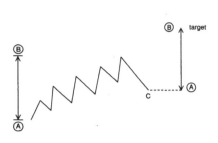

EXHIBIT 16.6. Swing Target

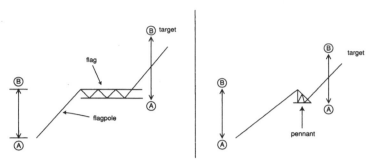

EXHIBIT 16.7. Bull Flag and Pennant

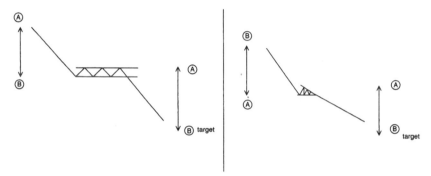

EXHIBIT 16.8. Bear Flag and Pennant

a clearly defined sharp advance or decline. This congestion band serves to relieve an overbought (in a rally) or oversold (in a decline) condition. If, after this short-term correction, the market resumes its prior trend, we then have a flag or pennant pattern.

The difference between flags and pennants is that in a flag, the "flag" portion is a horizontal box range. In a pennant pattern, the "flag" portion (i.e., the congestion band) looks like a pennant because it has lower highs and higher lows.

Exhibits 16.7 and 16.8 show the measurements of the bull and bear flags and pennants. Their measuring implications are built on the same concept as that of the swing target. For the flag or pennant pattern, we use the vertical height of the initial advance or decline—nicknamed the "flagpole."

In Exhibit 16.7 we see bull flag and pennant's price targets are derived by adding the height of the initial sharp advance (the flagpole) from A to B onto the bottom end of the congestion band (which is either a flag or pennant shape). The more traditional method is adding this flagpole's height to the top of the flag or pennant. I prefer to err on exiting too early rather than missing the last few ticks. As such, my measurement starts from the bottom of the flag or pennant rather than the top.

As shown in Exhibit 16.8, the bear flag or pennant objective is forecasted by subtracting the flagpole (A–B) range from the top of the congestion band. (Again, this is my subjective conservative target—others will use the more classic measurement from the bottom of the congestion band.)

In Exhibit 16.9 there is an almost vertical rally from 1 to 2 that took the stock from $22.50 to $27.50. The decline from 2 to A was almost exactly a Fibonacci 61.8% correction of this rally. (See Chapter 12 for discussions on retracements.) The stock started its advance from A.

Using the 1 to 2 rally and the correction to A, we can obtain a swing target by taking the $5 move from 1 to 2 and adding that to the correction low of A at $ 24.50. This gives a potential target to $29.50.

While measured moves do not only normally become resistance or support, in this example we see how a bearish engulf-

© CQG Inc. Used by permission.

EXHIBIT 16.9. Cisco Systems—Daily (Swing Target)

ing pattern (at B) on February 1 and 2 emerged at this project-
ed $29.50 price target.

In Exhibit 16.10 we see that after the ascent from A to B, the
stock took a breather for about a week. During this time the
market moved into a box range between $36.50 and $37.75. A
rising window opened on July 11 (after candle line C) and propelled the stock above the aforementioned lateral trading
range.

From a candlestick perspective, this rising window did two
things: First, it turns the trend north, and second, this window
now becomes potential support. While this window gives us a
positive bias, it does not provide an upside target. For this, we
shift to the Western technicals. Looking at the rally from A to B
and the correction to C, we have a bull flag pattern. Now we
can get a target by adding the "flagpole" portion (A to B) to the
bottom of the "flag" (at C). The A to B rally is about $ 5.50.
Putting this onto the low at C gives an upside target toward
$42. (As mentioned above, most books on Western technical
analysis will add this $5.50 to the top of the flag portion [near

© CQG Inc. Used by permission.

EXHIBIT 16.10. Transocean Sedco Forex—Daily (Bull Flag)

EXHIBIT 16.11. Internet Index—Daily (Bear Pennant)

$38], but I use the more conservative measurement of the bottom of the flag [$36.50] portion of a bull flag.)

As the stock approached our conservative $42 target, a shooting star arose overhead, making the target a resistance area. The black candle after the shooting star completed the third line needed for an evening star pattern. The descent from there found support in late July near $37.75. This was a support area defined by the rising window on July 14 with the inverted hammers. The rally that started the week of July 28 hesitated at the high of the aforementioned evening star pattern at around $42. As discussed with an evening star (and many other candle patterns), I normally look at resistance based on the close. Thus, when the stock pushed above the evening star's resistance intraday, but failed to close above it, this resistance remained intact.

Exhibit 16.11 highlights two shooting stars at A. This denotes hesitation near the 925–950 area. The steep fall from A to B hesitated with a long-legged doji at B. From there, the index ascended slightly. This helped mitigate what was an oversold

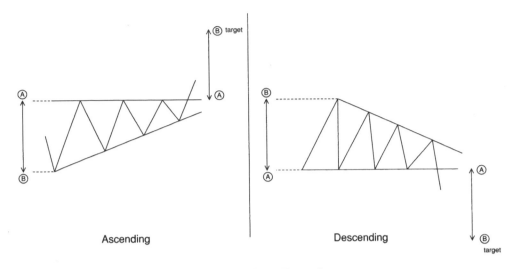

EXHIBIT 16.12. Ascending and Descending Triangles

condition. By looking at the A to B decline as a flagpole and the triangular range at B and C as a pennant, we have a bear pennant formation.

Once the bottom end of the pennant was broken, we can derive a target by taking the decline from A to B from the minor correction high at C near 775. This gives a downside target toward 525 which was exceeded.

A variation of a piercing pattern arose near 500 at P. It was a variation because the white candle did not get more than halfway into the black real body. However, since this was the first white candle and higher close of the entire decline from C, I would still view this variation as important as a classic piercing pattern. This outlook was validated the following week by the successful defense of the piercing pattern's support.

There are many types of triangles in Western technicals: symmetrical triangles, wedges, and so on. As shown in Exhibit 16.12, there are ascending and descending triangles.

The *ascending triangle* has a horizontal resistance area tested numerous times. Moves down from this resistance are at sequentially higher lows. This exemplifies that, although there is supply at the resistance line, demand is getting more aggressive as the market pulls back from this resistance area. If the bulls can then push the market over the horizontal resistance, we have an ascending triangle. The measurement is the height from the horizontal resistance area (A) to the widest part of the triangles (at B) added to the just-broken resistance area.

The *descending triangle* is a pattern wherein a horizontal support area is successfully defended, but each rally from there meets with successively lower highs. These lower highs reflect how the bears are keeping the bulls well in check. With a penetration of support, we take the widest point of the descending triangle and add that measurement from the prior support line.

Exhibit 16.13 displays a classic descending triangle. The horizontal line at 137 shows it was a clearly defined multitested support. This was the bottom part of the descending triangle. The upper part of the descending triangle was a downward sloping resistance line.

Once the bears had the wherewithal to pull the market under the 137 support area (at the arrow), we now use the ascending triangle projection. The highest point of the triangle is when it began at 138.25. The bottom end of the triangle is 137. This provides us with a target toward 135.75.

© Aspen Graphics. Used by permission.

EXHIBIT 16.13. S&P Depository Receipts—5 Minutes (Descending Triangle)

One of the attractive aspects of the descending triangle is that we can use the prior support area as new resistance (the change of polarity). Consequently, once the bears pulled prices under 137 (at the arrow), we then know that 137—if the market is indeed weak—should become resistance.

Further corroboration of trouble with the move under 137 was the falling window the next session. Consequently, we have a convergence of factors for resistance near 137: the prior support and the falling window.

CHAPTER 17

THE BEST OF THE EAST AND WEST: THE POWER OF CONVERGENCE

棚からぼた餅

If heaven drops a fig, open your mouth.

This chapter illustrates a classic example of how I used the principle of convergence to forecast significant trouble in the NASDAQ.

Exhibits 17.1 and 17.1a reveal the techniques—both Eastern and Western—that signaled a major high in the NASDAQ. It is rare to get so many signals emerging near one area. As we will see, while the converging of many candle and Western signals increased the likelihood of a top reversal, these techniques did not project the extent of correction after the market turned down.

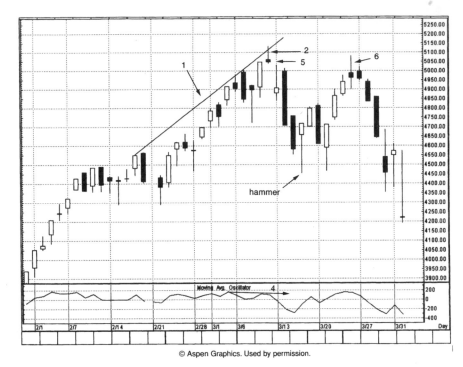

© Aspen Graphics. Used by permission.

EXHIBITS 17.1 and 17.1a. NASDAQ Composite—Daily (Convergence)

Let's look at these signals (and the chapters where these techniques were discussed) individually. This discussion refers to Exhibit 17.1 except for point 3, which uses Exhibit 17.1a.

1. An ascending resistance line obtained by connecting the highs from the week of February 14 to the highs in early March (this technique is discussed in Chapter 11). Since the NASDAQ was in uncharted territory, this rising resistance line was a useful mechanism to obtain a potential supply area as the market ascended.

2. A shooting star (Chapter 4) on March 10 was a candlestick signal confirming the potential resistance at the rising resistance line discussed above.

3. See Exhibit 17.1a. This is an hourly chart that shows a bearish engulfing pattern (Chapter 4) on March 10 (at 3). This bearish engulfing pattern emerged early the same day as the shooting star of the daily chart (discussed in point 2 above).

4. Returning to Exhibit 17.1, at the time the NASDAQ made new highs at the shooting star at 2, the oscillator (Chapter 14) made a lower high. This was bearish divergence.

5. A very small falling window opened between the sessions of March 10 and 13 (Chapter 7). This falling window is more evident in Exhibit 17.1a on the hourly chart. Once this falling window opened, it turned the trend southward. It then becomes potential resistance. The decline from this falling window found some stabilization at a hammer (Chapter 4) on March 16. This hammer became support a few days later, from where a rally ensued.

6. The rally that began on March 21 stalled at the window's resistance (from point 5 above) with a high-wave candle (Chapter 8). Although the upper shadow of the candle line at 6 moved over the window's resistance, the failure to close above this window reinforced the major resistance area between 5050 and 5150.

Based on the above, we have the major convergence of candle signals, including the shooting star, bearish engulfing pattern, falling window, and high-wave candle, with the Western signals of a rising resistance line and bearish divergence. This cluster of signals converging in the 5050–5150 area greatly strengthened the prognosis that the NASDAQ had reached a ceiling.

CONCLUSION

千里の道も一歩より始まる

Step after step the ladder is ascended.

After spending some time with candles, I am sure that you will not trade without the insights they offer. If a picture is worth a thousand words, then a candle chart sends out volumes.

Candle charts are so popular and powerful that they are replacing bar charts, but that does not mean I only use candle indicators. While candles techniques are powerful, they are more potent when joined with other charting tools. This is the advantage of candle charts. With them you can use candle techniques, Western techniques, or a combination of both. Experienced technicians will find that the union of Eastern and Western techniques creates a wonderfully exciting synergy.

Be flexible about chart reading. Where you stand in relation to the overall technical evidence may be more important than an individual candle pattern. For example, a bullish candle signal in a major bear market should not be used as a buy signal. A bullish candle formation, especially when confirmed by other technical signals in a bull market, would be a buying point.

Also consider the risk/reward aspect of a potential trade. Just because there is a candle signal does not mean one should trade on it.

Candles, as all other charting methods, require subjectivity. You are a doctor of the market. How you read and react to the symptoms of the market's health through candles techniques may not be the same as another candle practitioner. How you trade with candles will depend on your trading philosophy, your risk adversity, and your temperament. There are very individual aspects.

May the candles light your trading path!

GLOSSARY A

CANDLESTICK TERMS AND VISUAL DICTIONARY

The descriptions and illustrations below explain and show ideal examples of what the pattern should be like. These "ideal" patterns rarely unfold; therefore, use this glossary as a guidepost, since some subjectivity is required.

Abandoned baby—A very rare top or bottom reversal signal. It is comprised of a doji star that gaps away (including shadows) from the prior and following sessions' candlesticks. This is the same as a Western island top or bottom in which the island session is also a doji.

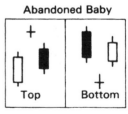

Abandoned Baby

Top   Bottom

Advance block—A variation of the three white soldiers in which the last two soldiers (i.e., white real bodies) display weakening upside drive. This weakness could be in the form of tall upper shadows or progressively smaller real bodies. It signifies a diminution of buying force or an increase in selling pressure.

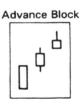

Advance Block

Belt-Hold Lines

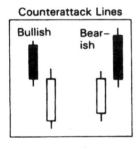

Candlestick Line

Counterattack Lines

Dark–Cloud Cover

Long-legged   Gravestone   Dragonfly

Bearish belt-hold—See *Belt-hold lines.*

Bearish engulfing pattern—See *Engulfing patterns.*

Belt-hold line—There are bullish and bearish belt-holds. A *bullish belt-hold* is a tall white candlestick that opens on, or near, its low and closes well above the opening price. It is also called a white opening shaven bottom. A *bearish belt-hold* is a long black candlestick that opens on, or near, its high and closes well off its open. Also referred to as a black opening shaven head.

Box range—The Japanese expression for a market in a horizontal trading range.

Bullish belt-hold—See *Belt-hold lines.*

Bullish engulfing pattern—See *Engulfing patterns.*

Candlestick lines and charts—Traditional Japanese charts whose individual lines look like candles, hence their name. Candlestick charts are also called "candle charts." The candlestick line is comprised of a real body and shadows. See *Real body* and *Shadows.*

Counterattack lines—Following a black (white) candle in a downtrend (uptrend), the market gaps sharply lower (higher) on the opening and then closes unchanged from the prior session's close. A pattern that reflects a stalemate between the bulls and bears and thus lessens the force in place before the emergence of the counterattack line.

Dark-cloud cover—A bearish reversal signal. In an uptrend a long white candlestick is followed by a black candlestick that opens above the prior white candlestick's high (or close) and then closes well into the white candlestick's real body— preferably more than halfway. The bullish counterpart of the dark-cloud cover is the *piercing pattern.*

Dead cross—A bearish signal given when a short-term moving average crosses under a longer-term moving average. Its bullish counterpart is the *golden cross.*

Deliberation pattern—See *Stalled pattern.*

Doji—A session in which the open and close are the same (or almost the same). There are different varieties of doji lines (see *Gravestone, Dragonfly,* and *Long-legged doji*) depending on where the opening and closing are in relation to the entire range. Doji lines are among the most important individual candlestick lines. They are also components of candlestick patterns. *Northern doji* are doji that appear during a rally. *Southern doji* are doji during declines.

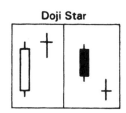

Doji Star

Doji star—A doji that gaps from a long white or black candle's real body.

Downside gap tasuki—See *Tasuki gaps.*

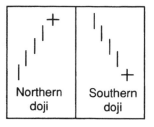

Northern doji   Southern doji

Dragonfly doji—— A doji with a long lower shadow and where the open, high, and close are at the session's high. See the illustration under *Doji*. The opposite version of this is the *gravestone doji.*

Dumpling tops—Similar to the Western rounding top. A window to the downside is needed to confirm this as a top. Its bullish opposite is the *frypan bottom.*

Dumpling Top

Window

Engulfing patterns—A *bullish engulfing pattern* is comprised of a large white real body that engulfs a small black real body in a downtrend. A *bearish engulfing pattern* occurs when selling pressure overwhelms buying force as reflected by a long black real body engulfing a small white real body in an uptrend.

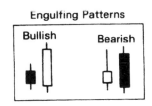

Engulfing Patterns

Bullish   Bearish

Evening doji star—See *Evening star.*

Evening star—A top reversal pattern formed by three candle lines. The first is a tall white real body, the second is a small real body (white or black) that gaps above the first real body to form a *star*, and the third is a black candle that closes well into the first session's white real body. If the middle portion of this pattern is a doji instead of a spinning top, it is an *evening doji star*. The opposite of the evening star is the *morning star* pattern.

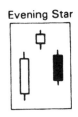

Evening Star

Falling three methods—See *Three methods.*

Falling window—See *Windows.*

Frypan bottom—Similar to a Western rounding bottom. A window to the upside confirms this pattern. It is the counterpart of the *dumpling top.*

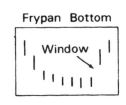

Frypan Bottom

Window

Gapping plays—There are two kinds of gapping plays: 1. *High-price gapping play*—After a sharp advance, the market consol-

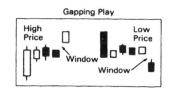

Gapping Play

High Price   Low Price

Window   Window

idates via a series of small real bodies near the recent highs. If prices gap above this consolidation area, it becomes a high-price gapping play. 2. *Low-price gapping play*—After a sharp price decline, the market consolidates via a series of small real bodies near the recent lows. If prices gap under this consolidation, it is a sell signal.

Golden cross—A bullish signal in which a shorter-term moving average crosses above a longer-term moving average. It is the opposite of the *dead cross.*

Gravestone doji—A doji in which the opening and closing are at the low of the session. It is a reversal signal at tops. See the illustration under *Doji.* The opposite of this doji is the *dragonfly doji.*

Hammer

Hammer—An important bottoming candlestick line. The hammer and the hanging man are both the same lines that are generally called *umbrella lines;* that is, a small real body (white or black) at the top of the session's range and a very long lower shadow with little or no upper shadow. When this line appears during a downtrend, it becomes a bullish hammer. For a classic hammer, the lower shadow should be at least twice the height of the real body.

Hanging Man

Hanging man—A top reversal that requires confirmation. The hanging man and the hammer are both the same type of candlestick line (i.e., a small real body [white or black], with little or no upper shadow, at the top of the session's range and a very long lower shadow). But when this line appears during an uptrend, it becomes a bearish hanging man. It signals the market has become vulnerable, but there should be bearish confirmation the next session with an open, and better is a close, under the hanging man's real body. In principle, the hanging man's lower shadow should be two or three times the height of the real body.

Harami

Harami—A two-candlestick pattern in which a small real body holds within the prior session's unusually large real body. The harami implies the immediately preceding trend is concluded, and the bulls and bears are now in a state of truce. The color of the second real body can be white or black. Most often the second real body is the opposite color of the first real body.

Harami cross—A harami with a doji on the second session instead of a small real body. An important top (bottom) reversal signal especially after a tall white (black) candlestick line. It is also called a *petrifying pattern.*

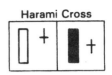

Harami Cross

High-price gapping play—See *Gapping plays.*

High-wave candle—A candle with very long upper and lower shadows and a small real body. It shows that the market is losing its direction bias that it had before this candle appeared. If the real body is a doji instead of a small real body, it is a *long-legged doji.*

High Waves

In-neck line—A small white candlestick in a downtrend whose close is slightly above the previous black candlestick's low of the session. After this white candlestick's low is broken, the downtrend should continue. Compare to *on-neck line, thrusting line,* and *piercing pattern.*

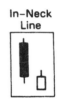

In-Neck Line

Inverted hammer—Following a downtrend, this is a candlestick line that has a long upper shadow and a small real body at the lower end of the session. There should be no, or very little, lower shadow. It has the same shape as the bearish shooting star, but when this line occurs in a downtrend, it is a bullish bottom reversal signal with confirmation the next session (i.e., a candlestick with a higher open and especially a higher close compared to the inverted hammer's close).

Inverted Hammer

Inverted three Buddha pattern—See *Three Buddha pattern.*

Long-legged doji—A doji with very long shadows. If the opening and closing of a long-legged doji session are in the middle of the session's range, the line is called a *rickshaw man.* See illustration under *Doji.*

Low-price gapping play—See *Gapping plays.*

Lower shadow—See *Shadows.*

Morning attack—The Japanese expression for a large buy or sell order on the opening that is designed to significantly move the market.

Morning doji star—See *Morning star.*

Morning star—A bottom reversal pattern formed by three candlesticks. The first is a long black real body, the second is a small real body (white or black) that gaps lower to form a

Morning Star

star, and the third is a white candlestick that closes well into the first session's black real body. Its opposite is the *evening star*. If the middle candle (the star portion) is a doji instead of a spinning top, the pattern becomes a *morning doji star*.

Night attack—The Japanese expression for a large order placed at the close to try to affect the market.

Northern Doji—See *Doji*.

On-neck line—A black candlestick in a downtrend is followed by a small white candlestick whose close is near the low of the session of the black candlestick. It is a bearish continuation pattern. The market should continue to move lower after the white candlestick's low is broken. Compare to an *in-neck line*, a *thrusting line*, and a *piercing pattern*.

Petrifying pattern—The nickname for the *harami cross*.

Piercing Pattern

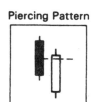

Piercing pattern—A bottom reversal signal. In a downtrend, a long black candlestick is followed by a gap lower open during the next session. This session finishes as a strong white candlestick that closes more than halfway into the prior black candlestick's real body. Compare to the *on-neck line*, the *in-neck line*, and the *thrusting line*.

Raindrop—See *Star*.

Real body—The rectangular part of the candlestick line. It is defined by the closing and opening prices of the session. When the close is higher than the open, the real body is white (or empty). A black (or filled-in) real body is when the close is lower than the opening. See the illustration under *Candlestick lines and charts*.

Rickshaw man—The nickname for the *long-legged doji*.

Rising three methods—See *Three methods*.

Rising window—See *Windows*.

Separating Lines

Bullish   Bearish

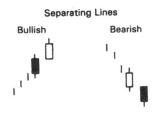

Separating lines—When, in an uptrend (downtrend), the market opens at the same opening as the previous session's opposite color candlestick and then closes higher (lower). The prior trend should resume after this line.

Shadows—The thin lines above and below the real body of the candlestick line. They represent the extremes of the session.

The lower shadow is the line under the real body. The bottom of the lower shadow is the low of the session. The upper shadow is the line on top of the real body. The top of the upper shadow is the high of the session. See the illustration under *Candlestick lines and charts.*

Shaven bottom—A candlestick with no lower shadow.

Shaven head—A candlestick with no upper shadow.

Shooting star—A bearish candle with a long upper shadow, little or no lower shadow, and a small real body near the lows of the session that arises after an uptrend.

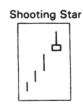

Shooting Star

Side-by-side white lines—Two consecutive white candlesticks that have the same open and whose real bodies are about the same size. In an uptrend, if these side-by-side white lines gap higher, it is a bullish continuation pattern. In a downtrend, these side-by-side white lines are still considered bearish (in spite of their white candles since they come after a falling gap).

Southern doji—See *Doji.*

Spinning tops—The nickname for candle lines with small real bodies.

Star—A small real body (white or black) that gaps away from the large real body preceding it. A star in a downtrend has the nickname *raindrop.*

Tasuki gaps—The *upward* (or *upside*) *gapping tasuki* is made of a rising window formed by a white candle and then a black candle. The black candle opens within the white real body and closes under the white candle's real body. The close on the black candle day is the fight point. A *downward* (or *downside*) *gapping tasuki* is when the market gaps down with a black candle followed by a white candle. The two candles of the tasuki should be about the same size. Both types of tasuki are rare.

Three Buddha patterns—A three Buddha top is the same as the Western head and shoulders top. In Japanese terms, the three Buddha top is a *three mountain top* in which the central mountain is the tallest. An inverted three Buddha is the same as the Western inverted head and shoulders. In Japanese terminol-

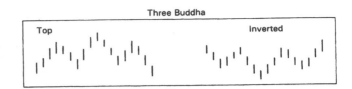

ogy, it is a *three river bottom* in which the middle river is the longest.

Three crows—Three relatively long consecutive black candles that close near or on their lows. It is a top reversal at a high-price level or after an extended rally.

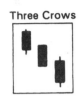

Three methods—There are two types. The first is the *falling three methods*, which is a bearish continuation pattern. It is ideally comprised of five lines. A long black real body is followed by three small, usually white, real bodies that hold within the first session's high–low range. Then a black candlestick closes at a new low for the move. The *rising three methods* is a bullish continuation pattern. A tall white candlestick precedes three small, usually black, real bodies that hold within the white candlestick's range. The fifth line of this pattern is a strong white candlestick that closes at a new high for the move.

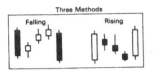

Three mountain top—A longer-term topping pattern in which prices stall at, or near, the same highs.

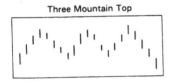

Three river bottom—When the market hits a bottom area three times.

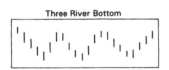

Three white or three advancing soldiers—This is a group of three white candlesticks with consecutively higher closes (with each closing near the highs of the session). These three white candles presage more strength if they appear after a period of stable prices or at a low price area.

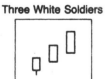

Thrusting line—A white candlestick that closes in the prior black real body, but still under the middle of the prior session's real body. The thrusting line is stronger than an in-neck line, but not so strong as a piercing line. In a downtrend, the thrusting line is viewed as bearish (unless two of these patterns appear within a few days of each other). As part of a rising market, it is considered bullish.

Towers—There is a *tower top* and a *tower bottom*. The *tower top*, a top reversal formation, is comprised of one or more tall white candles followed by congestion and then one or more long black candlesticks. It is a pattern that looks like it has towers on both sides of the congestion band. A *tower bottom* is a bottom reversal pattern. One or more long black candles are followed by lateral action. Then the market explodes to the upside via one or more long white candlesticks.

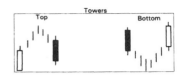

Tri-star—Three doji that have the same formation as a morning or evening star pattern. An extraordinarily rare pattern.

Tweezers top and bottom—When the same highs or lows are tested on back-to-back sessions. They are minor reversal signals that take on extra importance if the two candlesticks that comprise the tweezers pattern also form another candlestick indicator. For example, if both sessions of a harami cross have the same high, it could have more significance since there would be a tweezers top and a bearish harami cross made by the same two candlestick lines.

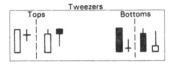

Umbrella lines—The generic name for the hammer and hanging man lines. The umbrella line looks like an umbrella since it is a candle with a long lower shadow and a small real body at, or near, the top of the trading range.

Upper shadow—See *Shadows*.

Upside gap tasuki—See *Tasuki gaps*.

Upside gap two crows—A three-candlestick pattern. The first line is a long white candlestick that is followed by a black real body that gaps over the white candle's real body. The third session is another black real body that opens above the second session's open and closes under the second session's close. It is very rare.

Window—The same as a Western gap. Windows are continuation patterns. When the market opens a window to the upside, it is a *rising window*. It is a bullish signal and the rising window should be support. If a window opens in a sell-off, it is a *falling window*. This is a bearish signal. The falling window is resistance.

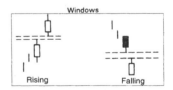

GLOSSARY B

WESTERN TECHNICAL TERMS

This glossary is to clarify the Western technical terms used in this book. It is not meant to be comprehensive or detailed, as this book focuses on Japanese candlesticks, not Western technicals.

Bar chart—A graphic representation of price activity. The high and low of the session define the top and bottom of a vertical line. The close for the period is marked with a short horizontal bar attached to the right of the vertical line. The open is marked with a short horizontal bar attached to the left of the vertical line. Price is on the vertical scale; time is on the horizontal scale.

Blow-offs—A top or bottom reversal. Blow-offs occur after an extended move. Prices sharply and quickly thrust strongly in the direction of the preceding trend. If the market reverses after this action, it is a blow-off.

Box range—The Japanese term for a market in a lateral trading range. See *Congestion zone or band*.

Breakaway gap—When prices gap away from a significant technical area (i.e., a trend line or a congestion zone).

Breakout—Overcoming a resistance or support level.

Change of polarity—When old support converts to new resistance, or when old resistance converts to new support.

Confirmation—When more than one indicator substantiates the action of another.

Congestion zone or band—A period of lateral price action within a relatively narrow price band. The Japanese call this a box range.

Consolidation—The same as a congestion zone. Consolidation, however, has the implication that the prior trend should resume.

Continuation pattern—A pattern whose implications are for a continuation of the prior trend. A flag, for instance, is a continuation pattern.

Crossover—When the faster indicator crosses above (bullish crossover) or below (bearish crossover) the slower indicator. For example, if a 5-day moving average crosses under a 13-day moving average, it is a bearish crossover.

Divergence—When related technical indicators fail to confirm a price move. For instance, if prices reach new highs and stochastics do not, this is negative divergence and is bearish. If prices establish new lows and stochastics do not make new lows, this is called positive divergence and is bullish.

Double bottom—Price action that resembles a W in which price declines twice stop at, or near, the same lows.

Double top—Price action that resembles an M in which price rallies twice stop at, or near, the same highs.

Downgap—When prices gap lower.

Downtrend—A market that is trending lower as shown by a series of lower highs and/or lower lows.

Exponential moving average—A moving average that is exponentially weighted.

Falling resistance line—A resistance line made by joining a series of lower highs.

Falling support line—A support line obtained by connecting a series of lower lows.

Fibonacci—Italian mathematician who formulated a series of numbers based on adding the prior two numbers. Popular Fibonacci ratios used by technicians include (rounding off) 38%, 50%, and 62%.

Flag or pennant—A continuation formation comprised of a sharp price move followed by a brief consolidation area. These are continuation patterns.

Gap—A price void (i.e., no trading), from one price area to another.

Inside session—When the entire session's high–low range is within the prior session's range.

Intraday—Any period shorter than daily. Thus, a 60-minute intraday chart is based on the high, low, open, and "close" on an hourly basis.

Islands—A formation at the extremes of the market when prices gap in the direction of the prior trend. Prices then stay there for one or more days, and then gaps in the opposite direction. Prices are thus surrounded by gaps that leave them isolated like an island.

Measured moves—A price target based on using measurements formulated on prior price action.

Momentum—The velocity of a price move. It compares the most recent close to the close a specific number of periods ago.

Moving average convergence–divergence (MACD) oscillator—A combination of three exponentially smoothed moving averages.

Neckline—A line connecting the lows of the head in a head and shoulders formation, or the highs of an inverse head and shoulders. A move under the neckline of a head and shoulders top is bearish; a move above the neckline of an inverse head and shoulders neckline is bullish.

Negative divergence—See *Divergence*.

Oscillator—A momentum line that fluctuates around a zero value line (or between 0% and 100%). Oscillators can help measure overbought/oversold levels, show negative and positive divergence, and measure a price move's velocity.

Overbought—When the market moves up too far, too fast. At this point the market is vulnerable to a downward correction.

Oversold—When the market declines too quickly. The market becomes susceptible to a bounce.

Paper trading—Not trading with real money. All transactions are only imaginary with a record of profit and loss on paper.

Pennant—See *Flag*.

Positive divergence—See *Divergence*.

Rally—An upward movement of prices.

Reaction—A price movement opposite of the prevailing trend.

Relative Strength Index (RSI)—The RSI compares the ratio of up closes to down closes over a specified time period.

Resistance level—A level where sellers are expected to enter.

Retracement—A price reaction from the prior move in percentage terms. The more common retracement levels are 38.2%, 50%, and 61.8%.

Reversal indicator—See *Trend reversals*.

Reversal session—A session when a new high is made for the move and the market then closes under the prior session's close.

Rising resistance line—A resistance line made by connecting higher highs.

Rising support line—A support line connecting higher lows.

Selling climax—When prices push sharply and suddenly lower on heavy volume after an extended decline. If the market reverses from this sharp sell-off, it is viewed as a selling climax.

Selloff—A downward movement of prices.

Simple moving average—A method of smoothing price data in which prices are added together and then averaged. It is a "moving" average because the average moves. As new price data is added, the oldest data is dropped.

Spring—When prices break under the support of a horizontal congestion band and then springs back above the "broken support" area. This is bullish and there is a measured price target to the upper end of the congestion band.

Stochastics—An oscillator that measures the relative position of the closing price as compared with its range over a chosen period. It is comprised of the faster moving %K line and the slower moving %D line.

Support level—An area where buyers are expected to enter.

Swing target—Using the height of a rally or decline to obtain a price target.

Trading range—When prices are locked between horizontal support and horizontal resistance levels.

Trend—The market's prevalent price direction.

Trend line—A line on a chart that connects a series of higher highs or lower lows. At least two points are needed to draw a trend line. The more often it is tested and the greater the volume on the tests, the more important the trend line.

Trend reversals—Also called *reversal indicators*. This is a misleading term. More appropriate, and more accurate, would be the term "trend change indicator." It means the prior trend should change. It does not mean prices are going to reverse. Prices might reverse after a trend reversal pattern, but they may not. For example, the trend could change from upwards to sideways. As long as the trend changes after a trend reversal pattern appears, that trend reversal worked. Thus, if a trend reversal appears during an uptrend and the market then trades sideways, the trend reversal pattern was successful.

Upgap—A gap that pushes prices higher.

Upthrust—When prices break above a resistance line from a laterally trading zone. If these new highs fail to hold and prices pull back under the "broken" resistance line, it is an upthrust. The target is for a retest of the lower end of the recent trading zone.

Uptrend—A market that is trending higher.

V bottom or top—When prices suddenly reverse direction, forming a price pattern that looks like the letter V for a bottom or an inverted V for a top.

Volume—The total of all contracts traded for a given period.

Weighted moving average—A moving average in which each previous price is assigned a weighting factor. Usually the most recent data is the more heavily weighted and thus considered more important.

BIBLIOGRAPHY

Analysis of Stock Price in Japan. Tokyo: Nippon Technical Analysts Association, 1986.

Buchanen, Daniel Crump. *Japanese Proverbs and Sayings.* Oklahoma City, OK: University of Oklahoma Press, 1965.

Chol-Kim Yong. *Proverbs East and West.* Elizabeth, NJ: Hollym Corp., 1991.

Dilts, Marion May. *The Pageant of Japanese History.* New York: David McKay Co., 1963.

Edwards, Robert D. and John Magee. *Technical Analysis of Stock Trends,* 5th ed. Boston: John Magee, 1966.

Galef, David. *Even a Stone Buddha Can Talk.* Boston: Tuttle Publishing, 2000.

Hill, Julie Skur. "That's not what I said," *Business Tokyo,* August 1990, 46–47.

Hirschmeier, Johannes and Tsunehiko Yui. *The Development of Japanese Business 1600–1973.* Cambridge, MA: Harvard University Press, 1975.

Hoshii, Kazutaka. *Hajimete Kabuka Chato wo Yomu Hito no Hon (A Book for Those Reading Stock Charts for the First Time).* Tokyo: Asukashuppansha, 1990.

Ifrah, Georges. *The Universal History of Numbers.* New York: John Wiley and Sons, 2000.

Ikutaro, Gappo. *Kabushikisouba no Technical Bunseki (Stock Market Technical Analysis).* Tokyo: Nihon Keizai Shinbunsha, 1985.

Ishii, Katsutoshi. *Kabuka Chato no Tashikana Yomikata (A Sure Way to Read Stock Charts).* Tokyo: Jiyukokuminsha, 1990.

Kaufman, Perry J. *The New Commodity Trading Systems and Methods.* New York: John Wiley and Sons, 1987.

Keisen Kyoshitsu Part 1 (Chart Classroom Part 1). Tokyo: Toshi Rader, 1989.

Kroll, Stanley. *Kroll on Futures Trading.* Homewood, IL: Dow Jones–Irwin, 1988.

Masuda, Koh, ed. *Kenkyusha's New School Japanese–English Dictionary.* Tokyo: Kenkyusha, 1968.

McCunn, Ruthanne Lum. *Chinese Proverbs.* San Francisco, CA: Chronicle Books, 1991.

Nihon Keisenshi (The History of Japanese Charts). Chapter 2 by Oyama Kenji, pp. 90–102. Tokyo: Nihon Keisai Shimbunsha, 1979.

Okasan Keisai Kenkyusho. *Shinpan Jissen Kabushiki Nyumon (Introduction to Stock Charts).* Tokyo: Diamond-sha, 1987.

Sakata Goho Wa Furinkazan (Sakata's Five Rules Are Wind, Forest, Fire and Mountain). Tokyo: Nihon Shoken Shimbunsha, 1969.

Schabacker, Richard W. *Technical Analysis and Stock Market Profits.* New York: The Schabacker Institute.

Seidensticker, Edward G. *Even Monkeys Fall from Trees and Other Japanese Proverbs.* Rutland, VA: Charles E. Tuttle, 1987.

Seward, Jack. *Japanese in Action.* New York: Weatherhill, 1983.

Shimizu, Seiki. *The Japanese Chart of Charts.* Trans. Gregory S. Nicholson. Tokyo: Tokyo Futures Trading Publishing Co., 1986.

Sklarew, Arthur. *Techniques of a Professional Commodity Chart Analyst.* New York: Commodity Research Bureau, 1980.

Smith, Adam. *The Money Game.* New York: Random House, 1968.

Tamarkin, Robert. *The New Gatsbys.* Chicago: Bob Tamarkin, 1985.

Taucher, Frank. *Commodity Trader's Almanac.* Tulsa, OK: Market Movements, 1988.

Technical Traders Bulletin. January 1990, May 1990, June 1990. Rolling Hill Estates, CA: Island View Financial Group Inc.

Wilder, J. Welles. *New Concepts in Technical Trading Systems.* Greensboro, NC: Trend Research, 1978.

Yong-Chol, Kim. *Proverbs East and West.* Seoul, Korea: Hollym International, 1991.

Yoshimi, Toshihiko. *Yoshimi Toshihiko no Chato Kyoshitsu (Toshihiko Yoshimi's Chart Classroom).* Tokyo: Nihon Chart, 1989.

ABOUT CANDLECHARTS.COM

Helping clients spot market turns *before* the competition™

Steve Nison, through his firm Candlecharts.com, is uniquely qualified to help you take advantage of the opportunities candle charts present to today's markets. Steve, the very first to reveal the startling strength of candle charts to the Western world, is the leading authority on the subject.

He has presented his trading strategies in 18 countries to traders from every financial firm, including the World Bank and the Federal Reserve Bank of New York.

A partial client list includes Spear; Leeds and Kellogg; Morgan Stanley; Knight Securities; J.P. Morgan; Fidelity; The Bank of New York; hedge funds, and numerous NASDAQ and NYSE market makers.

Candlecharts.com's services and products include:

- *Institutional Onsite Seminars*—Personalized training from Steve Nison at your place of business on candle charts and/or Western technical analysis. These seminars include such titles as "Harnessing the Power of Candle Charts to Spot the Early Reversal Signals" and "The Best of the East and West—merging the most potent tools of candle charts and Western technical analysis."

- *Private Workshops*—Come to Steve's intensive full-day workshop given once a year in Manhattan. Limited class size means personalized attention.
- *Six-Hour Video Workshop*—Learn at your own pace in the comfort of your home.
- *Interactive Products*—Extensive online and computer-based courses.
- *Custom Advisory Services*—Steve Nison will personally analyze your markets.

To learn all that Candlecharts.com has to offer visit Candlecharts.com's Web site. You can reach Candlecharts.com and Steve Nison at:

Web site: www.candlecharts.com

E-mail: nison@candlecharts.com

Telephone: 732.254-8660 (USA)

Fax: 732.390-6625

Address: Candlecharts.com
P.O. Box 6775
East Brunswick, NJ 08816
U.S.A.

INDEX

Page numbers appearing in italics refer to figures.